WEBSTER'S NEW WORLD™

French Grammar and Exercises

Grammar Compiled by
LEXUS
with
Raymond Perrez,
Noel Peacock
and
Sabrine Citron

Macmillan ■ USA

ISBN 0-02-861723-1

Library of Congress Number: 97-80034

A Webster's New World™ Book

Macmillan General Reference
A Simon & Schuster Macmillan Company
1633 Broadway
New York, NY 10019-6785

MACMILLAN is a registered trademark
of Macmillan Inc.

WEBSTER'S NEW WORLD DICTIONARY
is a registered trademark of
Simon & Schuster, Inc.

INTRODUCTION

This French grammar has been written to meet the new demands of language teaching in schools and colleges and is particularly suitable for exam review. The essential rules of the French language have been set in terms that are as accessible as possible to all users. Where technical terms have been used, full explanations of these terms have also been supplied. There is also a full glossary of grammatical terminology on pages 9–14. While literary aspects of the French language have not been ignored, the emphasis has been placed squarely on modern spoken French. This grammar, with its wealth of lively and typical illustrations of usage taken from the present-day language, is the ideal study tool for all levels—from the beginner who is starting to come to grips with the French language to the advanced user who requires a comprehensive and readily accessible work of reference.

Abbreviations used in the text:

fem	feminine
masc	masculine
plur	plural
sing	singular

The Exercises section of this book has been conceived to help you assess your knowledge of the essential grammar points of the French language. It comprises twelve comprehensive chapters, each dealing with a particular aspect of grammar. The exercises within each chapter have been designed to consolidate and extend your understanding of French grammar.

Every chapter focuses on a precise point of French grammar, and within the chapter the exercises take you gradually through various levels of grammatical difficulty. Every exercise has a key (these are given at the end of the book). After every test, a score is given, which allows you to assess your level.

We have tried to vary the types of exercises and the themes used, and we hope that this will make your study both enjoyable and stimulating. The vocabulary used is based on contemporary written and spoken French.

The obtained score for each test enables you to assess your level accurately. Do not worry if you do not obtain a good score the first time. If you have too many difficulties with a test or a chapter, and if, despite the keys, some points remain unclear, we advise you to go back to the grammar section and to redo the test or the chapter in question later on. If your score is:

- between 90 and 100% your knowledge is excellent;
- between 80 and 90% you have a good level;
- between 60 and 80% your level is not bad but we would recommend that you redo the test or the chapter after a while and that you review the particular points in the grammar section;
- under 60%: don't be discouraged, work quietly on the weak points using the grammar section and redo the tests several times if necessary.

We wish you good luck and hope that you will make good progress with your French and will enjoy working with this book.

CONTENTS

Part I

Grammar

1. GLOSSARY OF GRAMMATICAL TERMS

ADJECTIVE

A describing word, which adds information about a noun, telling us what something is like (e.g. *a **small** house, a **red** car, an **interesting** pastime*).

ADVERB

Adverbs are normally used with a verb to add extra information by indicating **how** the action is done (adverbs of manner), **when, where,** and **with how much intensity** the action is done (adverbs of time, place, and intensity), or **to what extent** the action is done (adverbs of quantity). Adverbs may also be used with an adjective or another adverb (e.g. *a **very** attractive girl, **very** well*).

AGREEMENT

In French, words such as adjectives, articles, and pronouns are said to agree in number and gender with the noun or pronoun they refer to. This means that their spelling changes according to the **number** of the noun (singular or plural) and according to its **gender** (masculine or feminine).

ANTECEDENT

The antecedent of a relative pronoun is the word or words to which the relative pronoun refers. The antecedent is usually found directly before the relative pronoun (e.g. in the sentence *I **know the man** who did this, the man* is the antecedent of *who*).

APPOSITION

A word or a clause is said to be in apposition with another when it is placed directly after it without any joining word (e.g. *Mr. Jones, **our bank manager**, phoned today*).

ARTICLE	See DEFINITE ARTICLE, INDEFINITE ARTICLE and PARTITIVE ARTICLE.
AUXILIARY	The French auxiliary verbs, or 'helping' verbs, are **avoir** (*to have*) and **être** (*to be*). They are used to make up the first part of compound tenses, the second part being a past participle (e.g. *I have eaten*).
CARDINAL	Cardinal numbers are numbers such as *one, two, ten, fourteen*, as opposed to **ordinal** numbers (e.g. *first, second*).
CLAUSE	A clause is a group of words that contains at least a subject and a verb: *he said* is a clause. A clause often contains more than this basic information, e.g. *he said this to her yesterday*. Sentences can be made up of several clauses, e.g. *he said / he'd call me / if he were free*. See SENTENCE.
COMPARATIVE	The comparative forms of adjectives and adverbs allow us to compare two things, persons, or actions. In English, *more . . . than, . . . er than, less . . . than*, and *as . . . as* are used for comparison.
COMPOUND	Compound tenses are verb tenses consisting of more than one element. In French, the compound tenses of a verb are formed by the **auxiliary** verb and the **past participle**: *j'ai visité, il est venu*.
CONDITIONAL	This mood is used to describe what someone would do, or something that would happen if a condition were fulfilled (e.g. *I would come if I were well; the chair would have broken if he had sat on it*).
CONJUGATION	The conjugation of a verb is the set of different forms used in the particular tenses of that verb.
CONJUNCTION	Conjunctions are linking words. They may be coordinating or subordinating. Coordinating conjunctions are words like *and, but, or*; subordinating conjunctions are words like *because, after, although*.

DEFINITE ARTICLE	The definite article is *the* in English and *le, la, l'*, and *les* in French.
DEMONSTRATIVE	Demonstrative adjectives (e.g. *this, that, these*) and pronouns (e.g. *this one, that one*) are used to point out a particular person or object.
DIRECT OBJECT	A noun or a pronoun that, in English, follows a verb without any linking preposition, e.g. *I met **a friend**.*
ELISION	Elision is the replacing of the last letter of certain words (*le, la, je, me, te, se, de, que*) with an apostrophe (') before a word starting with a **vowel** or **silent h** (e.g. *l'eau, l'homme, j'aime*).
ENDING	The ending of a verb is determined by the **person** (1st/2nd/3rd) and **number** (singular/plural) of its subject. In French, most tenses have six different endings. See PERSON and NUMBER.
EXCLAMATION	Words or sentences used to express surprise, wonder (e.g. *what!, how!, how lucky!, what a nice day!*).
FEMININE	See GENDER.
GENDER	The gender of a noun indicates whether the noun is **masculine** or **feminine** (all French nouns are either one or the other).
IDIOMATIC	Idiomatic expressions (or idioms), are expressions that cannot normally be translated word for word. For example, *it's raining cats and dogs* can be translated by *il pleut des cordes*.
IMPERATIVE	A mood used for giving orders (e.g. *eat!, don't go!*).
INDEFINITE	Indefinite pronouns and adjectives are words that do not refer to a definite person or object (e.g. *each, someone, every*).
INDEFINITE ARTICLE	The indefinite article is *a/an* in English and *un, une*, and *des* in French.
INDICATIVE	The normal form of a verb, as in *I like, he came, we are trying*. It differs from the subjunctive, conditional, and imperative.

INDIRECT OBJECT	A pronoun or noun that follows a verb indirectly, with a linking preposition (usually **to**), e.g. *I spoke to my friend/him.*
INFINITIVE	The infinitive is the basic form of the verb, as found in dictionaries. Thus *to eat, to finish, to take* are infinitives. In French, the infinitive is recognized by its ending: *manger, finir, prendre.*
INTERROGATIVE	Interrogative words are used to ask a question. This may be a direct question (*when will you arrive?*) or an indirect question (*I don't know when he'll arrive*). See QUESTION.
MASCULINE	See GENDER.
MOOD	The name given to the four main areas within which a verb is conjugated. See INDICATIVE, SUBJUNCTIVE, CONDITIONAL, IMPERATIVE.
NOUN	A naming word, which can refer to living creatures, things, places, or abstract ideas, e.g. *postman, cat, shop, passport, life.*
NUMBER	The number of a noun indicates whether the noun is **singular** or **plural**. A singular noun refers to one single thing or person (e.g. *boy, train*) and a plural noun, to several (e.g. *boys, trains*).
ORDINAL	Ordinal numbers are *first, second, third, fourth*, and all other numbers that end in **-th**. In French, all ordinal numbers, except for *premier* (first) and *second* (second), end in **-ième**.
PARTITIVE ARTICLE	The partitive articles are *some* and *any*, in English, and *du, de la, de l'*, and *des* (as in *du pain, de la confiture, des bananes*) in French.
PASSIVE	A verb is used in the passive when the subject of the verb does not perform the action but is subjected to it. The passive is formed with the verb **to be** and the past participle of the verb, e.g. *he was rewarded.*

PAST PARTICIPLE

The past participle of a verb is the form used after **to have** in English, e.g. *I have **eaten**, I have **said**, you have **tried***.

PERSON

In any tense, there are three persons in the singular (1st: *I . . .* , 2nd: *you . . .* , 3rd: *he / she / it . . .*), and three in the plural (1st: *we . . .* , 2nd: *you . . .* , 3rd: *they . . .*). See also ENDING.

PERSONAL PRONOUNS

Personal pronouns stand for a noun. They usually accompany a verb and can be either the subject (*I, you, he / she / it, we, they*) or the object of the verb (*me, you, him / her / it, us, them*).

PLURAL

See NUMBER.

POSSESSIVE

Possessive adjectives and pronouns are used to indicate possession or ownership. They are words like *my / mine, your / yours, our / ours*.

PREPOSITION

Prepositions are words such as *with, in, to, at*. They are followed by a noun or a pronoun, and express a certain relation to it.

PRESENT PARTICIPLE

The present participle is the verb form that ends in **-ing** in English (**-ant** in French).

PRONOUN

A word that stands for a noun. The main categories of pronouns are:
- **Relative pronouns** (e.g. *who, which, that*)
- **Interrogative pronouns** (e.g. *who?, what?, which?*)
- **Demonstrative pronouns** (e.g. *this, that, these*)
- **Possessive pronouns** (e.g. *mine, yours, his*)
- **Personal pronouns** (e.g. *you, him, us*)
- **Reflexive pronouns** (e.g. *myself, himself*)
- **Indefinite pronouns** (e.g. *something, all*)

QUESTION

There are two question forms: **direct** questions stand on their own and call for a question mark at the end (e.g. *when will he come?*); **indirect** questions are introduced by a clause and do not require a question mark (e.g. *I wonder when he will come*).

REFLEXIVE

Reflexive verbs 'reflect' the action back onto the subject (e.g. *I dressed myself*). They are always found with a reflexive pronoun and are much more common in French than in English.

SENTENCE

A sentence is a group of words made up of one or more clauses (see CLAUSE). The end of a sentence is indicated by a punctuation mark (usually a period, a question mark, or an exclamation mark).

SILENT H

The name 'silent **h**' is actually mis-leading since an **h** is never pronounced in French. The point is that, when a silent **h** occurs, any pre-ceding vowel is not pronounced either. For example, the **h** in *j'habite* is silent (note the *j'*). The **h** in *je hurle* is not silent (note the **je**).

SIMPLE TENSE

Simple tenses are tenses in which the verb consists of one word only, e.g. *j'habite, Maurice partira.*

SINGULAR

See NUMBER.

SUBJECT

The subject of a verb is the noun or pronoun that performs the action. In the sentences *the train left early* and *she bought a record, the train* and *she* are the subjects.

SUBJUNCTIVE

The subjunctive is a verb form that is rarely used in English (e.g. *if I were you, God forbid!*), but common in French.

SUPERLATIVE

The form of an adjective or an adverb, which, in English, is marked by *the most . . . , the . . . est,* or *the least . . . .*

TENSE

Verbs are used in tenses, which tell us when an action takes place, e.g. in the present, the imperfect, the future.

VERB

A 'doing' word, which usually describes an action (e.g. *to sing, to work, to watch*). Some verbs describe a state (e.g. *to be, to have, to hope*).

2. ARTICLES

A. THE DEFINITE ARTICLE

1. Forms

In English, there is only one form of the definite article: **the.** In French, there are three forms, depending on the gender and number of the noun following the article:

- with a masculine singular noun: **le**
- with a feminine singular noun: **la** } the
- with a plural noun (masc or fem): **les**

MASC SING	FEM SING	PLURAL
le chauffeur the driver	**la demoiselle** the young lady	**les étudiants** the students
le salon the lounge	**la cuisine** the kitchen	**les chambres** the bedrooms

Note: **le** and **la** both change to **l'** before a vowel or a silent **h**:

	MASCULINE	FEMININE
BEFORE VOWEL	**l'avion** the plane	**l'odeur** the smell
BEFORE SILENT H	**l'homme** the man	**l'hôtesse** the hostess

Pronunciation: the **s** of **les** is pronounced **z** when the noun following it begins with a vowel or a silent **h**.

2. Forms with the prepositions 'à' and 'de'

When the definite article is used with **à** or **de**, the following spelling changes take place:

a) *with à (to, at)*

à + le → **au**
à + les → **aux**
à + la and à + l' do not change

au restaurant at/to the restaurant

aux enfants to the children

à la plage	**àl'aéroport**
at/to the beach	at/to the airport

Pronunciation: the **x** of **aux** is pronounced **z** when the noun following it begins with a vowel or a silent **h**.

b) *with de (of, from)*

de + le	→	**du**
de + les	→	**des**
de + la and **de + l'** do not change		

du directeur	**des chômeurs**
of/from the manager	of/from the unemployed
de la région	**de l'usine**
of/from the area	of/from the factory

Pronunciation: the **s** of **des** is pronounced **z** when the noun following it begins with a vowel or a silent **h**.

3. Use

As in English, the definite article is used when referring to a particular person or thing, or particular persons or things:

les amis dont je t'ai parlé	**le café est prêt**
the friends I told you about	the coffee is ready

However, the definite article is used far more frequently in French than in English. It is used in particular in the following cases where English uses no article:

a) *when the noun is used in a general sense*

i) to refer to all things of a kind:

vous acceptez les chèques?
do you accept checks?

le sucre est mauvais pour les dents
sugar is bad for the teeth

ii) to refer to abstract things:

le travail et les loisirs	**la musique classique**
work and leisure	classical music

iii) when stating likes and dislikes:

j'aime la viande, mais je préfère le poisson
I love meat, but I like fish better

je déteste les tomates
I hate tomatoes

b) *with geographical names*

i) continents, countries, and areas:

le Canada	**la France**	**l'Europe**
Canada	France	Europe
la Bretagne	**l'Afrique**	**les Etats-Unis**
Brittany	Africa	the United States

But: the article **la** is omitted with the prepositions **en** (to, in) and **de** (from):

j'habite en France
I live in France

il vient d'Italie
he comes from Italy

ii) mountains, lakes, and rivers:

le mont Everest
Mount Everest

le Mississippi
the Mississippi

c) *with names of seasons*

l'automne   autumn, fall
l'hiver   winter
le printemps spring
l'été   summer

But: **en automne/été/hiver**
in the fall/summer/winter

au printemps un jour d'été
in the spring   a summer's day

d) *with names of languages*

j'apprends le français
I'm learning French

But: **ce film est en anglais**
this film is in English

elle parle chinois
she speaks Chinese

e) *with parts of the body*

j'ai les cheveux roux
I have red hair

ouvrez la bouche
open your mouth

les mains en l'air!
hands up!

l'homme à la barbe noire
the man with the black beard

f) *with names following an adjective*

le petit Pierre
little Pierre

la pauvre Isabelle
poor Isabelle

g) *with titles*

le docteur Coste
Doctor Coste

le commandant Cousteau
Captain Cousteau

h) *with days of the week to express regular occurrences*

que fais-tu le samedi?
what do you do Saturdays?

i) *with names of subjects or leisure activities*

les maths
math

l'histoire et la géographie
history and geography

la natation, la lecture, le tennis
swimming, reading, tennis

11

j) *in expressions of price, quantity, etc.*

> **c'est combien le kilo/la douzaine/la bouteille?**
> how much is it for a kilo/dozen/bottle?

B. THE INDEFINITE ARTICLE

1. Forms

In French, there are three forms of the indefinite article, depending on the number and gender of the noun it accompanies:

– with a masculine singular noun: **un** a/an
– with a feminine singular noun: **une** a/an
– with a plural noun (masc or fem): **des** some

Note: **des** is often not translated in English:

> **il y a des nuages dans le ciel**
> there are clouds in the sky

2. Use

a) On the whole, the French indefinite article is used in the same way as its English equivalent:

un homme	**une femme**	**des hommes/femmes**
a man	a woman	(some) men/women
un article	**une tasse**	**des articles/tasses**
an article	a cup	(some) articles/cups

b) However, the English indefinite article is not always translated in French:

i) when stating someone's profession or occupation:

> **mon père est architecte**
> my father is an architect

> **elle est médecin**
> she is a doctor

But: the article is used after **c'est, c'était**, etc:

> **c'est un acteur célèbre**
> he's a famous actor

> **ce sont des fraises**
> those are strawberries

ii) with nouns in apposition:

> **Madame Leclerc, employée de bureau**
> Mrs. Leclerc, an office worker

iii) after **quel** in exclamations:

> **quel dommage!**   **quelle surprise!**
> what a pity!   what a surprise!

c) In negative sentences, **de** (or **d'**) is used instead of **un, une, des**:

je n'ai pas d'amis
I don't have any friends

je n'ai plus de voiture
I don't have a car any more

d) In French (but not in English), the indefinite article is used with abstract nouns followed by an adjective:

avec une patience remarquable
with remarkable patience

elle a fait des progrès étonnants
she's made amazing progress

But: the article is not used when there is no adjective:

avec plaisir
with pleasure

sans hésitation
without hesitation

C. THE PARTITIVE ARTICLE

1. Forms

There are three forms of the French partitive article, which corresponds to 'some'/'any' in English:

– with a masculine singular noun: **du**
– with a feminine singular noun: **de la**
– with plural nouns (masc or fem): **des**

du vin
some wine

de la bière
some beer

des fruits
some fruit

Note: **de l'** is used in front of masculine or feminine singular nouns beginning with a vowel or a silent **h**:

de l'argent
some money

de l'eau
some water

2. Use

a) On the whole, the French partitive article is used as in English. However, English tends to omit the partitive article where French does not:

achète du pain
buy (some) bread

vous avez du beurre?
do you have (any) butter?

je voudrais de la viande
I'd like some meat

tu veux de la soupe?
do you want (any/some) soup?

tu dois manger des légumes
you must eat (some) vegetables

as-tu acheté des poires?
did you buy any/some pears?

b) The partitive article is replaced by **de** (or **d'**) in the following cases:

   i) in negative expressions:

      il n'y a plus de café   **je n'ai pas de verres**
      there isn't any coffee left   I don't have any glasses

But: **ce n'est pas du cuir, c'est du plastique**
       it's not leather, it's plastic

       je n'ai que de l'argent français
       I have only French money

   ii) after expressions of quantity (see also pp. 219–20):

      il boit trop de café   **il gagne assez d'argent**
      he drinks too much coffee he earns enough money

   iii) after **avoir besoin de:**

      j'ai besoin d'argent   **tu as besoin de timbres?**
      I need (some) money   do you need (any) stamps?

   iv) where an adjective is followed by a plural noun:

      de grands enfants   **de petites villes**
      (some) tall children   (some) small towns

But: if the adjective comes after the noun, **des** does not change:

      des résultats encourageants
      encouraging results

3. Partitive or definite article?

When no article is used in English, be careful to use the right article in French: **le/la/l'/les** or **du/de la/de l'/des**?

If **some/any** can be inserted before the English noun, the French partitive article should be used. But if the noun is used in a general sense, and if inserting **some/any** in front of the English noun does not make sense, the definite article must be used:

     did you buy fish? (*i.e. any fish*)
     tu as acheté *du* poisson?

     yes, I did; I like fish (*i.e. fish in general*)
     oui; j'aime *le* poisson

3. NOUNS

Nouns are naming words, which refer to persons, animals, things, places, or abstract ideas.

A. GENDER

All French nouns are either masculine or feminine; there is no neuter as in English. Though no absolute rule can be stated, the gender can often be determined either by the meaning or the ending of the noun.

1. Masculine

a) *by meaning*

    i) names of people and animals:

un homme a man	**le boucher** the butcher	**le tigre** the tiger

    ii) names of common trees and shrubs:

le chêne the oak	**le sapin** the fir tree	**le laurier** the laurel

But: **une aubépine**   **la bruyère**
        a hawthorn   the heather

    iii) days, months, seasons:

lundi Monday	**mars** March	**le printemps** spring

    iv) languages:

le français French	**le polonais** Polish	**le russe** Russian

    v) rivers and countries not ending in a silent **e**:

le Nil the Nile	**le Portugal** Portugal	**le Danemark** Denmark

But: **le Danube**   **le Rhône**   **le Mexique**
        the Danube   the Rhone   Mexico

b) *by ending*

    -acle   **le spectacle** (show)
                 But: **une débâcle** (breakdown, collapse)
    -age   **le fromage** (cheese)
                 But: **la cage** (cage), **une image** (picture), **la nage** (swimmming), **la page** (page), **la plage** (beach), **la rage** (rage; rabies)

-é	**le marché** (market) *But:* nouns ending in **-té** and **-tié** (see p. 26)
-eau	**le chapeau** (hat) *But:* **l'eau** (water), **la peau** (skin)
-ège	**le piège** (trap), **le collège** (secondary school)
-ème	**le thème** (theme, topic) *But:* **la crème** (the cream)
-isme, -asme	**le communisme** (communism), **le tourisme** (tourism), **l'enthousiasme** (enthusiasm)
-o	**le numéro** (the number) *But:* **la dynamo** (dynamo) and most abbreviated expressions: **une auto** (car), **la météo** (weather forecast), **la photo** (photograph), **la radio** (radio), **la sténo** (shorthand), **la stéréo** (stereo)

Nouns ending in a *consonant* are usually *masculine*.

Notable exceptions are:

i) most nouns ending in **-tion**, **-sion**, **-ation**, **-aison**, **-ison**
ii) most abstract nouns ending in **-eur** (see p. 26)
iii) the following nouns ending in a consonant:

la clef (key)	**la nef** (nave)
la soif (thirst)	**la faim** (hunger)
la fin (end)	**la façon** (manner)
la leçon (lesson)	**la boisson** (drink)
la moisson (harvest)	**la rançon** (ransom)
la mer (sea)	**la cuiller** (spoon)
la chair (flesh)	**la basse-cour** (farmyard)
la cour (yard)	**la tour** (tower)
la brebis (ewe)	**la fois** (time, occurrence)
la vis (screw)	**la souris** (mouse)
la part (share)	**la plupart** (majority, most)
la dent (tooth)	**la dot** (dowry)
la forêt (forest)	**la jument** (mare)
la mort (death)	**la nuit** (night)
la croix (cross)	**la noix** (nut)
la paix (peace)	**la perdrix** (partridge)
la toux (cough)	**la voix** (voice)

2. Feminine

a) *by meaning*

i) names of females (people and animals):

la mère the mother	**la bonne** the maid	**la génisse** the heifer

ii) names of rivers and countries ending in a silent **e**:

la Seine the Seine	**la Russie** Russia	**la Belgique** Belgium

iii) saints' days and festivals:

la Toussaint All Saints' Day	**la Pentecôte** Pentecost

But: **Noël** (Christmas) is masculine except with the definite article: **à la Noël** (at Christmas)

b) *by ending*

-ace	**la place** (city square; seat) *But:* **un espace** (space)
-ade	**la salade** (salad) *But:* **le grade** (degree, rank), **le stade** (stadium)
-ance, -anse	**la puissance** (power), **la danse** (dancing)
-ée	**la soirée** (evening) *But:* **le musée** (museum), **le lycée** (secondary school)
-ence, -ense	**une évidence** (evidence), **la défense** (defense) *But:* **le silence** (silence)
-ère	**la lumière** (light) *But:* **le mystère** (mystery), **le caractère** (character)
-eur	**la peur** (fear) *But:* **le bonheur** (happiness), **le chœur** (choir), **le cœur** (heart), **un honneur** (honor), **le labeur** (toil), **le malheur** (misfortune)
-ie	**la pluie** (rain) *But:* **le génie** (genius), **un incendie** (fire), **le parapluie** (umbrella)
-ière	**la bière** (beer) *But:* **le cimetière** (cemetery)
-oire	**la gloire** (glory) *But:* **le laboratoire** (laboratory), **le pourboire** (tip, gratuity)
-tion, -sion, -ation, -aison, -ison	**la fiction** (fiction), **la nation** (nation), **la raison** (reason), **la prison** (prison)
-té	**la bonté** (goodness) *But:* **le côté** (side), **le comté** (county), **le traité** (treaty), **le pâté** (pâté)
-tié	**la moitié** (half), **la pitié** (pity)

17

Most nouns ending in a silent **e** following two consonants:

> **la botte** (boot), **la couronne** (crown), **la terre** (earth),
> **la masse** (mass), **la lutte** (struggle)

But: **le verre** (glass), **le parterre** (flower-bed), **le tonnerre** (thunder),
un intervalle (interval), **le carosse** (carriage)

3. Difficulties

a) Some nouns may have either gender depending on the sex of the person to whom they refer:

un artiste a (male) artist	**une artiste** a (female) artist
le Russe the Russian (man)	**la Russe** the Russian (woman)

similarly:

un aide/une aide	an assistant
un camarade/une camarade	a friend
un domestique/une domestique	a servant
un enfant/une enfant	a child
un malade/une malade	a patient
un propriétaire/une propriétaire	an owner

b) Others have only one gender for both sexes:

un ange an angel	**un amateur** an amateur	**un auteur** an author
une connaissance an acquaintance	**la dupe** the dupe	**un écrivain** a writer
la bête the beast	**le médecin** the doctor	**le peintre** the painter
une personne a person	**le poète** the poet	**le professeur** the teacher
la recrue the recruit	**le sculpteur** the sculptor	**la sentinelle** the sentry
le témoin the witness	**la victime** the victim	**la vedette** the (film) star

c) The following nouns change meaning according to gender:

	MASCULINE	FEMININE
aide	male assistant	assistance; female assistant
crêpe	mourning band	pancake
critique	critic	criticism
faux	forgery	scythe

	MASCULINE	FEMININE
livre	book	pound
manche	handle	sleeve
manœuvre	laborer	maneuver
mémoire	thesis	memory
mode	method, way	fashion
mort	dead man	death
moule	mould	mussel
page	pageboy	page
pendule	pendulum	clock
physique	physique	physics
poêle	stove	frying pan
poste	post (*job*); set	post office
somme	nap	sum
tour	trick; tour	tower
trompette	trumpeter	trumpet
vapeur	steamer	steam
vase	vase	sludge
voile	veil	sail

d) **Gens** is regarded as feminine when it follows an adjective, and masculine when it precedes it:

de bonnes gens	**des gens ennuyeux**
good people	bores

B. THE FORMATION OF FEMININES

The feminine of nouns may be formed in the following ways:

1. Add an 'e' to the masculine

un ami	**une amie**
a (male) friend	a (female) friend
un Hollandais	**une Hollandaise**
a Dutchman	a Dutch woman

a) Nouns that end in e in the masculine do not change:

un élève	**une élève**
a (male) pupil	a (female) pupil

b) The addition of e often requires a change in the masculine form:

   i) nouns ending in **t** and **n** double the final consonant:

le chien	**la chienne** (dog/bitch)
le chat	**la chatte** (cat)

19

ii) nouns ending in **-er** add a grave accent to the **e** before the silent **e**:

un ouvrier **une ouvrière** (workman/female worker)

iii) nouns ending in **-eur** change to **-euse**:

le vendeur **la vendeuse** (male/female salesperson)

a few nouns ending in **-eur** change to **-eresse**:

le pécheur **la pécheresse** (sinner)

iv) nouns ending in **-teur** change to **-teuse** or **-trice** according to the following guidelines:

if the stem of the word is also that of a present participle, the feminine form is in **-euse**:

le chanteur **la chanteuse** (male/female singer)

but if the stem is not that of a present participle, the feminine form is in **-trice**:

le lecteur **la lectrice** (male/female reader)

v) nouns ending in **f** change to **-ve**:

le veuf **la veuve** (widower/widow)

vi) nouns ending in **x** change to **-se**:

un époux **une épouse** (husband/wife)

vii) nouns ending in **-eau** change to **-elle**:

le jumeau **la jumelle** (male/female twin)

2. Use a different word (as in English)

le beau-fils	la belle-fille (son/daughter-in-law)
le beau-père	la belle-mère (father/mother-in-law)
le bélier	la brebis (ram/ewe)
le bœuf	la vache (ox/cow)
le canard	la cane (drake/duck)
le cheval	la jument (horse/mare)
le cerf	la biche (stag/hind)
le coq	la poule (rooster/hen)
le fils	la fille (son/daughter)
le frère	la sœur (brother/sister)
un homme	une femme (man/woman)
un jars	une oie (gander/goose)
le mâle	la femelle (male/female)
le neveu	la nièce (nephew/niece)
un oncle	une tante (uncle/aunt)
le parrain	la marraine (godfather/godmother)
le père	la mère (father/mother)
le porc	la truie (pig/sow)
le roi	la reine (king/queen)

3. Add the word 'femme' (or 'femelle' for animals)

une **femme** poète (poetess)
un perroquet **femelle** (female parrot)

4. Irregular plurals

un **abbé**	une **abbesse** (abbot/abbess)
un **âne**	une **ânesse** (donkey)
le **comte**	la **comtesse** (count/countess)
le **dieu**	la **déesse** (god/goddess)
le **duc**	la **duchesse** (duke/duchess)
un **Esquimau**	une **Esquimaude** (Eskimo)
le **fou**	la **folle** (madman/madwoman)
un **héros**	une **héroïne** (hero/heroine)
un **hôte**	une **hôtesse** (host/hostess)
le **maître**	la **maîtresse** (master/mistress)
le **prêtre**	la **prêtresse** (priest/priestess)
le **prince**	la **princesse** (prince/princess)
le **tigre**	la **tigresse** (tiger/tigress)
le **Turc**	la **Turque** (Turk)
le **vieux**	la **vieille** (old man/old woman)

C. THE FORMATION OF PLURALS

1. Most nouns form their plural by adding s to the singular:

le **vin**	les **vins**	wine
un **étudiant**	des **étudiants**	student

2. Nouns ending in 's', 'x', or 'z' remain unchanged:

le **bras**	les **bras**	arm
la **voix**	les **voix**	voice
le **nez**	les **nez**	nose

3. Nouns ending in -au, -eau, and -eu add x to the singular:

le **tuyau**	les **tuyaux**	pipe, tube
le **bateau**	les **bateaux**	boat
le **jeu**	les **jeux**	game
But: le **landau**	les **landaus**	baby carriage
le **bleu**	les **bleus**	bruise
le **pneu**	les **pneus**	tire

4. Nouns ending in -al change to -aux:

le **journal**	les **journaux**	newspaper

21

But: **le bal**	**les bals**	dance
le carnaval	**les carnavals**	carnival
le festival	**les festivals**	festival

5. Nouns ending in **-ail** change to **-aux**:

le bail	**les baux**	lease
le travail	**les travaux**	work
le vitrail	**les vitraux**	stained-glass window

Common exceptions in which the plural is formed in **-ail**:

le chandail	**les chandails**	sweater
le détail	**les détails**	detail
l'épouvantail	**les épouvantails**	scarecrow
l'éventail	**les éventails**	fan
le rail	**les rails**	rail

6. Nouns ending in **-ou**:

a) Seven nouns ending in **-ou** add **x** in the plural:

le bijou	**les bijoux**	jewel
le caillou	**les cailloux**	pebble
le chou	**les choux**	cabbage
le genou	**les genoux**	knee
le hibou	**les hiboux**	owl
le joujou	**les joujoux**	toy
le pou	**les poux**	louse

b) Other nouns ending in **-ou** add **s**:

le clou	**les clous**	nail

7. Plural of compound nouns

Each noun should be checked individually in a dictionary:

e.g. **le chou-fleur**	**les choux-fleurs**	cauliflower
le beau-père	**les beaux-pères**	father-in-law
But: **un essuie-glace**	**des essuie-glaces**	windshield wiper
le tire-bouchon	**les tire-bouchons**	corkscrew

8. Irregular plurals:

un œil	**des yeux**	eye
le ciel	**les cieux**	sky
Monsieur	**Messieurs**	Mr.
Madame	**Mesdames**	Mrs.
Mademoiselle	**Mesdemoiselles**	Miss

9. Collective nouns

a) *Singular in French but plural in English*

le bétail	cattle
la famille	family
la police	police

la police *a* **arrêté certains grévistes**
the police *have* arrested some strikers

b) *Plural in French but singular in English*

> **les nouvelles sont bonnes**
> the news is good

10. Proper nouns

a) Ordinary family names are invariable:

> **j'ai rencontré les Leblanc**
> I met the Leblancs

b) Historical names add **-s**:

les Stuarts	**les Bourbons**	**les Tudors**
the Stuarts	the Bourbons	the Tudors

4. ADJECTIVES

Adjectives are describing words that usually accompany a noun (or a pronoun) and tell us what someone or something is like:

une *grande* ville
a *large* city

un passe-temps *intéressant*
an *interesting* hobby

elle est *espagnole*
she is *Spanish*

c'était *ennuyeux*
it was *boring*

A. AGREEMENT OF ADJECTIVES

In French, adjectives agree in number and gender with the noun or pronoun they refer to. This means that, unlike English adjectives, which don't change, French adjectives have four different forms that are determined by the noun they go with:

- **masculine singular** for masculine singular words (basic form, found in the dictionary)
- **feminine singular** for feminine singular words
- **masculine plural** for masculine plural words
- **feminine plural** for feminine plural words

un passeport *vert*
a green passport

une voiture *verte*
a green car

des gants *verts*
green gloves

des chaussettes *vertes*
green socks

Note: If two singular words share the same adjective, the adjective will be in the plural:

un foulard et un chapeau *rouges*
a red scarf and (a red) hat

If one of these words is feminine, one masculine, the adjective will be masculine plural:

une robe et un manteau *noirs*
a black dress and (a black) coat

B. FEMININE FORMS OF ADJECTIVES

1. General rule

Add the letter **e** to the masculine singular form:

MASCULINE	FEMININE
grand	**grande**
amusant	**amusante**

américain	**américaine**
bronzé	**bronzée**
un livre amusant	**une histoire amusante**
an amusing book	an amusing story
il est bronzé	**elle est bronzée**
he is suntanned	she is suntanned

2. Adjectives already ending in 'e'

These do not change:

MASCULINE	FEMININE
rouge	**rouge**
jeune	**jeune**
malade	**malade**
mon père est malade	**ma mère est malade**
my father is sick	my mother is sick

3. Others

The spelling of some adjectives changes when the **e** is added:

a) The following masculine endings generally double the final consonant before adding **e**:

MASCULINE ENDING	FEMININE ENDING
-el	**-elle**
-eil	**-eille**
-en	**-enne**
-on	**-onne**
-as	**-asse**
-et	**-ette**

MASCULINE		FEMININE
réel	(real)	**réelle**
cruel	(cruel)	**cruelle**
pareil	(similar)	**pareille**
ancien	(old)	**ancienne**
italien	(Italian)	**italienne**
bon	(good)	**bonne**
gras	(greasy)	**grasse**
bas	(low)	**basse**
muet	(silent)	**muette**
net	(clear)	**nette**

25

un problème actuel	**la vie actuelle**
a current problem	present-day life
un bon conseil	**c'est une bonne recette**
good advice	it's a good recipe

But: the feminine ending of some common adjectives in **-et** is **-ète** instead of **-ette**:

MASCULINE		FEMININE
complet	(complete)	**complète**
incomplet	(incomplete)	**incomplète**
concret	(concrete)	**concrète**
discret	(discreet)	**discrète**
inquiet	(worried)	**inquiète**
secret	(secret)	**secrète**

b) MASCULINE   FEMININE
IN **-er**   IN **-ére**

cher	(dear; expensive)	chère
fier	(proud)	**fière**
dernier	(last)	**dernière**

c) MASCULINE   FEMININE
IN **-x**   IN **-se**

heureux	(happy)	**heureuse**
malheureux	(unhappy)	**malheureuse**
sérieux	(serious)	**sérieuse**
jaloux	(jealous)	**jalouse**

But: | **doux** | (soft) | **douce** |
|---|---|---|
| **faux** | (false) | **fausse** |
| **roux** | (red-haired) | **rousse** |
| **vieux** | (old) | **vieille** |

d) MASCULINE   FEMININE
IN **-eur**   IN **-euse**

menteur	(lying)	**menteuse**
trompeur	(deceitful)	**trompeuse**

But: This rule applies only when the stem of the adjective is also the stem of a present participle (e.g. **mentant, trompant**). The following five adjectives simply add an e to the feminine, **-eur** becoming **-eure**:

MASCULINE		FEMININE
extérieur	(external)	**extérieure**
intérieur	(internal)	**intérieure**

inférieur	(inferior)	**inférieure**
supérieur	(superior)	**supérieure**
meilleur	(better)	**meilleure**

The feminine ending of the remaining adjectives in **-teur** is **-trice**:

MASCULINE		FEMININE
protecteur	(protective)	**protectrice**
destructeur	(destructive)	**destructrice**

e) MASCULINE   FEMININE
   IN -f   IN -ve

neuf	(new)	**neuve**
vif	(lively)	**vive**
naïf	(naive)	**naïve**
actif	(active)	**active**
passif	(passive)	**passive**
positif	(positive)	**positive**
bref	(brief)	**brève** (note the è!)

f) MASCULINE   FEMININE
   IN -c   IN -che or -que

blanc	(white)	**blanche**
franc	(frank)	**franche**
sec	(dry)	**sèche** (note the è!)
public	(public)	**publique**
turc	(Turkish)	**turque**
grec	(Greek)	**grecque** (note the c!)

g) The following five common adjectives have an irregular feminine form and two forms for the masculine singular; the second masculine form, based on the feminine form, is used before words starting with a vowel or a silent **h**:

MASCULINE	FEMININE	MASCULINE 2
beau (beautiful)	**belle**	**bel**
nouveau (new)	**nouvelle**	**nouvel**
vieux (old)	**vieille**	**vieil**
fou (mad)	**folle**	**fol**

27

mou (soft)	**molle**	**mol**
un beau lac a beautiful lake	**une belle vue** a beautiful view	**un bel enfant** a beautiful child
un nouveau disque a new record	**la nouvelle année** the new year	**un nouvel ami** a new friend
un vieux tableau an old painting	**la vieille ville** the old town	**un vieil homme** an old man

h) Other irregular feminines:

MASCULINE		FEMININE
favori	(favorite)	**favorite**
gentil	(nice)	**gentille**
nul	(no)	**nulle**
frais	(fresh, cool)	**fraîche**
malin	(shrewd)	**maligne**
sot	(foolish)	**sotte**
long	(long)	**longue**
aigu	(sharp)	**aiguë**
ambigu	(ambiguous)	**ambiguë**
chic	(elegant)	**chic**
châtain	(chestnut)	**châtain**

C. PLURALS OF ADJECTIVES

1. General rule

The masculine and feminine plural of adjectives is formed by adding an **s** to the singular form:

un vélo neuf a brand new bike	**des vélos neufs** brand new bikes
une belle fleur a beautiful flower	**de belles fleurs** beautiful flowers

2. Adjectives ending in 's' or 'x'

If the masculine singular ends in **s** or **x**, there is obviously no need to add the **s**:

il est heureux he's happy	**ils sont heureux** they are happy
un touriste québécois a Quebec tourist	**des touristes québécois** Quebec tourists

3. Others

A few masculine plurals are irregular (the feminine plurals are all regular):

a)

SINGULAR IN -al		PLURAL IN -aux
normal	(normal)	**normaux**
brutal	(brutal)	**brutaux**
loyal	(loyal)	**loyaux**

But:

fatal	(fatal)	**fatals**
final	(final)	**finals**
natal	(native)	**natals**
naval	(naval)	**navals**

b)

SINGULAR IN -eau		PLURAL IN -eaux
beau	(beautiful)	**beaux**
nouveau	(new)	**nouveaux**

D. POSITION OF ADJECTIVES

1. Unlike English adjectives, French adjectives usually follow the noun:

un métier intéressant	**des parents modernes**
an interesting trade	modern parents

Adjectives of color and nationality always follow the noun:

des chaussures rouges	**le drapeau américain**
red shoes	the American flag

2. However the following common adjectives generally come before the noun:

beau	beautiful
bon	good
court	short
gentil	nice
grand	big, tall
gros	fat
haut	high
jeune	young
joli	pretty
long	long
mauvais	bad

méchant	nasty, naughty (*child*)
meilleur	better
moindre	lesser, least
petit	small
pire	worse
vieux	old
vilain	nasty, ugly

3. Some adjectives have a different meaning according to their position:

	BEFORE NOUN	AFTER NOUN
ancien	former	ancient
brave	good	brave
certain	some	sure
cher	dear	expensive
dernier	last, final	last (= *latest*)
grand	great (*people only*)	big, tall
même	same	very, selfsame
pauvre	poor (*pitiable*)	poor (*not rich*)
propre	own	clean
seul	single, only	alone, lonely
simple	mere	simple
vrai	real	true

mon ancien métier my former trade	**un tableau ancien** an old painting
un brave type a nice guy	**un homme brave** a brave man
un certain charme a certain charm	**un fait certain** a definite fact
chère Brigitte dear Brigitte	**un cadeau cher** an expensive gift
la dernière classe the final class	**le mois dernier** last month
une grande vedette a great film star	**un homme assez grand** a fairly tall man
le même endroit the same place	**la vérité même** the truth itself
mon pauvre ami! my poor friend!	**des gens pauvres** poor people
mon propre frère my own brother	**une chambre propre** a clean room

mon seul espoir my only hope	**un homme seul** a lonely man
un simple employé an ordinary employee	**des goûts simples** simple tastes
un vrai casse-pieds a real bore	**une histoire vraie** a true story

4. If a noun is accompanied by several adjectives, the same rules apply to each of them:

le bon vieux temps
the good old days

un joli foulard rouge
a pretty red scarf

E. COMPARATIVE AND SUPERLATIVE OF ADJECTIVES

Persons or things can be compared by using:

1. *the comparative form of the adjective:*
   more ... than, ... er than, less ... than, as ... as
2. *the superlative form of the adjective:*
   the most ..., the ... est, the least ...

1. The comparative

The comparative is formed as follows:

plus ... (que) more ..., ... er (than)	**plus long** longer	**plus cher** more expensive
moins ... (que) less ... than	**moins long** less long	**moins récent** less recent
aussi ... (que) as ... (as)	**aussi bon** as good	**aussi important** as important

une plus grande maison
a bigger house

un village plus ancien
an older village

le baseball est-il plus populaire que le hockey?
is baseball more popular than hockey?

ces gants sont moins chauds que les autres
these gloves are less warm than the other ones

elle est beaucoup/bien moins patiente que lui
she's much less patient than he is

le problème de la pollution est tout aussi grave
the pollution problem is just as serious

2. The superlative

a) *Formation*

le/la/les plus . . .	the most . . . , the . . . est
le/la/les moins . . .	the least . . .
le plus grand pays the biggest country	**la plus grande ville** the biggest city
les plus grands acteurs the greatest actors	**les plus grandes voitures** the biggest cars

b) *Word order*

i) The normal rules governing word order of adjectives apply. When a superlative adjective comes after the noun, the article is used twice, before the noun and before the adjective:

le plat le plus délicieux
the most delicious dish

l'histoire la plus passionnante
the most exciting story

ii) When a possessive adjective is used, there are two possible constructions, depending on the position of the adjective:

ma plus forte matière
my best subject

or:

son besoin le plus urgent est de trouver un emploi
his most urgent need is to find a job

c) *'in' is normally translated by **de**:*

la plus jolie maison du quartier/de la ville
the prettiest house in the neighborhood/town

le restaurant le plus cher de France
the most expensive restaurant in France

Note: Verbs following the superlative usually take the subjunctive (see p. 92).

3. Irregular comparatives and superlatives

ADJECTIVE	COMPARATIVE	SUPERLATIVE
bon good	**meilleur** better	**le meilleur** best
mauvais bad	**pire** **plus mauvais** worse	**le pire** **le plus mauvais** the worst

petit	moindre	le moindre
small	plus petit	le plus petit
	smaller, lesser	the smallest, the least

Note: **–plus mauvais** is used in the sense of worse in quality, taste, etc.

–moindre usually means 'less in importance', and **plus petit** means 'less in size':

le moindre de mes soucis
the least of my worries

elle est plus petite que moi
she is smaller than I/me

5. ADVERBS

Adverbs are normally used with a verb to express:

		ADVERBS OF
how	⎫	manner
when	⎪	time
where	⎬ an action is done	place
with how much intensity	⎪	intensity
to what extent	⎭	quantity

A. ADVERBS OF MANNER

These are usually formed by adding **-ment** to the adjective (like **-ly** in English):

1. If the adjective ends in a consonant, **-ment** is added to its feminine form:

ADJECTIVE (masc, fem)	ADVERB
doux, douce (soft)	**doucement** (softly)
franc, franche (frank)	**franchement** (frankly)
final, finale (final)	**finalement** (finally)

2. If the adjective ends in a vowel, **-ment** is added to its masculine form:

ADJECTIVE	ADVERB
absolu (absolute)	**absolument** (absolutely)
désespéré (desperate)	**désespérément** (desperately)
vrai (true)	**vraiment** (truly)
simple (simple)	**simplement** (simply)

But:

gai (cheerful)	**gaiement** *or* **gaîment** (cheerfully)
nouveau (new)	**nouvellement** (newly)
fou (mad)	**follement** (madly)

3. Many adverbs have irregular forms:

a) Some change the **e** of the feminine form of the adjective to **é** before adding **-ment**:

ADJECTIVE	ADVERB
commun (common)	**communément** (commonly)
précis (precise)	**précisément** (precisely)

profond (deep)	**pronfondément** (deeply)
énorme (enormous)	**énormément** (enormously)
aveugle (blind)	**aveuglément** (blindly)

b) Adjectives that end in **-ent** and **-ant** change to **-emment** and **-amment** (*Note:* both endings are pronounced **-amant**):

ADJECTIVE	ADVERB
prudent (careful)	**prudemment** (carefully)
évident (obvious)	**évidemment** (obviously)
brillant (brilliant)	**brillamment** (brilliantly)
But: **lent** (slow)	**lentement** (slowly)
content (happy)	(*no corresponding adverb*)

4. Some adverbs are completely irregular, including some of the most commonly used ones:

ADJECTIVE	ADVERB
bon (good)	**bien** (well)
bref (brief)	**brièvement** (briefly)
gentil (kind)	**gentiment** (kindly)
mauvais (bad)	**mal** (badly)
meilleur (better)	**mieux** (better)

5. Some adjectives are also used as adverbs in certain set expressions, e.g.:

parler bas/haut *or* **fort**	to speak softly/loudly
coûter/payer cher	to cost/pay a lot
s'arrêter court	to stop short
couper court	to cut short
voir clair	to see clearly
marcher droit	to walk straight
travailler dur	to work hard
chanter faux/juste	to sing off key/in tune
sentir mauvais/bon	to smell bad/good
refuser net	to refuse point blank

6. After verbs of saying and looking in French an adverbial phrase is often preferred to an adverb, e.g.:

"tu m'écriras?" dit-il *d'une voix triste*
"will you write me?" he said *sadly*

elle nous a regardés *d'un air dédaigneux*
she looked at us *disdainfully*

7. English adverbs may be expressed in French by a preposition followed by a noun, e.g.:

sans soin	carelessly
avec fierté	proudly
avec amour	lovingly

B. ADVERBS OF TIME

These are not usually formed from adjectives. Here are the commonest ones:

alors	then
après	afterwards
aujourd'hui	today
aussitôt	right away, immediately
bientôt	soon
d'abord	first
déjà	already
demain	tomorrow
encore	still, again
pas encore	not yet
enfin	at last, finally
hier	yesterday
parfois	sometimes
rarement	seldom
souvent	often
tard	late
tôt	early
toujours	always
tout de suite	immediately

c'est déjà Noël!	**tu as déjà essayé?**
it's Christmas already!	have you tried before?
il mange encore!	**elle n'est pas encore arrivée**
he's still eating!	she hasn't arrived yet

C. ADVERBS OF PLACE

Here are the commonest ones:

ailleurs	somewhere else
ici	here
là	there
loin	far away
dessus	on top, on it
au-dessus	over, above
dessous	underneath
au-dessous	below
dedans	inside
dehors	outside
devant	in front, ahead
derrière	behind
partout	everywhere

ne restez pas dehors!	**mon nom est marqué dessus**
don't stay outside!	my name is written on it
qu'est-ce qu'il y a dedans?	**passez devant!**
what's inside?	you go first!

D. ADVERBS OF INTENSITY AND QUANTITY

These may be used with a verb, an adjective, or another adverb. Here are the commonest ones:

à peine	hardly
assez	enough, quite
autant	as much/many
beaucoup	a lot, much/many
combien	how much/many
comme	how
moins	less
plus	more
presque	nearly, almost
peu	little
seulement	only
si	so
tant	so much/many
tellement	so much/many
très	very
trop	too, too much/many
un peu	a little

vous avez assez bu!
you've had enough to drink!

il ne fait pas assez chaud
it's not warm enough

nous avons beaucoup ri
we laughed a lot

comme c'est amusant!
how funny!

je vais un peu mieux
I'm feeling a little better

c'est si fatigant!
it's so tiring!

elle parle trop
she talks too much

il est très timide
he's very shy

Note: All of these adverbs, except **à peine, comme, presque, si, très, seulement,** may be followed by **de** and a noun to express a quantity (see pp. 174–76).

E. POSITION OF ADVERBS

1. Adverbs usually follow verbs:

   je vais rarement au théâtre
   I seldom go to the theater

   comme vous conduisez prudemment!
   how carefully you drive!

2. With compound tenses, shorter adverbs usually come between the auxiliary and the past participle:

   j'ai enfin terminé
   I have finished at last

   nous y sommes souvent allés
   we've often gone there

37

il me l'a déjà dit
he's already told me so

elle avait beaucoup souffert
she had suffered a lot

3. But adverbs of place and many adverbs of time follow the past participle:

je l'ai rencontré hier
I met him yesterday

elle avait cherché partout
she had looked everywhere

mettez-le dehors
put it outside

tu t'es couché tard?
did you get to bed late?

4. Adverbs usually come before adjectives or other adverbs:

très rarement
very seldom

trop vite
too quickly

elle est vraiment belle
she is really beautiful

F. COMPARATIVE AND SUPERLATIVE OF ADVERBS

1. The comparative and superlative of adverbs are formed in the same way as adjectives:

ADVERB	COMPARATIVE	SUPERLATIVE
souvent often	**plus souvent (que)** more often (than)	**le plus souvent** (the) most often
	moins souvent (que) less often (than)	**le moins souvent** (the) least often
	aussi souvent (que) as often (as)	

Note: The superlative of the adverb always takes the masculine singular article **le**:

je le vois plus souvent qu'avant
I see him more often than I used to

il conduit moins prudemment que moi
he drives less carefully than I/me

c'est lui qui conduit le moins prudemment
he's the one who drives the least carefully

je sais cuisiner aussi bien que toi!
I know how to cook as well as you!

Note:

a) as ... as possible is translated either by **aussi ... que possible** or by **le plus ... possible**:

as far as possible
aussi loin que possible
le plus loin possible

b) after a negative, **aussi** is often replaced by **si**:

pas si vite!
not so fast!

c) In French, the idea of **not so, not as** is often expressed by **moins** (less):

parle moins fort!
don't talk so loud!

2. Irregular comparatives and superlatives

ADVERB	COMPARATIVE	SUPERLATIVE
beaucoup much, a lot	**plus** more	**le plus** (the) most
bien well	**mieux** better	**le mieux** (the) best
mal badly	**pis** or **plus mal** worse	**le pis** or **le plus mal** (the) worst
peu little	**moins** less	**le moins** (the) least

Note: i) **mieux/le mieux** must not be confused with **meilleur/le meilleur**, which are adjectives, used in front of a noun (though the adverbial forms are often used adjectivally in contemporary French, in certain cases).

ii) **pis/le pis** are only found in certain set expressions:

tant pis so much the worse, too bad	**de mal en pis** from bad to worse

6. PRONOUNS AND CORRESPONDING ADJECTIVES

A. DEMONSTRATIVES

1. Demonstrative adjectives

a) *CE*

ce is often used to point out a particular person or thing, or persons or things. It is followed by the noun it refers to and agrees in number and gender with that noun:

– with a masculine singular noun:	**ce (cet)**	this/that
– with a feminine singular noun:	**cette**	this/that
– with a plural noun (masc or fem):	**ces**	these/those

ce roman m'a beaucoup plu   **il a neigé ce matin**

I really liked that novel   it snowed this morning

cette chanson m'énerve   **cette fois, c'est fini!**

that song gets on my nerves   this time, it's over!

tu trouves que ces lunettes me vont bien?
do you think these glasses suit me?

cet is used instead of **ce** in front of a word that begins with a vowel or a silent **h**:

cet après-midi   **cet hôtel**

this afternoon   that hotel

b) *-CI and -LA*

French does not have separate words to distinguish between 'this' and 'that'. However, when a particular emphasis is being placed on a person or object, or when a contrast is being made between persons or objects, **-ci** and **-là** are added to the noun:

-ci translates the idea of	this/these
-là translates the idea of	that/those

je suis très occupé ces jours-ci
I'm very busy these days

que faisiez-vous ce soir-là?
what were you doing that evening?

d'où vient ce fromage-là?—ce fromage-ci, Monsieur?
where does that cheese come from?—this cheese, sir?

2. Demonstrative pronouns

Demonstrative pronouns are used instead of a noun with **ce/cette/ces**. They are:

a) **celui, celle, ceux, celles**
b) **ce**
c) **ceci, cela, ça**

a) *CELUI*

i) **celui** agrees in number and gender with the noun it refers to. It has four different forms:

	MASCULINE	FEMININE
SINGULAR	**celui**	**celle**
PLURAL	**ceux**	**celles**

ii) use of **celui**

celui, **celle**, **ceux**, and **celles** cannot be used by themselves. They are used:

- with **-ci** or **-là**, for emphasis or for contrast:

celui-ci	**celle-ci**	this (one)
celui-là	**celle-là**	that (one)
ceux-ci	**celles-ci**	these (here)
ceux-là	**celles-là**	those (there)

j'aime bien ce maillot, mais celui-là est moins cher
I like this swimsuit, but that one is cheaper

je voudrais ces fleurs—lesquelles? celles-ci ou celles-là?
I'd like these flowers—which ones? these or those?

- with **de** + noun, to express possession:

je préfère mon ordinateur à celui de Jean-Claude
I like my computer better than Jean-Claude's

range ta chambre plutôt que celle de ta sœur
clean up your own bedroom rather than your sister's

mes parents sont moins sévères que ceux de Nicole
my parents aren't as strict as Nicole's

les douches municipales sont mieux que celles du camping
the public showers are better than the ones at the campsite

- with the relative pronouns **qui, que, dont** to introduce a relative clause (for use of these relative pronouns, see pp. 62–67).

  celui/celle/ceux/celles qui   the one(s) who/which/that
  celui/celle/ceux/celles que   the one(s) whom/which/that
  celui/celle/ceux/celles dont   the one(s) of which/whose

  lequel est ton père? celui qui a une moustache?
  which one is your father? the one with the moustache?

  regarde cette voiture! celle qui est garée au coin
  look at that car! the one that's parked on the corner

  deux filles, celles qu'il avait rencontrées la veille
  two girls, the ones he had met the day before

  voilà mon copain, celui dont je t'ai parlé l'autre jour
  here's my friend, the one I told you about the other day

b) CE

i) **ce** (meaning 'it', 'that') is mostly found with the verb **être**:

c'est	**ce serait**	**c'était**
it's/that's	it/that would be	it/that was

Note: **ce** changes to **c'** before an **e** or an **é**.

ii) use of **ce**

- with a noun or pronoun, **ce** is used to identify people or things, or to emphasize them; it is translated in a variety of ways:

  qu'est-ce que c'est?—c'est mon billet d'avion
  what's that?—it's my plane ticket

qui est-ce?—c'est moi	**ce doit être lui**
who is it?—it's me	that must be him
c'est un artiste bien connu	**c'était une bonne idée**
he's a well-known artist	it was a good idea
ce sont mes amis	**c'est la dernière fois!**
they're my friends	it's the last time!
c'est elle qui l'a fait	**c'est celui que j'ai vu**
she's the one who did it	he's the one I saw

- before an adjective, **ce** is used to refer to an idea, an event, or a fact that has already been mentioned; it does not refer to any specific noun:

c'était formidable	**ce serait amusant**
it was great	it would be funny
oui, c'est vrai	**c'est sûr?**
yes, that's true	is that definite?
ce n'est pas grave	**c'est bon à entendre**
it doesn't matter	that's good to hear
or it's not serious	

Note: the translation of **it** often presents problems for students of French, since it is sometimes translated by **ce** and sometimes by **il/elle**; see pp. 192–93.

c) *CECI, CELA, ÇA*

ceci (this), **cela** (that), and **ça** (that) are used to refer to an idea, an event, a fact, or an object. They never refer to a specific noun already mentioned.

non, je n'aime pas ça!	**ah, bon? cela m'étonne**
no, I don't like that!	really? that surprises me
ça, c'est un acteur!	**souvenez-vous de ceci**
that's what I call an actor!	remember this
ça m'est égal	**cela ne vous regarde pas**
it's all the same to me	that's none of your business

buvez ceci, ça vous fera du bien
drink this, it'll do you good

ça alors!
well, really!

cela s'appelle comment, en anglais?
what do you call this in English?

Note: **ceci** is not very common in French; **cela** and **ça** are often used to translate 'this' as well as 'that'; **ça** is used far more frequently than **cela** in spoken French.

B. INDEFINITE ADJECTIVES AND PRONOUNS

1. Indefinite adjectives

They are:

MASCULINE	FEMININE	
autre(s)	**autre(s)**	other
certain(s)	**certaine(s)**	certain
chaque	**chaque**	each, every
même(s)	**même(s)**	same
plusieurs	**plusieurs**	several
quelque(s)	**quelque(s)**	some
tel(s)	**telle(s)**	such
tout (tous)	**toute(s)**	all, every

43

a) *CHAQUE* and *PLUSIEURS*

chaque (each) is always singular, **plusieurs** (several) always plural; the feminine form is the same as the masculine:

j'y vais chaque jour	**chaque personne**
I go there every day	each person
plusieurs années	**il a plusieurs amis**
several years	he has several friends

b) *AUTRE, MEME,* and *QUELQUE*

autre (other), **même** (same), and **quelque** (some) agree in number with the noun that follows; the feminine is the same as the masculine:

je voudrais un autre café	**d'autres couleurs**
I'd like another coffee	other colors
la même taille	**les mêmes touristes**
the same size	the same tourists
quelque temps après	**à quelques kilomètres**
some time later	a few kilometers away

Note: **même** has a different meaning when placed after the noun (see p. 30).

c) *CERTAIN, TEL,* and *TOUT*

certain (certain, some), **tel** (such), and **tout** (all) agree in number and gender with the noun; they have four different forms:

un certain charme	**une certaine dame**
a certain charm	a certain lady
à certains moments	**certaines personnes**
at (certain) times	some people
un tel homme	**une telle aventure**
such a man	such an adventure
de tels avantages	**de telles difficultés**
such advantages	such difficulties

quoi! tu as mangé tout le fromage et tous les fruits?
what! you've eaten all the cheese and all the fruit?

toute la journée	**toutes mes matières**
all day long	all my subjects

Note:

i) **tel**: the position of the article **un/une** with **tel** is not the same as in English: **un tel homme** = such a man.

ii) **tel** cannot qualify another adjective; when it is used as an adverb, 'such' is translated by **si** or **tellement** (so):

c'était un si bon repas/un repas tellement bon!
it was such a good meal!

iii) **tous les/toutes les** are often translated by 'every':

tous les jours	**toutes les places**
every day	all the seats, every seat

2. Indefinite pronouns

a) These are:

MASC	FEM	
aucun	aucune	none, not any
autre(s)	autre(s)	another one, other ones/others
certains	certaine(s)	certain, some
chacun	chacune	each one, everyone
on		one, someone, you, they, people, we
personne		nobody, no one
plusieurs	plusieurs	several (ones)
quelque chose		something, anything
quelqu'un		someone
quelques-uns	quelques-unes	some, a few
rien		nothing
tout (tous)	toute(s)	everything, every one, all

pas celui-là, l'autre	**où sont les autres?**
not that one, the other (one)	where are the others/other ones?
certains disent que . . .	**personne n'est venu**
some say that . . .	no one came
qui est là?—personne	**qu'as-tu?—rien**
who's there?—nobody	what's wrong?—nothing
plusieurs d'entre eux	**chacun pour soi!**
several of them	every man for himself!
il manque quelque chose?	**dis quelque chose!**
is anything missing?	say something!
quelqu'un l'a averti	**il y a quelqu'un?**
someone warned him	is anyone in?
j'ai tout oublié	**c'est tout, merci**
I've forgotten everything	that's all, thanks
elles sont toutes arrivées	**allons-y tous ensemble**
they've all arrived	let's all go there together

b) *Points to note*

i) **aucun(e), personne,** and **rien**: these can be used by themselves but are more often used with a verb and the negative word **ne** (see negative expressions, pp. 182–83):

personne n'habite ici
no one lives here

il n'y a rien à manger
there's nothing to eat

ii) **aucun(e), un(e) autre, d'autres, certain(e)s, plusieurs,** and **quelques-un(e)s**: when these pronouns are used as direct objects, the pronoun **en** must be used before the verb (or after, if the verb is an affirmative imperative):

je n'en ai lu aucun
I haven't read any (of them)

donne-m'en une autre
give me another one

j'en ai vu d'autres qui étaient moins chers
I saw other ones that were cheaper

j'en connais certains
I know some of them

il y en a plusieurs
there are several

tu m'en donnes quelques-uns?
will you give me a few?

achètes-en quelques-unes
buy a few

iii) **personne, quelque chose, rien, plusieurs**: when these are followed by an adjective, the preposition **de(d')** must be used in front of the adjective:

il n'y a personne de libre
there's no one available

quelque chose de mieux
something better

il y en avait plusieurs de cassés
several of them were broken

rien de grave
nothing serious

iv) **autre** is commonly used in the following expressions:

quelqu'un d'autre
someone else

quelque chose d'autre
something else

rien d'autre
nothing else

c) *ON*

This pronoun is used in a variety of ways in French. It can mean:

i) *one/you/they/people* in a general sense:

dans la plupart des pays on roule à droite
in most countries they drive on the right

on ne sait jamais
you/one never know(s)

on ne doit pas mentir
you shouldn't lie

ii) *someone* (an undefined person)

In this sense, **on** is often translated by the passive (see pp. 111–12):

on me l'a déjà dit
someone's already told me
I've already been told

on vous l'apportera
someone will bring it to you
it will be brought to you

iii) *we*

In spoken French, **on** is increasingly used instead of **nous**;
although it refers to a plural subject, it is followed by the third
person singular:

qu'est-ce qu'on fait?	**fais vite, on t'attend!**
what shall we do?	hurry up, we're waiting for you!

Note: in compound tenses with the auxiliary **être**, the agreement of the
past participle with **on** is optional:

on est allé au cinéma	**on est rentré en taxi**
on est allés au cinéma	**on est rentrées en taxi**
we went to the movies	we went home by taxi

C. INTERROGATIVE AND EXCLAMATORY ADJECTIVES AND PRONOUNS

1. The interrogative adjective QUEL?

a) *Forms*

quel (which, what) agrees in number and gender with the noun it
refers to. It has four forms:

—with a masc sing noun:	**quel?**
—with a fem sing noun:	**quelle?**
—with a masc plur noun:	**quels?**
—with a fem plur noun:	**quelles?**

b) *Direct questions*:

quel est votre passe-temps favori?
what's your favorite hobby?

quelle heure est-il?
what time is it?

quels jours as-tu de libres?
which days do you have free?

quelles affaires comptes-tu prendre avec toi?
what/which things do you plan to take with you?

c) *Indirect questions*:

je ne sais pas quelle cassette choisir
I don't know which tape to choose

il se demande quelle veste lui va le mieux
he's wondering which jacket fits him best

47

2. The exclamatory adjective QUEL!

quel! has the same forms as the interrogative adjective **quel?**:

quel dommage!
what a pity!

quelle belle maison!
what a beautiful house!

quels imbéciles!
what idiots!

3. Interrogative pronouns

These are:

lequel/laquelle/lesquel(le)s?	which (one(s))?
qui?	who?, whom?
que?	what?
quoi?	what?
ce qui	what
ce que	what

ce qui and **ce que** are used only in indirect questions; all other interrogative pronouns can be used both in direct and indirect questions.

a) *LEQUEL?*

i) forms

lequel (which?, which one?) agrees in gender and number with the noun it stands for:

—with a masc sing noun:	**lequel?**	which (one)?
—with a fem sing noun:	**laquelle?**	which (one)?
—with a masc plur noun:	**lesquels?**	which (ones)?
—with a fem plur noun:	**lesquelles?**	which (ones)?

after the prepositions **à** and **de**, the following changes occur:

à + lequel?	→	**auquel?**
à + lesquels?	→	**auxquels?**
à + lesquelles?	→	**auxquelles?**
de + lequel?	→	**duquel?**
de + lesquels?	→	**desquels?**
de + lesquelles?	→	**desquelles?**

à/de + laquelle? do not change

ii) direct questions:

je cherche un hôtel; lequel recommandez-vous?
I'm looking for a hotel; which one do you recommend?

nous avons plusieurs couleurs; vous préférez laquelle?
we have several colors; which one do you like best?

lesquels de ces livres sont à toi?
which of these books are yours?

je voudrais essayer ces chaussures—lesquelles?
I would like to try these shoes on—which ones?

iii) indirect questions:

demande-lui lequel de ces ordinateurs est le moins cher
ask him which (one) of these computers is the cheapest

c'est dans une de ces rues, mais je ne sais plus laquelle
it's on one of these streets, but I can't remember which one

b) *QUI?*

qui (who?, whom?) is used to refer to people; it can be both subject and object, and can be used after a preposition:

qui t'a accompagné?	**qui as-tu appelé?**
who accompanied you?	who(m) did you call?
tu y vas avec qui?	**c'est pour qui?**
who are you going there with?	who is it for?
pour qui vous prenez-vous?	**à qui l'as-tu donné?**
who do you think you are?	who did you give it to?

Note: **que** (not **qui**!) changes to **qu'** before a vowel or a silent **h**:

qui est-ce qu'elle attend?
who is she waiting for?

qui? can be replaced by **qui est-ce qui?** (subject) or **qui est-ce que?** (object) in direct questions:

qui est-ce qui veut du café? **qui est-ce que tu as vu?**
who wants coffee? who did you see?

avec qui est-ce que tu sors ce soir?
who are you going out with tonight?

But: **qui** cannot be replaced by **qui est-ce qui** or **qui est-ce que** in indirect questions:

j'aimerais savoir qui vous a dit ça
I'd like to know who told you that

elle se demandait de qui étaient les fleurs
she was wondering who the flowers were from

For more details on the use of **qui/que** as relative pronouns, see pp. 63–64.

c) *QUE?*

que (what?) is used to refer to things; it is only used in direct questions; it is always a direct object and cannot be used after prepositions:

que désirez-vous? **qu'a-t-il dit?**
what do you want? what did he say?

que? is rather formal and is usually replaced by **qu'est-ce qui?** or **qu'est-ce que?** in spoken French.

Note: **que** becomes **qu'** before a vowel or a silent **h**.

d) *QU'EST-CE QUI?*

qu'est-ce qui? (what?) is used as the subject of a verb; it cannot refer to a person:

qu'est-ce qui lui est arrivé?
what happened to him?

qu'est-ce qui la fait rire?
what makes her laugh?

e) *QU'EST-CE QUE?*

qu'est-ce que? (what?) replaces **que?** as the object of a verb; it becomes **qu'est-ce qu'** before a vowel or a silent **h**:

qu'est-ce que tu aimes lire?
what do you like to read?

qu'est-ce qu'il va faire pendant les vacances?
what's he going to do during the vacation?

f) *QUOI?*

quoi? (what?) refers to things; it is used:

i) instead of **que** or **qu'est-ce que** after a proposition:

à quoi penses-tu?   **dans quoi l'as-tu mis?**
what are you thinking about?   what did you put it in?

ii) in indirect questions:

demandez-lui de quoi il a besoin
ask him what he needs

je ne sais pas à quoi ça sert
I don't know what that's for

g) *CE QUI, CE QUE*

ce qui and **ce que** (what) are only used in indirect questions; they replace **qu'est-ce qui** and **(qu'est-ce) que**.

They are used in the same way as the relative pronouns **ce qui** and **ce que** (see pp. 66–67).

i) **ce qui** is used as the subject of the verb in the indirect question (**ce qui** is the subject of **s'est passé** in the following example):

nous ne saurons jamais ce qui s'est passé
we'll never know what happened

ii) **ce que**

ce que (**ce qu'** before a vowel or a silent **h**) is used as the object of the verb in the indirect question (**ce que** is the object of **il faisait** in the following example):

je n'ai pas remarqué ce qu'il faisait
I didn't notice what he was doing

D. PERSONAL PRONOUNS

There are four categories of personal pronouns:
— **subject** pronouns
— **object** pronouns
— **disjunctive** pronouns
— **reflexive** pronouns

For reflexive pronouns, see pp. 81–82.

1. Subject pronouns

PERSON	SINGULAR		PLURAL	
1st	**je (j')**	I	**nous**	we
2nd	**tu**	you	**vous**	you
3rd	**il**	he, it	**ils**	they
	elle	she, it	**elles**	they
	on	one, we, they		

Note:

a) **je** changes to **j'** before a vowel or a silent **h**:

j'ai honte   **j'adore les frites**
I'm ashamed   I love French fries

j'habite au Canada
I live in Canada

b) **tu** and **vous**

vous can be plural or singular; it is used when speaking to more than one person (plural), or to a stranger or an older person (singular):

vous venez, les gars?   **vous parlez (l')anglais, Monsieur?**
are you guys coming?   do you speak English, sir?

tu is used when speaking to a friend, a relative, a younger person, or someone you know well:

tu viens, Marc?
are you coming, Marc?

c) **il/ils, elle/elles** may refer to people, animals, or things, and must be of the same gender as the noun they replace:

ton stylo? *il* **est là**   **ta montre?** *elle* **est là**
your pen? there *it* is   your watch? there *it* is

tes gants? *ils* **sont là**   **tes lunettes?** *elles* **sont là**
your gloves? there *they* are   your glasses? there *they* are

When referring to several nouns of different genders, French uses the masculine plural **ils**:

> **tu as vu *le* stylo et *la* montre de Marie?—oui, *ils* sont dans son sac**
> have you seen Marie's pen and watch?—yes, *they*'re in her bag

d) on: see pp. 46–47.

2. Object pronouns

These include:
— direct object pronouns
— indirect object pronouns
— the pronouns **en** and **y**

a) *Forms*

	PERSON	DIRECT	INDIRECT
SING	1st	**me (m')**	**me (m')**
		me	(to) me
	2nd	**te (t')**	**te (t')**
		you	(to) you
	3rd	**le (l')**	**lui**
		him, it	(to) him
		la (l')	**lui**
		her, it	(to) her
PLUR	1st	**nous**	**nous**
		us	(to) us
	2nd	**vous**	**vous**
		you	(to) you
	3rd	**les**	**leur**
		them	(to) them

Note:

i) **me, te, le,** and **la** change to **m', t',** and **l'** before a vowel or a silent **h**:

> **il m'énerve!**   **je m'habituerai à lui**
> he gets on my nerves!   I'll get used to him

ii) **te** and **vous**: the same distinction should be made as between the subject pronouns **tu** and **vous** (see p. 51).

iii) **le** is sometimes used in an impersonal sense, when it refers to a fact, a statement, or an idea that has already been expressed; it is usually not translated in English:

> **j'irai en Afrique un jour; en tout cas je *l'*espère**
> I'll go to Africa some day; I hope so anyway

elle a eu un bébé—je *le* sais, elle me *l'*a dit
she's had a baby—I know, she told me

iv) **moi** and **toi** are used instead of **me** and **te** after an imperative, except when **en** follows:

écris-*moi* bientôt
write to me soon

donne-*m'*en
give me some

b) *Position*

In French, object pronouns come immediately before the verb they refer to. With a compound tense, they come before the auxiliary:

on *t'*attendra ici
we'll wait for you here

je *l'*ai rencontrée en ville
I met her in town

Note: When there are two verbs, the pronoun comes immediately before the verb it refers to:

j'aimerais lui demander
I'd like to ask him

tu l'as entendu chanter?
have you heard him sing?

In positive commands (affirmative imperative) the pronoun follows the verb and is joined to it by a hyphen:

regarde-*les*!
look at them!

parle-*lui*!
speak to him!

dis-*nous* ce qui s'est passé
tell us what happened

c) *Direct pronouns and indirect pronouns*

i) Direct object pronouns replace a noun that follows the verb directly. They answer the question 'who(m)?' or 'what'?

WHO(M) did you see?
qui as-tu vu?

I saw *my friend*; I saw *him*
j'ai vu *mon ami*; je *l'*ai vu

tu *me* connais
you know *me*

j'aime *le* voir danser
I like to see *him* dance

je *les* ai trouvés
I found *them*

ne *nous* ennuie pas!
don't bother *us*!

ii) Indirect object pronouns replace a noun that follows the verb with a linking preposition (usually **à** = 'to'). They answer the question to 'who(m)?':

WHO did you speak to?

à qui as-tu parlé?

I spoke *to Marc*; I spoke *to him*

j'ai parlé *à Marc*; je *lui* ai parlé

elle *lui* a menti
she lied *to him*

je *te* donne cette cassette
I'm giving you this tape

je ne *leur* parle plus
I'm not talking *to them* any more

iii) **le/la/les** or **lui/leur?**

Direct pronouns differ from indirect pronouns only in the 3rd person and great care must be taken with them:

- English indirect object pronouns often look like direct objects; their function becomes obvious when the object is placed at the end of the sentence:

  I showed him your photo =   I showed your photo to him
                                      je *lui* ai montré ta photo

This is particularly the case with the following verbs:

acheter to buy	**offrir** to offer
donner to give	**prêter** to lend
montrer to show	**vendre** to sell
je *lui* ai acheté un livre I bought him a book = I bought a book *for him*	**ne *leur* prête pas mes affaires** don't lend them my things = don't lend my things *to them*

- Some verbs take a direct object in English and an indirect object in French (see pp. 152–53):

je ne *lui* ai rien dit I didn't tell *him / her* anything	**je *leur* demanderai** I'll ask *them*
tu *lui* ressembles you look like *him / her*	**téléphone-*leur*** phone *them*

- Some verbs take a direct object in French and an indirect object in English (see p. 152):

je *l'*attends I'm waiting *for him / her*	**écoutez-*les*!** listen *to them*!

d) *Order of object pronouns*

When several object pronouns are used together, they come in the following order:

i) Before the verb:

1	**me**		**te**		**nous**		**vous**
2		**le**		**la**		**les**	
3			**lui**		**leur**		

il *me l'*a donné he gave it to me	**je vais *vous les* envoyer** I'll send them to you
ne *la leur* vends pas don't sell it to them	**je *le lui* ai acheté** I bought it for him

ii) After the verb:

With a positive command (affirmative imperative), the order is as follows:

1		le	la	les	
2	moi (m')		toi (t')	nous	vous
3			lui	leur	

apporte-*les-moi*!
bring them to me!

dites-*le-lui*!
tell it to him!

prête-*la-nous*!
lend it to us!

rends-*la-leur*!
give it back to them!

3. The pronoun *EN*

a) *Use*

en is used instead of **de** + noun. Since **de** has a variety of meanings, **en** can be used in a number of ways:

i) It means 'of it/them', but also 'with it/them', 'about it/them', 'from it/there', 'out of it/there':

tu es sûr *du prix*?—j'*en* suis sûr
are you sure of the price?—I'm sure *of it*

je suis content *de ce cadeau* ; j'*en* suis content
I'm pleased with this present; I'm pleased *with it*

elle est folle *des animaux* ; elle *en* est folle
she's crazy about animals; she's crazy *about them*

il est descendu *du train* ; il *en* est descendu
he got off the train; he got *off of it*

il revient *de Paris* ; il *en* revient
he's coming back from Paris; he's coming back *from there*

ii) Verb constructions

Particular care should be taken with verbs and expressions that are followed by **de** + noun. Since **de** is not always translated in the same way, **en** may have a number of meanings:

il a envie *de ce livre* ; il *en* a envie
he wants this book; he wants *it*

je te remercie *de ta carte* ; je t'*en* remercie
I thank you for your card; I thank you *for it*

tu as besoin *de ces papiers*? tu *en* as besoin?
do you need these papers? do you need *them*?

elle a peur *des chiens*; elle *en* a peur
she's afraid of dogs; she's afraid *of them*

tu te souviens *de ce film*? tu t'*en* souviens?
do you remember this film? do you remember *it*?

iii) 'some'/'any'

en replaces the partitive article (**du, de la, des**) + noun; it means 'some'/'any':

> **tu veux** *du café*?—**non, je n'en veux pas**
> do you want (some/any) coffee?—no, I don't want *any*

> **j'achète** *des fruits*?—**non, j' en ai chez moi**
> shall I buy (some) fruit?—no, I have *some* at home

> **il y a** *de la place*?—*en* **voilà là-bas**
> is there (any) room?—there's *some* over there

iv) Expressions of quantity

en must be used with expressions of quantity not followed by a noun. It replaces **de** + noun and means 'of it/them', but is seldom translated in English:

> **tu as pris assez** *d'argent*? **tu** *en* **as pris assez?**
> did you take enough money? did you take enough?

> **vous avez** *combien de frères*?—**j'***en* **ai deux**
> how many brothers do you have?—I have two

> **j'ai fini** *mes cigarettes*; **je vais** *en* **acheter un paquet**
> I've finished my cigarettes; I'm going to buy a pack

b) *Position*

Like object pronouns, **en** comes immediately before the verb, except with positive commands (affirmative imperative), where it comes after the verb and is linked to it by a hyphen:

> **j'en veux un kilo**   **j'en ai marre!**
> I want a kilo (of it/them)   I'm fed up (with it)!

> **prends-en assez!**   **laisses-en aux autres!**
> take enough (of it/them)!   leave some for the others!

When used in conjunction with other object pronouns, it always comes last:

> **ne** *m'en* **parlez pas!**   **je** *vous en* **donnerai**
> don't talk to me about it!   I'll give you some

> **prête-***lui-en***!**   **gardez-***nous-en***!**
> lend him some!   keep some for us!

4. The pronoun Y

a) *Use*

y is used instead of à + noun (not referring to a person). It is used:

i) As the indirect object of a verb. Since the preposition à is translated in a variety of ways in English, y may have various meanings (it, of it/them, about it/them, etc.):

tu joues *au bridge*?—non, j'y joue rarement
do you play bridge?—no, I seldom play (*it*)

je pense *à mes examens*; j'y pense souvent
I'm thinking *about* my exams; I often think *about them*

il s'intéresse *à la photo*; il s'y intéresse
he's interested in photography; he's interested *in it*

ii) Meaning 'there':

j'ai passé deux jours *à Washington*; j'y ai passé deux jours
I spent two days in Washington; I spent two days there

il est allé *en Grèce*; il y est allé
he went to Greece; he went there

Note: y must always be used with the verb **aller** (to go) when the place is not mentioned in the clause. It is often not translated in English:

comment vas-tu *à l'école*?—j'y vais en bus
how do you go to school?—I go (there) by bus

allons-y!   **on y va demain**
let's go!   we're going (there) tomorrow

iii) Replacing the prepositions **en, dans, sur** + noun; y then means 'there', 'in it/them', 'on it/them':

je voudrais vivre *en France*; je voudrais y vivre
I'd like to live in France; I'd like to live *there*

je les ai mis *dans ma poche*; je les y ai mis
I put them in my pocket; I put them *in there*

sur la table? non, je ne l'y vois pas
on the table? no, I don't see it *there*

b) *Position*

Like other object pronouns, y comes immediately before the verb, except with a positive command (affirmative imperative), where it must follow the verb:

j'y réfléchirai   **il s'y est habitué**
I'll think about it   he got used to it

pensez-y!   **n'y allez pas!**
think about it!   don't go!

57

When used with other object pronouns, **y** comes last:

il va *nous y* rencontrer   **je *l'y* ai vu hier**
he'll meet us there   I saw him there yesterday

5. Disjunctive pronouns

a) *Forms*

PERSON	SINGULAR	PLURAL
1st	**moi**	**nous**
	me	us
2nd	**toi**	**vous**
	you	you
3rd (masc)	**lui**	**eux**
	him	them
(fem)	**elle**	**elles**
	her	them
(impersonal)	**soi**	
	oneself	

Note:

   i) **toi/vous**: the same difference should be made as between **tu** and **vous** (see p. 51).

   ii) **soi** is used in an impersonal, general sense to refer to indefinite pronouns and adjectives (**on, chacun, tout le monde, personne, chaque**. etc.); it is mainly found in set phrases, such as:

   chacun pour soi
   every man for himself

b) *Use*

Disjunctive pronouns, also called emphatic pronouns, are used instead of object pronouns (only when referring to persons) in the following cases:

   i) In answer to a question, alone or in a phrase without a verb:

   qui est là?—moi   **j'aime les pommes; et toi?**
   who's there?—me   I love apples; do you?

   qui préfères-tu, lui ou elle?—elle, bien sûr
   who do you like better, him or her?—her, of course

   ii) After **c'est/ce sont, c'était/étaient**, etc:

   ouvrez, c'est moi!   **non, ce n'était pas lui**
   open up, it's me!   no, it wasn't him

   iii) After a preposition:

   vous allez chez lui?   **tu y vas avec elle?**
   are you going to his place?   are you going with her?

regarde devant toi!
look in front of you!

oh, c'est pour moi?
oh, is that for me?

iv) Verb constructions: special care should be taken with verbs followed by a preposition:

tu peux compter sur moi
you can count on me

quoi! tu as peur de lui?
what! you're afraid of him?

il m'a parlé de toi
he told me about you

je pense souvent à vous
I often think about you

Note: Emphatic pronouns are only used when referring to persons. Otherwise, use **y** or **en**.

v) For emphasis, particularly when two pronouns are contrasted. The unstressed subject pronoun is usually included:

vous, vous m'énervez!
you get on my nerves!

lui, il joue bien; elle, non
he plays well; *she* doesn't

moi, je n'aime pas l'hiver
I don't like winter

eux, ils sont partis
they've left

vi) In the case of multiple subjects (two pronouns, or one pronoun and one noun):

lui et son frère sont dans l'équipe
he and his brother are on the team

ma famille et moi allons très bien
my family and I are very well

vii) As the second term of comparisons:

il est plus sympa que toi
he's nicer than you

elle chante mieux que lui
she sings better than he does/him

viii) Before a relative pronoun:

c'est lui que j'aime
he's the one I love

c'est toi qui l'as dit
you're the one who said it

lui qui n'aime pas le vin blanc en a bu six verres
he, the one who doesn't like white wine, had six glasses

ix) With **-même(s)** (-self, -selves), **aussi** (too), **seul** (alone):

faites-le vous-mêmes
do it yourselves

j'irai moi-même
I'll go myself

lui aussi est parti
he went away too

elle seule le sait
she alone knows

x) To replace a possessive pronoun (see p. 84):

c'est *le mien*; il est à moi
it's mine; it belongs to me

59

E. POSSESSIVE ADJECTIVES AND PRONOUNS

1. Possessive adjectives

a) *Forms*

Possessive adjectives always come before a noun. Like other adjectives, they agree in gender and number with the noun; the masculine and feminine plural are identical:

SINGULAR		PLURAL	
MASC	FEM		
mon	ma	mes	my
ton	ta	tes	your
son	sa	ses	his/her/its/one's
notre	notre	nos	our
votre	votre	vos	your
leur	leur	leurs	their

j'ai mis mon argent et mes affaires dans mon sac
I put my money and my things in my bag

comment va ton frère? et ta sœur? et tes parents?
how's your brother? and your sister? and your parents?

notre rue est assez calme   **ce sont vos amis**
our street is pretty quiet   they're your friends

Note: **mon/ton/son** are used instead of **ma/ta/sa** when the next word starts with a vowel or silent **h**:

mon ancienne maison   **ton amie Christine**
my old house   your friend Christine

son haleine sentait l'alcool
his breath smelled of alcohol

b) *Use*

i) The possessive adjective is repeated before each noun and agrees with it:

mon père et ma mère sont sortis
my father and mother have gone out

ii) **son/sa/ses**

son, **sa**, and **ses** can all mean 'his', 'her', or 'its'. In French, the form of the adjective is determined by the gender and number of the noun that follows, and not by the possessor:

il m'a prêté sa mobylette et son casque
he lent me his moped and his helmet

elle s'entend bien avec sa mère, mais pas avec son père
she gets along well with her mother, but not with her father

il cire ses chaussures; elle repasse ses chemisiers
he's polishing his shoes; she's ironing her blouses

iii) **ton/ta/tes** and **votre/vos**

The two sets of words for 'your', **ton/ta/tes** and **votre/vos**, correspond to the two different forms **tu** and **vous**; they must not be used together with the same person:

Papa, tu as parlé à ton patron?
have you spoken to your boss, Dad?

Monsieur! votre veste! vous ne la prenez pas?
Sir! your jacket! aren't you taking it?

iv) In French, the possessive adjective is replaced by the definite article (**le/la/les**) with the following:

- parts of the body:

  il s'est essuyé les mains   **elle a haussé les épaules**
  he wiped his hands   she shrugged (her shoulders)

- descriptive phrases tagged on to the end of a clause, where English adds 'with':

  il marchait lentement, les main dans les poches
  he was walking slowly, with his hands in his pockets

  elle l'a regardé partir, les larmes aux yeux
  she watched him leave, with tears in her eyes

2. Possessive pronouns

MASC	FEM	PLURAL (MASC AND FEM)	
le mien	**la mienne**	**les mien(ne)s**	mine
le tien	**la tienne**	**les tien(ne)s**	yours
le sien	**la sienne**	**les sien(ne)s**	his/hers/its
le nôtre	**la nôtre**	**les nôtres**	ours
le vôtre	**la vôtre**	**les vôtres**	yours
le leur	**la leur**	**les leurs**	theirs

Possessive pronouns are used instead of a possessive adjective + noun. They agree in gender and in number with the noun they stand for, and not with the possessor (it is particularly important to remember this when translating 'his' and 'hers'):

j'aime bien ton chapeau, mais je préfère le mien
I like your hat, but I like mine better

on prend quelle voiture? la mienne ou la tienne?
which car shall we take? mine or yours?

comment sont vos profs? les nôtres sont sympas
what are your teachers like? ours are nice

j'ai pris mon passeport, mais Brigitte a oublié le sien
I brought my passport, but Brigitte forgot hers

j'ai gardé ma moto, mais Paul a vendu la sienne
I've kept my motorbike but Paul has sold his

à or de + possessive pronoun

The prepositions **à** or **de** combine with the articles **le** and **les** in the usual way:

à + le mien	→	au mien
à + les miens	→	aux miens
à + les miennes	→	aux miennes
de + le mien	→	du mien
de + les miens	→	des miens
de + les miennes	→	des miennes

demande à tes parents, j'ai déjà parlé aux miens
ask your parents, I've already spoken to mine

leur appartement ressemble beaucoup au nôtre
their apartment is a lot like ours

j'aime bien les chiens, mais j'ai peur du tien
I like dogs, but I'm afraid of yours

Note: after the verb **être**, the possessive pronoun is often replaced by **à** + emphatic (disjunctive) pronoun (see pp. 58–59):

à qui est cette écharpe?—elle est à moi
whose scarf is this?—it's mine

ce livre est à toi?—non, il est à elle
is this book yours?—no, it's hers

c'est à qui? à vous ou à lui?
whose is this? yours or his?

F. RELATIVE PRONOUNS

1. Definition

Relative pronouns are words that introduce a relative clause. In the following sentence:

I bought the book that you recommended

'that' is the relative pronoun, 'that you recommended' is the relative clause, and 'the book' is the antecedent (i.e. the noun the relative pronoun refers to).

2. Forms

Relative pronouns are:

qui	who, which, that	**lequel**	which
que	who(m), which, that	**dont**	of which, whose
quoi	what	**ce qui**	what
où	where	**ce que**	what

qui, que, quoi, lequel, ce qui, and **ce que** can also be used as interrogative pronouns (see pp. 48–50) and must not be confused with them.

3. Use

a) *QUI*

qui is used as the subject of a relative clause; it means:

i) 'who', 'that' (referring to people):

connaissez-vous le monsieur qui habite ici?
do you know the man who lives here?

ce n'est pas lui qui a menti
he's not the one who lied

ii) 'which', 'that' (referring to things):

tu as pris le journal qui était sur la télé?
did you take the paper that was on the television set?

b) *QUE*

que (written **qu'** before a vowel or a silent **h**) is used as the object of a relative clause; it is often not translated and means:

i) 'who(m)', 'that' (referring to people):

la fille que j'aime ne m'aime pas
the girl (that) I love doesn't love me

ii) 'which', 'that' (referring to things):

j'ai perdu le briquet qu'il m'a offert
I've lost the lighter (that) he gave me

c) *qui* or *que*?

qui (subject) and **que** (object) are translated by the same words in English (who, which, that). To use the correct pronoun in French, you have to know if a relative pronoun is the object or the subject of the relative clause:

i) when the verb of the relative clause has its own subject, the object pronoun **que** must be used:

c'est un passe-temps que j'adore
it's a pastime (that) *I* love (*the subject of 'adore' is 'je'*)

ii) otherwise the relative pronoun is the subject of the verb in the relative clause, and the subject pronoun **qui** must be used:

j'ai trouvé un manteau qui me plaît
I found a coat (that) I like (*the subject of 'plaît' is 'qui'*)

d) LEQUEL

i) forms

lequel (which) has four different forms, since it must agree with the noun it refers to:

	SINGULAR	PLURAL	
MASCULINE	**lequel**	**lesquels**	} which
FEMININE	**laquelle**	**lesquelles**	

lequel etc. combines with the prepositions **à** and **de** as follows:

à + lequel	→	**auquel**
à + lesquels	→	**auxquels**
à + lesquelles	→	**auxquelles**
de + lequel	→	**duquel**
de + lesquels	→	**desquels**
de + lesquelles	→	**desquelles**

à + laquelle and **de + laquelle** do not change.

quels sont les sports auxquels tu t'intéresses?
what are the sports (which/that) you are interested *in*?

voilà le village près duquel on campait
here's the village (that) we camped near (i.e., near which we camped)

ii) **qui** or **lequel** with a preposition?

When a relative pronoun follows a preposition, the pronoun used is either **qui** or **lequel**. In English, the relative pronoun is seldom used, and the preposition is frequently placed after the verb or at the end of the sentence, despite the objections of some grammarians.

qui is generally used after a preposition when referring to people:

où est la fille *avec* qui je dansais?
where's the girl I was dancing *with*?

montre-moi la personne à qui tu as vendu ton vélo
show me the person you sold your bike *to*

lequel is often used after a preposition when referring to things:

l'immeuble *dans* lequel j'habite est très moderne
the building (which/that) I live *in* is very modern

> **je ne reconnais pas la voiture *avec* laquelle il est venu**
> I don't recognize the car (that) he came *in*

lequel is also used when referring to persons after the prepositions **entre** (between), **parmi** (among), and **selon** (according to):

> **des touristes, parmi lesquels il y avait des Japonais**
> tourists, among whom were (some) Japanese people

> **il aimait deux filles, entre lesquelles il hésitait**
> he loved two girls that he couldn't decide between (i.e., between whom he couldn't decide)

e) *DONT*

dont (of which, of whom, whose) is frequently used instead of **de qui, duquel**, etc. It means:

i) *of which, of whom*:

> **un métier dont il est fier**
> a trade (which/that) he is proud of

Care must be taken with verbs that are normally followed by **de** + object: **de** is not always translated by 'of' in English, and is sometimes not translated at all (see section on verb constructions pp. 153–4):

> **voilà les choses *dont* j'ai besoin**
> here are the things (*which / that*) I need

> **les gens *dont* tu parles ne m'intéressent pas**
> I'm not interested in the people you're talking about

> **l'enfant *dont* elle s'occupe n'est pas le sien**
> the child she is looking *after* isn't hers

ii) *whose*

dont is also used to translate the English pronoun 'whose'. In French, the construction of the clause that follows **dont** differs from English in two ways:

* the noun that follows **dont** is used with the definite article (**le, la, l', les**):

> **mon copain, dont *le* père a eu un accident**
> my friend, whose father had an accident

* the word order in French is **dont** + subject + verb + object:

> **je te présente Hélène, dont tu connais déjà le frère**
> this is Helen, whose brother you already know

> **c'était dans une petite rue dont j'ai oublié le nom**
> it was on a small street whose name (i.e. the name of which) I've forgotten

Note: **dont** cannot be used after a preposition:

> **une jolie maison, *près* de laquelle il y a un petit lac**
> a pretty house, *next* to which there is a small lake

dont can also never be used for the interrogative (whose?).

f) OU

i) **où** generally means 'where':

l'hôtel où on a logé était très confortable
the hotel where we stayed was very comfortable

ii) **où** often replaces a preposition + lequel, meaning 'in/to/on/at which', etc:

c'est la maison où je suis né
that's the house I was born in (i.e., in which/where I was born)

une surprise-partie où il a invité tous ses amis
a party he invited all his friends to (i.e., to which he invited all his friends)

iii) **où** is also used to translate 'when' after a noun referring to time:

le jour où   **la fois où**   **le moment où**
the day when   the time when   the moment when

tu te rappelles le soir où on a raté le dernier métro?
do you remember the night (when) we missed the last train?

g) CE QUI, CE QUE

ce is used before **qui** and **que** when the relative pronoun does not refer to a specific noun. Both **ce qui** and **ce que** mean 'that which', 'the thing which', and are usually translated by 'what':

i) **ce qui**

ce qui is followed by a verb without a subject (**qui** is the subject):

ce qui s'est passé ne vous regarde pas
what happened is none of your business

ce qui m'étonne, c'est sa patience
what surprises me is his patience

Note the comma and the **c'**

ii) **ce que**

ce que (**ce qu'** before a vowel or a silent **h**) is followed by a verb with its own subject (**que** is the object):

fais ce que tu veux   **c'est ce qu'il a dit?**
do what you want   is that what he said?

ce que vous me demandez est impossible
what you're asking me is impossible

iii) **tout ce qui/que**

tout is used in front of **ce qui/que** in the sense of 'all that', 'everything that':

c'est tout ce que je veux   **tout ce que tu as fait**
that's all I want   everything you did

tu n'as pas eu de mal; c'est tout ce qui compte
you weren't hurt; that's all that matters

iv) **ce qui/que** are often used in indirect questions (see p. 50):

je ne sais pas ce qu'ils vont dire
I don't know what they'll say

v) when referring to a previous clause, **ce qui** and **ce que** are translated by 'which':

elle est en retard, ce qui arrive souvent
she's late, which happens often

vi) **ce qui/que** are used with a preposition (when the preposition refers to **ce**):

ce n'est pas étonnant, après ce qui lui est arrivé
it's not surprising, after what happened to him

il y a du vrai dans ce que vous dites
there is some truth in what you say

But: **QUOI** is used instead of **ce que** after a preposition when the preposition refers to **que**, and not to **ce**:

c'est ce à quoi je pensais
that's what I was thinking about

vii) **ce que** is used with the preposition **de** when **de** refers to **ce**:

je suis fier de ce qu'il a fait
I'm proud of what he did

But: **ce dont** is used instead of **de + ce que** when **de** refers to **que**, and not to **ce**:

c'est ce dont j'avais peur
that's what I was afraid of

tu as trouvé ce dont tu avais besoin?
did you find what you needed?

7. VERBS

A. REGULAR CONJUGATIONS

1. Conjugations

There are three main conjugations in French, which are determined by the infinitive endings. The first conjugation verbs, by far the largest category, end in **-er** (e.g. aim**er**) and will be referred to as **-er** verbs; the second conjugation verbs end in **-ir** (e.g. fin**ir**) and will be referred to as **-ir** verbs; the third conjugation verbs, the smallest category, end in **-re** (e.g. vend**re**) and will be referred to as **-re** verbs.

2. Simple tenses

The simple tenses in French are:

    a) present
    b) imperfect
    c) future
    d) conditional
    e) simple past
    f) present subjunctive
    g) imperfect subjunctive

For the use of the different tenses, see pp. 86–92.

Note: The simple past is called by a variety of names and will be designated in the following pages by its common French name, *passé simple.*

3. Formation of tenses

The tenses are formed by adding the following endings to the stem of the verb (mainly the stem of the infinitive) as presented in the following section:

a) *PRESENT:* stem of the infinitive + the following endings:

-er VERBS	-ir VERBS	-re VERBS
-e, -es, -e,	-is, -is, -it,	-s, -s, -,
-ons, -ez, -ent	-issons, -issez, -issent	-ons, -ez, -ent

AIMER	FINIR	VENDRE
j'aime	je finis	je vends
tu aimes	tu finis	tu vends
il aime	il finit	il vend
elle aime	elle finit	elle vend
nous aimons	nous finissons	nous vendons
vous aimez	vous finissez	vous vendez
ils aiment	ils finissent	ils vendent
elles aiment	elles finissent	elles vendent

b) *IMPERFECT*: stem of the first person plural of the present tense (i.e. the **'nous'** form minus **-ons**) + the following endings:

-ais, -ais, -ait, -ions, -iez, -aient

j'aimais	je finissais	je vendais
tu aimais	tu finissais	tu vendais
il aimait	il finissait	il vendait
elle aimait	elle finissait	elle vendait
nous aimions	nous finissions	nous vendions
vous aimiez	vous finissiez	vous vendiez
ils aimaient	ils finissaient	ils vendaient
elles aimaient	elles finissaient	elles vendaient

Note: the only irregular imperfect is **être: j'étais** etc.

c) *FUTURE*: infinitive + the following endings:

-ai, -as, -a, -ons, -ez, -ont

Note: Verbs ending in **-re** drop the final **e** of the infinitive

j'aimerai	je finirai	je vendrai
tu aimeras	tu finiras	tu vendras
il aimera	il finira	il vendra
elle aimera	elle finira	elle vendra
nous aimerons	nous finirons	nous vendrons
vous aimerez	vous finirez	vous vendrez
ils aimeront	ils finiront	ils vendront
elles aimeront	elles finiront	elles vendront

d) *CONDITIONAL*: infinitive + the following endings:

-ais, -ais, -ait, -ions, -iez, -aient

Note: Verbs ending in **-re** drop the final **e** of the infinitive

j'aimerais	je finirais	je vendrais
tu aimerais	tu finirais	tu vendrais
il aimerait	il finirait	il vendrait
elle aimerait	elle finirait	elle vendrait
nous aimerions	nous finirions	nous vendrions
vous aimeriez	vous finiriez	vous vendriez
ils aimeraient	ils finiraient	ils vendraient
elles aimeraient	elles finiraient	elles vendraient

e) *'PASSÉ SIMPLE'*: stem of the infinitive + the following endings:

-er VERBS	-ir VERBS	-re VERBS
-ai, -as, -a, -âmes, -âtes, -èrent	-is, -is, -it, -îmes, -îtes, -irent	-is, -is, -it, -îmes, -îtes, -irent
j'aim**ai**	je fin**is**	je vend**is**
tu aim**as**	tu fin**is**	tu vend**is**
il aim**a**	il fin**it**	il vend**it**
elle aim**a**	elle fin**it**	elle vend**it**
nous aim**âmes**	nous fin**îmes**	nous vend**îmes**
vous aim**âtes**	vous fin**îtes**	vous vend**îtes**
ils aim**èrent**	ils fin**irent**	ils vend**irent**
elles aim**èrent**	elles fin**irent**	elles vend**irent**

f) *PRESENT SUBJUNCTIVE*: stem of the first person plural of the present indicative + the following endings:

-es, -es, -e, -ions, -iez, -ent

j'aim**e**	je fin**isse**	je vend**e**
tu aim**es**	tu fin**isses**	tu vend**es**
il aim**e**	il fin**isse**	il vend**e**
elle aim**e**	elle fin**isse**	elle vend**e**
nous aim**ions**	nous fin**issions**	nous vend**ions**
vous aim**iez**	vous fin**issiez**	vous vend**iez**
ils aim**ent**	ils fin**issent**	ils vend**ent**
elles aim**ent**	elles fin**issent**	elles vend**ent**

g) *IMPERFECT SUBJUNCTIVE*: stem of the first person singular of the *passé simple* + the following endings:

-er VERBS	-ir VERBS	-re VERBS
-asse, -asses, -ât, -assions, -assiez, -assent	-isse, -isses, -ît, -issions, -issiez, -issent	-isse, -isses, -ît, -issions, -issiez, -issent
j'aim**asse**	je fin**isse**	je vend**isse**
tu aim**asses**	tu fin**isses**	tu vend**isses**
il aim**ât**	il fin**ît**	il vend**ît**
elle aim**ât**	elle fin**ît**	elle vend**ît**
nous aim**assions**	nous fin**issions**	nous vend**issions**
vous am**assiez**	vous fin**issiez**	vous vend**issiez**
ils aim**assent**	ils fin**issent**	ils vend**issent**
elles aim**assent**	elles fin**issent**	elles vend**issent**

B. STANDARD SPELLING IRREGULARITIES

Spelling irregularities affect only **-er** verbs.

1. Verbs ending in *-cer* and *-ger*

a) Verbs ending in **-cer** require a cedilla under the **c** (**ç**) before an **a** or an **o** to preserve the soft sound of the **c**: e.g. **commencer** (to begin).

b) Verbs ending in **-ger** require an **-e** after the **g** before an **a** or an **o** to preserve the soft sound of the **g**: e.g. **manger** (to eat).

Changes in **-cer** and **-ger** verbs occur in the following tenses: present, imperfect, *passé simple*, imperfect subjunctive, and present participle.

COMMENCER	MANGER
PRESENT	
je commence	je mange
tu commences	tu manges
il commence	il mange
elle commence	elle mange
nous **commençons**	nous **mangeons**
vous commencez	vous mangez
ils commencent	ils mangent
elles commencent	elles mangent
IMPERFECT	
je **commençais**	je **mangeais**
tu **commençais**	tu **mangeais**
il **commençait**	il **mangeait**
elle **commençait**	elle **mangeait**
nous commencions	nous mangions
vous commenciez	vous mangiez
ils **commençaient**	ils **mangeaient**
elles **commençaient**	elles **mangeaient**
'PASSÉ SIMPLE'	
je **commençai**	je **mangeai**
tu **commenças**	tu **mangeas**
il **commença**	il **mangea**
elle **commença**	elle **mangea**
nous **commençâmes**	nous **mangeâmes**
vous **commençâtes**	vous **mangeâtes**
ils commencèrent	ils mangèrent
elles commencèrent	elles mangèrent

71

IMPERFECT SUBJUNCTIVE

je **commençasse**	je **mangeasse**
tu **commençasses**	tu **mangeasses**
il **commençât**	il **mangeât**
elle **commençât**	elle **mangeât**
nous **commençassions**	nous **mangeassions**
vous **commençassiez**	vous **mangeassiez**
ils **commençassent**	ils **mangeassent**
elles **commençassent**	elles **mangeassent**

PRESENT PARTICIPATE

commençant	**mangeant**

2. Verbs ending in *-eler* and *-eter*

a) Verbs ending in **-eler**

Verbs ending in **-eler** double the **l** before a silent **e** (i.e. before **-e, -es, -ent** of the present indicative and subjunctive, and throughout the future and conditional): e.g. **appeler** (to call).

PRESENT INDICATIVE / *PRESENT SUBJUNCTIVE*

j'**appelle**	j'**appelle**
tu **appelles**	tu **appelles**
il **appelle**	il **appelle**
elle **appelle**	elle **appelle**
nous appelons	nous appelions
vous appelez	vous appeliez
ils **appellent**	ils **appellent**
elles **appellent**	elles **appellent**

FUTURE / *CONDITIONAL*

j'**appellerai**	j'**appellerais**
tu **appelleras**	tu **appellerais**
il **appellera**	il **appellerait**
elle **appellera**	elle **appellerait**
nous **appellerons**	nous **appellerions**
vous **appellerez**	vous **appelleriez**
ils **appelleront**	ils **appelleraient**
elles **appelleront**	elles **appelleraient**

But: some verbs in **-eler**, including the following, are conjugated like **acheter** (see pp. 74–75):

celer	to conceal
congeler	to (deep-) freeze
déceler	to detect, reveal
dégeler	to defrost
geler	to freeze
harceler	to harass

marteler	to hammer
modeler	to model
peler	to peel

b) Verbs ending in **-eter**

Verbs ending in **-eter** double the **t** before a silent **e** (i.e. before **-e**, **-es**, **-ent** of the present indicative and subjunctive, and throughout the future and conditional): e.g. **jeter** (to throw).

PRESENT INDICATIVE	*PRESENT SUBJUNCTIVE*
je **jette**	je **jette**
tu **jettes**	tu **jettes**
il **jette**	il **jette**
elle **jette**	elle **jette**
nous jetons	nous jetions
vous jetez	vous jetiez
ils **jettent**	ils **jettent**
elles **jettent**	elles **jettent**

FUTURE	*CONDITIONAL*
je **jetterai**	je **jetterais**
tu **jetteras**	tu **jetterais**
il **jettera**	il **jetterait**
elle **jettera**	elle **jetterait**
nous **jetterons**	nous **jetterions**
vous **jetterez**	vous **jetteriez**
ils **jetteront**	ils **jetteraient**
elles **jetteront**	elles **jetteraient**

But: some verbs in **-eter**, including the following, are conjugated like **acheter** (see pp. 74–75):

crocheter	to pick (*lock*)
fureter	to ferret about
haleter	to pant
racheter	to buy back, redeem

c) Verbs ending in **-oyer** and **-uyer**

In verbs ending in **-oyer** and **-uyer** the y changes to **i** before a silent **e** (i.e. before **-e**, **-es**, **-ent** of the present indicative and subjunctive, and throughout the future and conditional): e.g. **employer** (to use) and **ennuyer** (to bore).

PRESENT INDICATIVE	*PRESENT SUBJUNCTIVE*
j'**emploie**	j'**emploie**
tu **emploies**	tu **emploies**

il **emploie**	il **emploie**
elle **emploie**	elle **emploie**
nous employons	nous employons
vous employez	vous employiez
ils **emploient**	ils **emploient**
elles **emploient**	elles **emploient**

FUTURE	*CONDITIONAL*
j'**emploierai**	j'**emploierais**
tu **emploieras**	tu **emploierais**
il **emploiera**	il **emploierait**
elle **emploiera**	elle **emploierait**
nous **emploierons**	nous **emploierions**
vous **emploierez**	vous **emploieriez**
ils **emploieront**	ils **emploieraient**
elles **emploieront**	elles **emploieraient**

Note: **envoyer** (to send) and **renvoyer** (to dismiss) have an irregular future and conditional: **j'enverrai, j'enverrais; je renverrai, je renverrais.**

d) Verbs ending in **-ayer**

In verbs ending in **-ayer**, e.g. **balayer** (to sweep), **payer** (to pay), **essayer** (to try), the change from **y** to **i** is optional, though common:

e.g.	je **balaie**	*or*	je **balaye**
	je **paie**	*or*	je **paye**
	j'**essaie**	*or*	j'**essaye**

e) Verbs in **e** + consonant + **er**

Verbs like **acheter, enlever, mener, peser** change the (last) **e** of the stem to **è** before a silent e (i.e. before **-e, -es, -ent** of the present indicative and subjunctive, and throughout the future and conditional):

PRESENT INDICATIVE	*PRESENT SUBJUNCTIVE*
j'**achète**	j'**achète**
tu **achètes**	tu **achètes**
il **achète**	il **achète**
elle **achète**	elle **achète**
nous achetons	nous achetions
vous achetez	vous achetiez
ils **achètent**	ils **achètent**
elles **achètent**	elles **achètent**

FUTURE	*CONDITIONAL*
j'**achèterai**	j'**achèterais**
tu **achèteras**	tu **achèterais**
il **achètera**	il **achèterait**
elle **achètera**	elle **achèterait**

nous **achèterons**	nous **achèterions**
vous **achèterez**	vous **achèteriez**
ils **achèteront**	ils **achèteraient**
elles **achèteront**	elles **achèteraient**

Verbs conjugated like **acheter** include:

achever to complete	**haleter** to pant
amener to bring	**harceler** to harass
celer to conceal	**lever** to lift
crever to burst	**marteler** to hammer
crocheter to pick (*lock*)	**mener** to lead
élever to raise	**modeler** to model
emmener to take away	**peler** to peel
enlever to remove	**peser** to weigh
étiqueter to label	**se promener** to go for a walk
fureter to ferret about	**semer** to sow
geler to freeze	**soulever** to lift

f) Verbs in **é** + consonant + **er**

Verbs like **espérer** (to hope) change **é** to **è** before a silent e in the present indicative and subjunctive. **BUT** in the future and conditional **é** is retained.

PRESENT *INDICATIVE*	*PRESENT* *SUBJUNCTIVE*
j'**espère**	j'**espère**
tu **espères**	tu **espères**
il **espère**	il **espère**
elle **espère**	elle **espère**
nous espérons	nous espérions
vous espérez	vous espériez
ils **espèrent**	ils **espèrent**
elles **espèrent**	elles **espèrent**

FUTURE	*CONDITIONAL*
j'**espérerai**	j'**espérerais**
tu **espéreras**	tu **espérerais**
il **espérera**	il **espérerait**
elle **espérera**	elle **espérerait**
nous **espérerons**	nous **espérerions**
vous **espérerez**	vous **espéreriez**
ils **espéreront**	ils **espéreraient**
elles **espéreront**	elles **espéreraient**

Verbs conjugated like **espérer** include verbs in **-éder, -érer, -éter,** etc.:

accéder	to accede to
céder	to yield
célébrer	to celebrate
compléter	to complete
considérer	to consider

décéder	to die
digérer	to digest
gérer	to manage
inquiéter	to worry
libérer	to free
opérer	to operate
pénétrer	to penetrate
persévérer	to persevere
posséder	to possess
précéder	to precede
préférer	to prefer
protéger	to protect
récupérer	to recover
refréner	to curb
régler	to rule
régner	to reign
répéter	to repeat, to rehearse
révéler	to reveal
sécher	to dry
succéder	to succeed
suggérer	to suggest
tolérer	to tolerate

C. AUXILIARIES AND THE FORMATION OF COMPOUND TENSES

1. Formation

a) The two auxiliary verbs **AVOIR** and **ETRE** are used with the past participle of a verb to form compound tenses.

b) *The past participle*
The regular past participle is formed by taking the stem of the infinitive and adding the following endings:

-er	**-ir**	**-re**
aim(**er**) + é	fin(**ir**) + i	vend(**re**) + u
aim**é**	fin**i**	vend**u**

For the agreement of past participles see pp. 109–11.

c) *Compound tenses*
In French there are seven compound tenses, the first two usually designated by their French names: 'passé composé', 'plus-que-parfait', future perfect, past conditional, past anterior, past subjunctive, pluperfect subjunctive.

2. Verbs conjugated with AVOIR

a) 'PASSÉ COMPOSÉ'
present of **avoir** +
past participle

j'ai aimé
tu as aimé
il a aimé
elle a aimé
nous avons aimé
vous avez aimé
ils ont aimé
elles ont aimé

b) 'PLUS-QUE-PARFAIT'
imperfect of **avoir** +
past participle

j'avais aimé
tu avais aimé
il avait aimé
elle avait aimé
nous avions aimé
vous aviez aimé
ils avaient aimé
elles avaient aimé

c) FUTURE PERFECT
future of **avoir** +
past participle

j'aurai aimé
tu auras aimé
il aura aimé
elle aura aimé
nous aurons aimé
vous aurez aimé
ils auront aimé
elles auront aimé

d) PAST CONDITIONAL
conditional of **avoir** +
past participle

j'aurais aimé
tu aurais aimé
il aurait aimé
elle aurait aimé
nous aurions aimé
vous auriez aimé
ils auraient aimé
elles auraient aimé

e) PAST ANTERIOR
passé simple of **avoir** +
past participle

j'eus aimé
tu eus aimé
il eut aimé
elle eut aimé
nous eûmes aimé
vous eûtes aimé
ils eurent aimé
elles eurent aimé

f) PAST SUBJUNCTIVE

present subjunctive of
avoir + past participle

j'aie aimé
tu aies aimé
il ait aimé
elle ait aimé
nous ayons aimé
vous ayez aimé
ils aient aimé
elles aient aimé

g) PLUPERFECT
SUBJUNCTIVE
pluperfect subjunctive of
avoir + past participle

j'eusse aimé
tu eusses aimé
il eût aimé
elle eût aimé
nous eussions aimé
vous eussiez aimé
ils eussent aimé
elles eussent aimé

3. Verbs conjugated with ETRE

a) 'PASSÉ COMPOSÉ'
present of être +
past participle

je suis arrivé(e)
tu es arrivé(e)
il est arrivé
elle est arrivée
nous sommes arrivé(e)s
vous êtes arrivé(e)(s)
ils sont arrivés
elles sont arrivées

b) 'PLUS-QUE-PARFAIT'
imperfect of être +
past participle

j'étais arrivé(e)
tu étais arrivé(e)
il était arrivé
elle était arrivée
nous étions arrivé(e)s
vous étiez arrivé(e)s
ils étaient arrivés
elles étaient arrivées

c) FUTURE PERFECT
future of être +
past participle

je serai arrivé(e)
tu seras arrivé(e)
il sera arrivé
elle sera arrivée
nous serons arrivé(e)s
vous serez arrivé(e)(s)
ils seront arrivés
elles seront arrivées

d) PAST CONDITIONAL
conditional of être +
past participle

je serais arrivé(e)
tu serais arrivé(e)
il serait arrivé
elle serait arrivée
nous serions arrivé(e)s
vous seriez arrivé(e)(s)
ils seraient arrivés
elles seraient arrivées

e) PAST ANTERIOR
passé simple of être +
past participle

je fus arrivé(e)
tu fus arrivé(e)
il fut arrivé
elle fut arrivée
nous fûmes arrivé(e)s
vous fûtes arrivé(e)(s)
ils furent arrivés
elles furent arrivées

f) PAST SUBJUNCTIVE
present subjunctive of
être + past participle

je sois arrivé(e)
tu sois arrivé(e)
il soit arrivé
elle soit arrivée
nous soyons arrivé(e)s

g) PLUPERFECT
SUBJUNCTIVE
imperfect subjunctive of
être + past participle

je fusse arrivé(e)
tu fusses arrivé(e)
il fût arrivé
elle fût arrivée
nous fussions arrivé(e)s

vous soyez arrivé(e)(s)	**vous fussiez arrivé(e)(s)**
ils soient arrivés	**ils fussent arrivés**
elles soient arrivées	**elles fussent arrivées**

4. AVOIR or ETRE?

a) *Verbs conjugated with* **avoir**

The compound tenses of most verbs are formed with **avoir**:

j'ai marqué un but	**elle a dansé toute la nuit**
I scored a goal	she danced all night

b) *Verbs conjugated with* **être**

i) all reflexive verbs (see p. 82):

je me suis baigné
I took a bath

ii) the following verbs (mainly of motion):

aller	to go
arriver	to arrive
descendre	to go/come down
entrer	to go/come in
monter	to go/come up
mourir	to die
naître	to be born
partir	to leave
passer	to go through, to drop in
rester	to remain
retourner	to return
sortir	to go/come out
tomber	to fall
venir	to come

and most of their compounds:

revenir	to come back
devenir	to become
parvenir	to reach, to manage to
rentrer	to return home
remonter	to go up again
redescendre	to go down again

But: **prévenir** (to warn) and **subvenir** (to provide for) take a direct object and are conjugated with **avoir**.

Note: **passer** can also be conjugated with **avoir**:

il a passé par Paris
he went via Paris

Some of the verbs listed above can take a direct object. In such cases they are conjugated with **avoir** and can take on a different meaning:

descendre	to take/bring down, to go down (*the stairs, a slope*)

monter	to take/bring up, to go up (*the stairs, a slope*)
rentrer	to take/bring/put in
retourner	to turn over
sortir	to take/bring out

les élèves sont sortis à midi
the pupils came out at noon

les élèves ont sorti leurs livres
the pupils took out their books

elle n'est pas encore descendue
she hasn't come down yet

elle a descendu un vieux tableau du grenier
she brought an old painting down from the attic

elle a descendu l'escalier
she came down the stairs

les prisonniers sont montés sur le toit
the prisoners climbed up on the roof

le garçon a monté les bouteilles de vin de la cave
the waiter brought the bottles of wine up from the cellar

nous sommes rentrés tard
we got home late

j'ai rentré la voiture dans le garage
I put the car in the garage

je serais retourné à Paris
I would have gone back to Paris

le jardinier a retourné le sol
the gardener turned over the soil

ils sont sortis de la piscine
they got out of the swimming pool

le gangster a sorti un revolver
the gangster pulled out a revolver

D. REFLEXIVE VERBS

1. Definition

Reflexive verbs are so called because they 'reflect' the action back onto the subject. Reflexive verbs are always accompanied by a reflexive pronoun; e.g. in the following sentence:

I looked at myself in the mirror

'myself' is the reflexive pronoun.

> **je lave la voiture**
> I'm washing the car
>
> **je *me* lave**
> I'm washing *myself*
>
> **j'ai couché le bébé**
> I put the baby to bed
>
> **je *me* suis couché**
> I went to bed (I put *myself* to bed)

2. Reflexive pronouns

They are:

PERSON	SINGULAR	PLURAL
1st	**me(m')** myself	**nous** ourselves
2nd	**te(t')** yourself	**vous** yourself/selves
3rd	**se(s')** himself, herself, itself, oneself	**se(s')** themselves

Note:

a) **m'**, **t'**, and **s'** are used instead of **me**, **te**, and **se** in front of a vowel or a silent **h**:

> **tu t'amuses?—non, je m'ennuie**
> are you enjoying yourself?—no, I'm bored

> **il s'habille dans la salle de bain**
> he gets dressed in the bathroom

b) French reflexive pronouns are often not translated in English:

> **je me demande si . . .**
> I wonder if . . .
>
> **ils se moquent de moi**
> they're making fun of me

c) Plural reflexive pronouns can also be used to express reciprocal actions; in this case they are translated by 'each other' or 'one another':

> **nous nous détestons**
> we hate one another
>
> **ils ne se parlent pas**
> they're not talking to each other

d) **se** can mean 'ourselves' or 'each other' when it is used with the pronoun **on** meaning 'we' (see pp. 46–47):

> **on s'est perdu**
> we got lost
>
> **on se connaît**
> we know each other

3. Position of reflexive pronouns

Reflexive pronouns are placed immediately before the verb, except in positive commands, where they follow the verb and are linked to it by a hyphen:

> **tu te dépêches?**
> will you hurry up?
>
> **dépêchons-nous!**
> let's hurry!

ne t'inquiète pas   ne vous fiez pas à lui
don't worry   don't trust him

Note: reflexive pronouns change to emphatic (disjunctive) pronouns in positive commands:

elle doit se reposer   repose-toi
she needs to rest   take a rest

4. Conjugation of reflexive verbs

a) *Simple tenses*

These are formed in the same way as for non-reflexive verbs, except that a reflexive pronoun is used.

b) *Compound tenses*

These are formed with the auxiliary **être** followed by the past participle of the verb.

A full conjugation table is given on p. 78.

5. Agreement of the past participle

a) In most cases, the reflexive pronoun is a direct object, and the past participle of the verb agrees in number and in gender with the reflexive pronoun:

il s'est trompé   elle s'est endormie
he made a mistake   she fell asleep

ils se sont excusés   elles se sont assises
they apologized   they sat down

b) When the reflexive pronoun is used as an indirect object, the past participle does not change:

nous nous sommes écrit   elle se l'est acheté
we wrote to each other   she bought it for herself

When the reflexive verb has a direct object, the reflexive pronoun is the indirect object of the reflexive verb and the past participle does not agree with it:

Caroline s'est tordu la cheville
Caroline sprained her ankle

vous vous êtes lavé les mains, les filles?
did you girls wash your hands?

6. Common reflexive verbs

s'en aller
to go away

s'amuser
to have fun

s'appeler
to be called

s'approcher (de)
to come near

s'arrêter
to stop

s'asseoir
to sit down

s'attendre à
to expect

se baigner
to take a bath

se battre
to fight

se blesser
to hurt oneself

se coucher
to go to bed

se débarrasser de
to get rid of

se demander
to wonder

se dépêcher
to hurry

se déshabiller
to undress

se diriger vers
to move towards

s'éloigner (de)
to move away (from)

s'endormir
to fall asleep

s'ennuyer
to be bored

s'étonner (de)
to be surprised (at)

s'excuser (de)
to apologize (for)

se fâcher
to get angry

s'écrier
to cry out/exclaim

s'habiller
to get dressed

se hâter
to hurry

s'inquiéter
to worry

s'installer
to settle down

se laver
to wash

se lever
to get up

se mêler de
to meddle with

se mettre à
to start

se mettre en route
to set out

se moquer de
to make fun of

s'occuper de
to take care of

se passer
to happen

se passer de
to do without

se promener
to go for a walk

se rappeler
to remember

se raser
to shave

se renseigner
to make inquiries

se ressembler
to look alike

se retourner
to turn around

se réveiller
to wake up

se sauver
to run away

se souvenir (de)
to remember

se taire
to be/keep quiet

se tromper
to be mistaken

se trouver
to be (situated)

E. IMPERSONAL VERBS

1. Conjugation

Impersonal verbs are used only in the third person singular and in the infinitive. The subject is always the impersonal pronoun **il** = it.

il neige
it's snowing

il y a du brouillard
it's foggy

2. List of impersonal verbs

a) *verbs describing the weather:*

   i) **faire** + adjective:

il fait beau/chaud	**il fait frais/froid**
it's nice/warm	it's cool/cold
il fera beau demain	**il va faire très froid**
the weather will be good tomorrow	it will be very cold

   ii) **faire** + noun:

il fait beau temps	**il fait mauvais temps**
the weather is nice	the weather is bad

   Note: **il fait jour**   **il fait nuit**
   it's day(light)   it's dark

   iii) other impersonal verbs and verbs used impersonally to describe the weather:

il gèle	**(geler)**	it's freezing
il grêle	**(grêler)**	it's hailing
il neige	**(neiger)**	it's snowing
il pleut	**(pleuvoir)**	it's raining
il tonne	**(tonner)**	it's thundering

   Note: some of these verbs may be used personally:

   je gèle   I am freezing

   iv) **il y a** + noun:

il y a des nuages	it's cloudy
il y a du brouillard	it's foggy
il y a du verglas	it's icy

b) *être*

   i) **il est** + noun:

il est cinq heures	it's five o'clock
il était une fois un géant	there was once a giant

   ii) **il est** + adjective + **de** + infinitive:

il est difficile de	it's difficult to
il est facile de	it's easy to
il est nécessaire de	it's necessary to
il est inutile de	it's useless to
il est possible de	it's possible to

   il est difficile d'en parler
   it is difficult to talk about it

   Note: the indirect object pronoun in French corresponds to the English 'for me, for him' etc.:

   il m'est difficile d'en parler
   it is difficult for me to talk about it

iii) **il est + adjective + que:**

il est douteux que	it's doubtful that
il est évident que	it's clear that
il est possible que	it's possible that
il est probable que	it's probable that
il est peu probable que	it's unlikely that
il est vrai que	it's true that

Note: que may be followed by the indicative or the subjunctive (see p. 92):

il est probable qu'il ne viendra pas
he probably won't come

il est peu probable qu'il vienne
it's unlikely that he'll come

c) *arriver, se passer* (to happen)

il est arrivé une chose curieuse
a strange thing happened

que se passe-t-il?
what's happening?

d) *exister* (to exist), *rester* (to remain), *manquer* (to be missing)

il existe trois exemplaires de ce livre
there are three copies of this book

il me restait six francs
I had six francs left

il me manque vingt francs
I am twenty francs short

e) *paraître, sembler* (to seem)

il paraîtrait/semblerait qu'il ait changé d'avis
it would appear that he has changed his mind

il paraît qu'il va se marier
it seems he's going to get married

il me semble que le professeur s'est trompé
it seems to me (that) the teacher made a mistake

f) *other common impersonal verbs*

i) **s'agir** (to be a matter of):

may be followed by a noun, a pronoun, or an infinitive:

il s'agit de ton avenir
it's about your future

de quoi s'agit-il?
what is it about?

il s'agit de trouver le coupable
we must find the culprit

ii) **falloir** (to be necessary):

may be followed by a noun, an infinitive, or the subjunctive:

il faut six heures pour aller de New-York à Paris
it takes six hours to get from New York to Paris

il me faut plus de temps
I need more time

il faudra rentrer plus tôt ce soir
we'll have to come home earlier tonight

il faut que tu parles à ta maman
you('ll) have to speak to your mom

iii) **suffire** (to be enough):

may be followed by a noun, an infinitive, or the subjunctive:

il suffit de peu de chose pour être heureux
it doesn't take a lot to be happy

il suffit de passer le pont
you only have to cross the bridge

il suffira qu'ils te donnent le numéro de téléphone
they will only have to give you the phone number

iv) **valoir mieux** (to be better):

may be followed by an infinitive or the subjunctive:

il vaudrait mieux prendre le car
it would be better to take the bus

il vaut mieux que vous ne sortiez pas seule le soir
you'd better not go out alone at night

F. TENSES

For the formation of the different tenses, see pp. 68–70 and 76–79.

Note: French has no progressive tenses (as in 'I am eating', 'I was going', 'I will be arriving'). The 'be' and '-ing' parts of English progressive tenses are not translated as separate words. Instead, the equivalent tense is used in French:

ENGLISH	FRENCH
I am eating	**je mange**
I will be eating	**je mangerai**

1. Present

The present is used to describe what someone does/something that happens regularly, or what someone is doing/something that is happening at the time of speaking.

a) *regular actions*

il travaille dans un bureau
he works in an office

je lis rarement le journal
I seldom read the paper

b) *continuous actions*

ne le dérangez pas, il travaille
don't disturb him, he's working

je ne peux pas venir, je garde mon petit frère
I can't come, I'm taking care of my kid brother

Note: the continuous nature of the action can also be expressed by using the phrase **être en train de** (to be in the act of) + infinitive:

je suis en train de cuisiner
I'm (busy) cooking

c) *immediate future*

je pars demain
I'm leaving tomorrow

But: the present cannot be used after **quand** and other conjunctions of time when the future is implied (see p. 92):

je le ferai quand j'aurai le temps
I'll do it when I have (the) time

d) *general truths*

la vie est dure
life is hard

2. Imperfect

The imperfect is a past tense used to express what someone was doing or what someone used to do, or to describe something in the past. The imperfect refers particularly to something that *continued* over a period of time, as opposed to something that happened at a specific point in time.

a) *continuous actions*

the imperfect describes an action that was happening, e.g. when something else took place (imperfect means unfinished):

il prenait un bain quand le téléphone a sonné
he was taking a bath when the phone rang

excuse-moi, je pensais à autre chose
I'm sorry, I was thinking of something else

Note: the continuous nature of the action can be emphasized by using **être en train de** + infinitive:

j'étais en train de faire le ménage
I was (busy) doing the housework

b) *regular actions in the past*

je le voyais souvent quand il habitait dans le quartier
I used to see him often when he lived in this neighborhood

quand il était plus jeune il voyageait beaucoup
when he was younger he used to travel a lot

c) *description in the past*

il faisait beau ce jour-là   **c'était formidable!**
the weather was fine that day   it was great!

elle portait une robe bleue   **elle donnait sur la rue**
she wore a blue dress   it looked out onto the street

3. Passé composé

The *passé composé* is a compound past tense, used to express *single* actions that have been completed, i.e. what someone did or what someone has done/has been doing, or something that has happened or has been happening:

je l'ai envoyé lundi I sent it on Monday	**on est sorti hier soir** we went out last night
tu t'es bien amusé? did you have a good time?	**je ne l'ai pas vu** I didn't see him
j'ai lu toute la journée I've been reading all day	**tu as déjà mangé?** have you eaten?

Note: 'Passé composé' or imperfect?

In English, the simple past ('did', 'went', 'prepared') is used to describe both single and repeated actions in the past. In French, the *passé composé* only describes single actions in the past, while repeated actions are expressed by the imperfect (they are sometimes indicated by 'used to'). Thus 'I went' should be translated 'j'allais' or 'je suis allé' depending on the nature of the action:

après dîner, je suis allé en ville
after dinner I went downtown

l'an dernier, j'allais plus souvent au théâtre
last year, I went to the theater more often

4. Passé simple

This tense is used in the same way as the *passé composé* to describe a single, completed action in the past (what someone did or something that happened). It is a literary tense, not common in everyday spoken French; it is found mainly as a narrative tense in written form:

le piéton ne vit pas arriver la voiture
the pedestrian didn't see the car coming

5. Plus-que-parfait

This compound tense is used to express what someone had done/had been doing, or something that had happened or had been happening:

il n'avait pas voulu aller avec eux
he hadn't wanted to go with them

elle était essoufflée parce qu'elle avait couru
she was out of breath because she'd been running

However, the *plus-que-parfait* is not used as in English with **depuis** (for, since), or with **venir de** + infinitive (to have just done something). For details see pp. 90–91

il neigeait depuis une semaine
it had been snowing for a week

les pompiers venaient d'arriver
the firemen had just arrived

6. Future

This tense is used to express what someone will do or will be doing, or something that will happen or will be happening:

je ferai la vaisselle demain   j'arriverai tard
I'll do the dishes tomorrow   I'll be arriving late

Note: the future and not the present, as in English, is used in time clauses introduced by quand (when) or other conjunctions of time where the future is implied (see p. 92):

il viendra quand il le pourra
he'll come when he can

French makes frequent use of **aller** + infinitive (to be about to do something) to express the immediate future:

je vais vous expliquer ce qui s'est passé
I'll explain to you what happened

il va déménager la semaine prochaine
he's moving next week

7. Future perfect

This compound tense is used to describe what someone will have done/will have been doing in the future, or to describe something that will have happened in the future:

j'aurai bientôt fini
I will have finished soon

In particular, it is used instead of the English present perfect in time clauses introduced by **quand** or other conjunctions of time where the future is implied (see p. 92):

appelle-moi quand tu auras fini
call me when you've finished

on rentrera dès qu'on aura fait les courses
we'll come back as soon as we've done our shopping

8. Past anterior

This tense is used instead of the *plus-que-parfait* to express an action that preceded another action in the past (i.e. a past in the past). It is usually introduced by a conjunction of time (translated by 'when', 'as soon as', 'after' etc.) and the main verb is in the *passé simple*:

il se coucha dès qu'ils furent partis
he went to bed as soon as they'd left

à peine eut-elle raccroché que le téléphone sonna
she'd hardly hung up when the phone rang

9. Use of tenses with 'depuis' (for, since)

a) The present must be used instead of the *passé composé* to describe actions that started in the past and have continued up to the present:

il habite ici depuis trois ans
he's been living here for three years

elle l'attend depuis ce matin
she's been waiting for him since this morning

But: The *passé composé*, not the present, is used when the clause is negative or when the action has been completed:

il n'a pas pris de vacances depuis longtemps
he hasn't taken a vacation in a long time

j'ai fini depuis un bon moment
I've been finished for quite a while

Note:

i) **il y a ... que** or **voilà ... que** are also used with the present tense to translate 'for':

it's been ringing for ten minutes
ça sonne depuis dix minutes
il y a dix minutes que ça sonne
voilà dix minutes que ça sonne

ii) **depuis que** is used when 'since' introduces a clause, i.e. when there is a verb following **depuis**:

elle dort depuis que vous êtes partis
she's been sleeping since you left

iii) do not confuse **depuis** (for, since) and **pendant** (for, during): **depuis** refers to the starting point of an action that is still going on, and **pendant** refers to the duration of an action that is over, and is used with the *passé composé*:

il vit ici depuis deux mois
he's been living here for two months

il a vécu ici pendant deux mois
he lived here for two months

b) the imperfect must be used instead of the *plus-que-parfait* to describe an action that had started in the past and was still going on at a given time:

> **elle le connaissait depuis son enfance**
> she had known him since her childhood

> **il attendait depuis trois heures quand on est arrivé**
> he had been waiting for three hours when we arrived

But: if the sentence is negative or if the action has been completed, the *plus-que-parfait* and not the imperfect is used:

> **je n'étais pas allé au théâtre depuis des années**
> I hadn't gone to the theater in years

> **il était parti depuis peu**
> he'd been gone for a little while

Note:

i) **il y avait ... que** + imperfect is also used to translate 'for':
> she'd been living alone for a long time
> **elle habitait seule depuis longtemps**
> **il y avait longtemps qu'elle habitait seule**

ii) **depuis que** is used when 'since' introduces a clause; if it describes an action that was still going on at the time, it can be followed by the imperfect, otherwise it is followed by the *plus-que-parfait*:

> **il pleuvait depuis que nous étions en vacances**
> it had been raining the whole time we were on vacation

> **il pleuvait depuis que nous étions arrivés**
> it had been raining since we arrived

iii) do not confuse **depuis** and **pendant**: **depuis** refers to the starting point of an action that is still going on and **pendant** refers to the duration of an action that is over; **pendant** is used with the *plus-que-parfait*:

> **j'y travaillais depuis un an**
> I had been working there for a year

> **j'y avais travaillé pendant un an**
> I had worked there for a year

10. Use of tenses with 'venir de'

> **venir de** + infinitive means 'to have just'.

a) if it describes something that has just happened, it is used in the present instead of the *passé composé*:

> **l'avion vient d'arriver**   **je viens de te le dire!**
> the plane has just arrived   I've just told you!

b) if it describes something that had just happened, it is used in the imperfect instead of the *plus-que-parfait*:

> **le film venait de commencer**   **je venais de rentrer**
> the film had just started   I'd just gotten home

11. Use of tenses after conjunctions of time

quand	when
tant que	as long as
dès/aussitôt que	as soon as
lorsque	when
pendant que	while

Verbs that follow these conjunctions must be used in the following tenses:

a) *future instead of present*:

je te téléphonerai quand je serai prêt
I'll phone you when I am ready

on ira dès qu'il fera beau
we'll go as soon as the weather is nice

b) *future perfect instead of passé composé* when the future is implied:

on rentrera dès qu'on aura fini les courses
we'll come back as soon as we've done our shopping

je t'appellerai dès qu'il sera arrivé
I'll call you as soon as he has arrived

c) *present/past conditional instead of passé composé/plus-que-parfait* in indirect speech:

il a dit qu'il sortirait quand il aurait fini
he said he would come out when he had finished

For the tenses of the subjunctive and conditional, see pp. 92–96 and 97–98.

G. MOODS

1. The subjunctive

In spoken everyday French, the only two subjunctive tenses that are used are the present and the past. The imperfect and the pluperfect subjunctive are found mainly in literature or in texts of a formal nature.

The subjunctive is practically always preceded by the conjunction **que** and is used in subordinate clauses when the subject of the subordinate clause is different from the subject of the main verb.

Some clauses introduced by **que** take the indicative. But the subjunctive must be used after the following:

a) *Verbs of emotion*

être content que	to be pleased that
être désolé que	to be sorry that
être étonné que	to be surprised that
être heureux que	to happy that

être surpris que	to be surprised that
être triste que	to be sad that
avoir peur que ... ne	to be afraid/to fear that
craindre que ... ne	to be afraid/to fear that
regretter que	to be sorry that

ils étaient contents que j'aille les voir
they were pleased (that) I went to visit them

je serais très étonné qu'il mente
I'd be very surprised to find (that) he was lying

on regrette beaucoup que tu n'aies pas pu vendre ta voiture
we're very sorry (that) you couldn't sell your car

Note: **ne** is used after **craindre que** or **avoir peur que,** but does not have a negative meaning in itself, and is not translated in English:

je crains que l'avion *ne* soit en retard
I'm afraid (that) the plane will be late

b) *Verbs of wishing and desiring:*

aimer que	to like
désirer que	to wish (that)
préférer que	to prefer (that)
souhaiter que	to wish (that)
vouloir que	to want

Note: In English, such verbs are often used in the following type of construction: verb of desiring + object + infinitive (e.g. I'd like you to listen); this type of construction is impossible in French, where a subjunctive clause has to be used:

je souhaite que tu réussisses
I hope (that) you (will) succeed

il aimerait que je lui écrive plus souvent
he'd like me to write him more often

voulez-vous que je vous y amène en voiture?
would you like me to drive you there?

préférez-vous que je rappelle demain?
would you rather I call back tomorrow?

c) *Impersonal constructions* (expressing necessity, possibility, doubt, denial, preference):

il faut que	it is necessary (that) (*must*)
il est nécessaire que	it is necessary that (*must*)
il est important que	it is important (that)
il est possible que	it is possible that (*may*)
il se peut que	it is possible that (*may*)
il est impossible que	it is impossible (that) (*can't*)
il est douteux que	it is doubtful whether/that
il est peu probable que	it is unlikely that

93

il semble que	it seems (that)
il est préférable que	it is preferable (that)
il vaut mieux que	it is better (that) (*had better*)
c'est dommage que	it is a pity (that)

Note: these expressions may be used in any appropriate tense:

il faut qu'on se dépêche
we must hurry

il était important que tu le saches
it was important for you to know it

il se pourrait qu'elle change d'avis
she might change her mind

il est peu probable qu'ils s'y intéressent
they're unlikely to be interested in it

il semble qu'elle ait raison
she appears to be right

il vaudrait mieux que tu ne promettes rien
you'd better not promise anything

c'est dommage que vous vous soyez manqués
it's a pity you missed each other

d) *Some verbs and impersonal constructions expressing doubt or uncertainty* (mainly used negatively or interrogatively):

douter que	to doubt (that)
(ne pas) croire que	(not) to believe (that)
(ne pas) penser que	(not) to think (that)
(ne pas) être sûr que	(not) to be sure that
il n'est pas certain que	it isn't certain that
il n'est pas évident que	it isn't obvious that
il n'est pas sûr que	it isn't certain that
il n'est pas vrai que	it isn't true that

je doute fort qu'il veuille t'aider
I doubt very much that he'll want to help you

croyez-vous qu'il y ait des places de libres?
do you think there are any seats available?

on n'était pas sûr que ce soit le bon endroit
we weren't sure that it was the right place

il n'était pas certain qu'elle puisse gagner
it wasn't certain that she could win

e) *attendre que* (to wait until, to wait for someone to do something):

attendons qu'il revienne
let's wait until he comes back/for him to come back

f) *Some subordinating conjunctions*:

bien que	although
quoique	although
sans que	without
pour que	so that
afin que	so that
à condition que	provided that
pourvu que	provided that
jusqu'à ce que	until
en attendant que	until
avant que ... (ne)	before
à moins que ... (ne)	unless
de peur que ... (ne)	for fear that
de crainte que ... ne	for fear that
de sorte que	so that
de façon que	so that
de manière que	so that

Note: When **ne** is shown in parentheses, it may be used with the conjunction, though it is seldom used in spoken French; it does not have a negative meaning, and is not translated in English.

il est allé travailler bien qu'il soit malade
he went to work even though he was sick

elle est entrée sans que je la voie
she came in without me/my seeing her

voilà de l'argent pour que tu puisses aller au cinéma
here's some money so (that) you can go to the movies

d'accord, pourvu que tu me promettes de ne pas le répéter
all right, as long as you promise me not to tell anyone

tu l'as revu avant qu'il (ne) parte?
did you see him again before he left?

je le ferai demain, à moins que ce (ne) soit urgent
I'll do it tomorrow, unless it's urgent

elle n'a pas fait de bruit de peur qu'il (ne) se réveille
she didn't make any noise, for fear he might wake up

parle moins fort de sorte qu'elle ne nous entende pas
don't talk so loud, so (that) she won't hear us

Note: when **de façon/manière que** (so that) express a result, as opposed to a purpose, the indicative is used instead of the subjunctive:

il a fait du bruit, de sorte qu'elle l'*a* entendu
he made some noise, so that (as a result) she heard him

g) *A superlative, or adjectives like* **premier** *(first),* **dernier** *(last),* **seul** *(only), followed by* **qui** *or* **que**:

c'était le coureur le plus rapide que j'aie jamais vu
he was the fastest runner I ever saw

But: the indicative is used with a statement of fact rather than the expression of an opinion:

> **c'est le coureur le plus rapide qui a gagné**
> it was the fastest runner who won (i.e. the fastest runner is the one who won)

h) *Negative and indefinite pronouns (e.g.* **rien, personne, quelqu'un**) *followed by* **qui** *or* **que**:

> **je ne connais personne qui sache aussi bien chanter**
> I don't know anyone who can sing so well

> **il n'y a aucune chance qu'il réussisse**
> he doesn't have a chance of succeeding

> **ils cherchent quelqu'un qui puisse garder le bébé**
> they're looking for someone who can take care of the baby

2. Avoiding the subjunctive

The subjunctive can be avoided, as is the tendency in modern spoken French, as long as both verbs in the sentence have the same subject. It is replaced by an infinitive introduced by the preposition **de**, the preposition **à**, or by no preposition at all (see pp. 101–6).

a) *de + infinitive replaces the subjunctive after*:

i) verbs of emotion:

> **j'ai été étonné d'apprendre la nouvelle**
> I was surprised to hear the news

> **il regrette de ne pas avoir vu cette émission**
> he's sorry he didn't see that program

> **tu as peur de ne pas avoir assez d'argent?**
> are you worried you won't have enough money?

ii) **attendre** (to wait) and **douter** (to doubt):

> **j'attendrai d'avoir bu mon café**
> I'll wait until I've drunk my coffee

iii) most impersonal constructions:

> **il serait préférable de déclarer ces objets**
> it would be better to declare these things

> **il est important de garder votre billet**
> it's important to keep your ticket

iv) most conjunctions:

> **il est resté dans la voiture afin de ne pas se mouiller**
> he stayed in the car so as not to get wet

> **j'ai lu avant de m'endormir**
> I read before I fell asleep

> **tu peux sortir, à condition de rentrer avant minuit**
> you can go out, as long as you're back before midnight

b) à + *infinitive replaces the subjunctive after*:

   i) **de façon/manière**

      mets la liste sur la table de manière à ne pas l'oublier
      put the list on the table so that you won't forget it

   ii) **premier, seul, dernier**

      il a été le seul à s'excuser
      he was the only one who apologized

c) the infinitive without any linking preposition replaces the subjunctive after:

   i) verbs of wishing and desiring:

      je voudrais sortir avec toi
      I'd like to go out with you

   ii) **il faut, il vaut mieux**:

      il vous faudra prendre des chèques de voyage
      you'll have to take some traveler's checks

      Il lui a fallu recommencer à zéro
      he had to start all over again

      il vaudrait mieux lui apporter des fleurs que des bonbons
      it would be better to bring her some flowers rather than candy

   Note: an indirect object pronoun is often used with **il faut** to indicate the subject (who has to do something).

   iii) verbs of thinking:

      je ne crois pas le connaître
      I don't think I know him

      tu penses être chez toi à cinq heures?
      do you think you'll be home by five?

   iv) **pour** and **sans**:

      le car est reparti sans nous attendre
      the bus left without waiting for us

      j'économise pour pouvoir acheter une moto
      I'm saving up to buy a motorbike

3. The conditional

a) *The present conditional*

   i) The present conditional is used to describe what someone would do or would be doing, or what would happen (if something else were to happen):

      si j'étais riche, j'*achèterais* un château
      if I were rich, I *would buy* a castle

   Note: when the main verb is in the present conditional, the verb after **si** is in the imperfect.

ii) It is also used in indirect questions or reported speech instead of the future:

> **il ne m'a pas dit s'il *viendrait***
> he didn't tell me whether/if he *would come*

b) *The past conditional*

The past conditional is used to express what someone would have done or would have been doing, or what would have happened:

> **si j'avais su, je n'aurais rien dit**
> if I had known, I wouldn't have said anything

> **qu'aurais-je fait sans toi?**
> what would I have done without you?

Note: if the main verb is in the past, the verb introduced by **si** is in the *plus-que-parfait*.

c) *Tenses after **si**:*

The tense of the verb introduced by **si** is determined by the tense of the verb in the main clause:

MAIN VERB		VERB FOLLOWING 'SI'
present conditional	→	imperfect
past conditional	→	*plus-que-parfait*

> **je te le dirais si je le savais**
> I would tell you if I knew

> **je te l'aurais dit si je l'avais su**
> I would have told you if I had known

Note: never use the conditional (or the future) with **si** unless **si** means whether (i.e. when it introduces an indirect question):

> **je me demande si j'y serais arrivé sans toi**
> I wonder if (= *whether*) I would have managed without you

4. The imperative

a) *Definition*

The imperative is used to give commands, or polite instructions, or to make requests or suggestions; these can be positive (affirmative imperative: 'do!') or negative ('don't!'):

mange ta soupe! eat your soup	**n'aie pas peur!** don't be afraid!
partons! let's leave!	**entrez!** come in!
faites attention! be careful!	**n'hésitez pas!** don't hesitate!
tournez à droite à la poste turn right at the post office	

b) *Forms*

The imperative has only three forms, which are the same as the **tu, nous,** and **vous** forms of the present tense, but without the subject pronoun:

	-ER VERBS	-IR VERBS	-RE VERBS
'TU' FORM:	**regarde** watch	**choisis** choose	**attends** wait
'NOUS' FORM:	**regardons** let's watch	**choisissons** let's choose	**attendons** let's wait
'VOUS' FORM:	**regardez** watch	**choisissez** choose	**attendez** wait

i) the **-s** of the **tu** form of **-er** verbs is dropped, except when **y** or **en** follow the verb:

parle-lui! talk to him!	*But*	**parles-en avec lui** talk with him about it
achète du sucre! buy some sugar!	*But*	**achètes-en un kilo** buy a kilo (of it)

ii) the distinction between the subject pronouns **tu** and **vous** (see p. 51) applies to the **tu** and **vous** forms of the imperative:

prends ta sœur avec toi, Alain
take your sister with you, Alain

prenez le plat du jour, Monsieur; c'est du poulet rôti
have today's special, sir; it's roast chicken

les enfants, prenez vos imperméables: il va pleuvoir
take your raincoats, children; it's going to rain

c) *Negative commands*

In negative commands, the verb is placed between **ne** and **pas** (or the second part of other negative expressions):

ne fais pas ça! don't do that!	**ne dites rien!** don't say anything!

d) *Imperative with object pronouns*

In positive commands, object pronouns come after the verb and are attached to it by a hyphen. In negative commands, they come before the verb (see pp. 53, 55, 56, and 57):

dites-moi ce qui s'est passé tell me what happened	**attendons-les!** let's wait for them!

prends-en bien soin, ne l'abîme pas!
be careful with it, don't damage it!

ne le leur dis pas! don't tell it to them	**ne les écoutez pas** don't listen to them

e) *Imperative of reflexive verbs*

The position of the reflexive pronoun of reflexive verbs is the same as that of object pronouns:

tais-toi!
keep quiet!

levez-vous!
get up!

méfiez-vous de lui
don't trust him

arrêtons-nous ici
let's stop here

ne nous plaignons pas
let's not complain

ne t'approche pas plus!
don't come any closer!

f) *Alternatives to the imperative*

i) infinitive

the infinitive is often used instead of the imperative in written instructions and in recipes:

s'adresser au concierge
see the caretaker

ne pas fumer
no smoking

verser le lait et bien mélanger
pour in the milk and stir well

ii) subjunctive

as the imperative has no third person (singular or plural), **que** + subjunctive is used for giving orders in the third person:

que personne ne me dérange!
don't let anyone disturb me!

qu'il entre!
have him (come) in!

qu'elle parte, je m'en fiche!
Let her leave, I couldn't care less!

g) *Idiomatic usage*

The imperative is used in spoken French in many set phrases. Here are some of the most common ones:

allons donc!
you don't say!
come now!

dis/dites donc!
by the way!
hey! (*protest*)

tiens/tenez!
here you are!

tiens! voilà le facteur
ah! here comes the postman

tiens (donc)!
(oh) really?

tiens! tiens!
well, well! (imagine that!)

voyons!
come (on) now!

voyons donc!
let's see now

H. THE INFINITIVE

1. Forms of the infinitive

The infinitive is the basic form of the verb. It is recognized by its ending, which is found in three forms corresponding to the three conjugations: -er, -ir, -re.

These endings give the verb the meaning 'to. . . .':

acheter	**choisir**	**vendre**
to buy	to choose	to sell

Note: although this applies as a general rule, the French infinitive will often be translated by a verb form in *-ing* (see p. 191–2).

2. Uses of the infinitive

The infinitive can follow a preposition, a verb, a noun, a pronoun, an adverb, or an adjective.

a) *After a preposition*

The infinitive can be used after some prepositions (**pour, avant de, sans, au lieu de, afin de, etc.**):

sans attendre	**avant de partir**
without waiting	before leaving

b) *After a verb*

There are three main constructions when a verb is followed by an infinitive:

i) with no linking preposition
ii) with the linking preposition **à**
iii) with the linking preposition **de**

i) Verbs followed by the infinitive with no linking preposition:

verbs of wishing and desiring, e.g.:

vouloir	to want
souhaiter	to wish
désirer	to wish, to want
espérer	to hope

voulez-vous manger maintenant ou plus tard?
do you want to eat now or later?

je souhaite parler au directeur
I want to speak to the manager

- verbs of seeing, hearing, and feeling, e.g.:

voir	to see
écouter	to listen to
regarder	to watch

sentir	to feel, to smell
entendre	to hear

je l'ai vu jouer   **tu m'as regardé danser?**
I've seen him play   did you watch me dance?

j'ai entendu quelqu'un crier
I heard someone shout

- verbs of motion, e.g.:

aller	to go
monter	to go/come up
venir	to come
entrer	to go/come in
rentrer	to go/come home
sortir	to go/come out
descendre	to go/come down

je viendrai te voir demain
I'll come (and) see you tomorrow

il est descendu laver la voiture
he went down to wash the car

va acheter le journal
go (and) buy the paper

Note: in English, 'to come' and 'to go' may be linked to the verb
that follows by 'and'; 'and' is not translated in French.

aller + infinitive can be used to express a future action, e.g.
what someone is going to do:

qu'est-ce que tu vas faire demain?
what are you going to do tomorrow?

- modal verbs (see pp. 113–15)
- verbs of liking and disliking, e.g.:

aimer	to like
adorer	to love
aimer mieux	to prefer
détester	to hate
préférer	to prefer

tu aimes voyager?   **j'aime mieux attendre**
do you like traveling?   I'd rather wait

je déteste aller à la campagne
I hate going to the country

j'adore faire la grasse matinée
I love staying in bed late

- some impersonal verbs (see pp. 84–6)
- a few other verbs, e.g.:

compter	to intend
sembler	to seem
laisser	to let, to allow

| **faillir** | 'to nearly' (do) |
| **oser** | to dare |

ils l'ont laissé partir
they let him go

je n'ose pas le lui demander
I don't dare ask him

tu sembles être malade
you seem to be sick

je compte partir demain
I intend to leave tomorrow

j'ai failli manquer l'avion
I nearly missed the plane

- in the following set expressions:

aller chercher	to go (and) get
envoyer chercher	to send for
entendre dire (que)	to hear (that)
entendre parler de	to hear about
laisser tomber	to drop
venir chercher	to come (and) get
vouloir dire	to mean

va chercher ton argent
go get your money

j'ai entendu dire qu'il était journaliste
I heard that he was a journalist

tu as entendu parler de ce film?
have you heard about this film?

ne le laisse pas tomber!
don't drop it!

ça veut dire "demain"
that means 'tomorrow'

ii) Verbs followed by **à** + infinitive

A list of these is given on p. 150:

je dois aider ma mère à préparer le déjeuner
I have to help my mother get lunch ready

il commence à faire nuit
it's beginning to get dark

alors, tu t'es décidé à y aller?
so you've made up your mind to go?

je t'invite à venir chez moi pour les vacances de Noël
I invite you to come to my place for the Christmas vacation

je passe mon temps à lire et à regarder la télé
I spend my time reading and watching TV

cela sert à nettoyer les fenêtres
this is used for cleaning windows

iii) Verbs followed by **de** + infinitive

A list of these is given on pp. 150–2:

je crois qu'il s'est arrêté de pleuvoir
I think it's stopped raining

tu as envie de sortir?
do you feel like going out?

le médecin a conseillé à Serge de rester au lit
the doctor advised Serge to stay in bed

j'ai décidé de rester chez moi
I decided to stay home

essayons de faire du stop let's try and hitch-hike	**tu as fini de m'ennuyer?** will you stop bothering me?
demande à Papa de t'aider ask Dad to help you	**je t'interdis d'y aller** I forbid you to go there
n'oublie pas d'en acheter! don't forget to buy some!	**j'ai refusé de le faire** I refused to do it
je vous prie de m'excuser please forgive me	**il vient de téléphoner** he's just phoned

c) *After a noun, a pronoun, an adverb, or an adjective*

There are two possible constructions: with **à** or with **de**.

i) with the linking preposition **à**:

il avait plusieurs clients à voir
he had several customers to see

c'est difficile à dire
it's hard to say

ii) with the linking preposition **de**:

je suis content de te voir
I'm glad to see you

iii) **à** or **de** with pronouns, adverbs, or nouns?

- **à** conveys the idea of something to do or to be done after the following:

beaucoup	a lot
plus	more
tant	so much
trop	too much
assez	enough
moins	less
rien	nothing
tout	everything
quelque chose	something

une maison à vendre a house for sale	**j'ai des examens à préparer** I have exams to get ready for

il nous a indiqué la route à suivre
he showed us the road to follow

il y a trop de livres à lire
there are too many books to read

il n'y a pas de temps à perdre
there's no time to lose

c'était une occasion à ne pas manquer
it was an opportunity not to be missed

- **de** is used after nouns of an abstract nature, usually with the definite article, e.g.;

l'habitude de	the habit of
l'occasion de	the opportunity/chance to
le temps de	the time to
le courage de	the courage to
l'envie de	the desire to
le besoin de	the need to
le plaisir de	the pleasure of
le moment de	the time to

il n'avait pas l'habitude d'être seul
he wasn't used to being alone

je n'ai pas le temps de lui parler
I don't have (the) time to talk to him

avez-vous eu l'occasion de la rencontrer?
did you have the chance to meet her?

ce n'est pas le moment de le déranger
now is not the time to bother him

je n'ai pas eu le courage de le lui dire
I didn't have the courage to tell him so

iv) **à** or **de** with adjectives?

- **à** is used in a passive sense (something to be done) and after **c'est**:

un livre agréable à lire
a pleasant book to read

il est facile à satisfaire
he is easily satisfied

c'est intéressant à savoir
that's interesting to know

c'était impossible à faire
that wasn't possible to do

- **de** is used after **il est** in an impersonal sense (see p. 84):

il est intéressant de savoir que . . .
it's interesting to know that . . .

Note: for the use of **c'est** and **il est**, see p. 193.

- **de** is used after many adjectives, especially those where the idea 'of' is present in English, e.g.:

certain/sûr de	certain of/to
capable de	capable of/able to
incapable de	incapable of/unable to
coupable de	guilty of

  j'étais sûr de réussir
  I was sure of succeeding

  il est incapable d'y arriver seul
  he's unable to manage on his own

- **de** is also used with adjectives of emotion, feeling, and generally with adjectives denoting a state of mind, e.g.:

content de	glad/happy to
surpris/étonné de	surprised/amazed to
fier de	proud to
heureux de	happy to
fâché de	annoyed to/at
triste de	sad to
gêné de	embarrassed to
désolé de	sorry for/to

  j'ai été très content de recevoir ta lettre
  I was very glad to get your letter

  elle sera surprise de vous voir
  she will be surprised to see you

  nous avons été très tristes d'apprendre la nouvelle
  we were very sad to hear the news

  But: à is used with **prêt à** (ready to) and **disposé à** (willing to):

  es-tu prête à partir?
  are you ready to go?

  je suis tout disposé à vous aider
  I'm very willing to help you

d) *faire* + *infinitive*

faire is followed by an infinitive without any linking preposition to express the sense of 'having someone do something' or 'having something done'; two constructions are possible:

i) with one object
ii) with two objects

i) when only one object is used, it is a direct object:

  je dois le faire réparer
  I have to get it fixed

  il veut faire repeindre sa voiture
  he wants to have his car repainted

  je ferai nettoyer cette veste; je la ferai nettoyer
  I'll have this jacket cleaned; I'll have it cleaned

tu m'as fait attendre!	je le ferai parler
you made me wait!	I'll make him talk

Note the following set expressions:

faire entrer	to show in
faire venir	to send for
faites entrer ce monsieur	je vais faire venir le
show this gentleman in	docteur
	I'll send for the doctor

ii) when both **faire** and the following infinitive have an object, the object of **faire** is indirect:

elle lui a fait prendre une douche
she made him take a shower

je leur ai fait ranger leur chambre
I made them clean up their room

e) *Infinitive used as subject of another verb:*

trouver un emploi n'est pas facile
finding a job isn't easy

3. The past infinitive

a) *Form*

The past infinitive is formed with the infinitive of the auxiliary **avoir** or **être** as appropriate (see pp. 79–80), followed by the past participle of the verb, e.g.:

avoir mangé	être allé	s'être levé
to have eaten	to have gone	to have gotten up

b) *Use*

i) after the preposition **après** (after):

après avoir attendu une heure, il est rentré chez lui
after waiting for an hour, he went back home

il s'en est souvenu après s'être couché
he remembered it after going to bed

ii) after certain verbs:

se souvenir de	to remember
remercier de	to thank for
regretter de	to regret, to be sorry for
être désolé de	to be sorry for

je vous remercie de m'avoir invité
I thank you for inviting me

il regrettait de leur avoir menti
he was sorry for lying/having lied to them

tu te souviens d'avoir fait cela?
do you remember doing this?

I. PARTICIPLES

1. The present participle

a) *Formation*

Like the imperfect, the present participle is formed by using the stem of the first person plural of the present tense (the **nous** form less the **-ons** ending):

-ons is replaced by **-ant** (= English *-ing*)

Exceptions:

INFINITIVE	PRESENT PARTICIPLE
avoir to have	**ayant** having
être to be	**étant** being
savoir to know	**sachant** knowing

b) *Use as an adjective*

Used as an adjective, the present participle agrees in number and in gender with its noun or pronoun:

un travail étonnant	**la semaine suivante**
astonishing work	the following week
ils sont très exigeants	**des nouvelles surprenantes**
they're very demanding	surprising news

c) *Use as a verb*

The present participle is used much less frequently in French than in English, and English present participles in *-ing* are often not translated by a participle in French (see pp. 191–2).

i) used by itself, the present participle corresponds to the English present participle:

ne voulant plus attendre, ils sont partis sans moi
not wanting to wait any longer, they left without me

pensant bien faire, j'ai insisté
thinking I was doing the right thing, I insisted

ii) **en** + present participle

When the subject of the present participle is the same as that of the main verb, this structure is often used to express simultaneity (i.e. 'while doing something'), manner (i.e. 'by doing something'), or to translate English phrasal verbs.

- simultaneous actions

In English this structure is translated by:
–while/when/on/upon + present participle (e.g. 'on arriving')
–while/when/as + subject + verb (e.g. 'as he arrived')

il est tombé en descendant l'escalier
he fell as he was going down the stairs

en le voyant, j'ai éclaté de rire
when I saw him, I burst out laughing

elle lisait le journal en attendant l'autobus
she was reading the paper while waiting for the bus

Note: the adverb **tout** is often used before **en** to emphasize the fact that both actions are simultaneous, especially when there is an element of contradiction:

elle écoutait la radio tout en faisant ses devoirs
she was listening to the radio while doing her homework

tout en protestant, je les ai suivis
despite my protests, I followed them

- manner

  when expressing how an action is done, **en** + participle is translated by: 'by' + participle, e.g.:

  il gagne sa vie en vendant des voitures d'occasion
  he earns his living (by) selling second-hand cars

  j'ai trouvé du travail en lisant les petites annonces
  I found work by reading the classified ads

- phrasal verbs of motion

  en + present participle is often used to translate English phrasal verbs expressing motion, where the verb expresses the means of motion and a preposition expresses the direction of movement (e.g. 'to run out', 'to swim across').

  In French, the English preposition is translated by a verb, while the English verb is translated by **en** + present participle:

  il est sorti du magasin *en courant*
  he *ran* out of the shop

  elle a traversé la route *en titubant*
  she *staggered* across the road

2. The past participle

a) *Forms*

For the formation of the past participle see p. 76.

b) *Use*

The past participle is used mostly as a verb in compound tenses or in the passive, but it can also be used as an adjective. In either case, there are strict rules of agreement to be followed.

c) *Rules of agreement of the past participle*

i) When used as an adjective, the past participle always agrees with the noun or pronoun it refers to:

un pneu crevé	**une pomme pourrie**
a blown-out tire	a rotten apple

ils étaient épuisés	**trois assiettes cassées!**
they were exhausted	three broken plates!

Note: in French, the past participle is used as an adjective to describe postures or attitudes of the body, where English uses the present participle. The most common of these are:

accoudé	leaning on one's elbows
accroupi	squatting
agenouillé	kneeling
allongé	lying (down)
appuyé (contre)	leaning (against)
assis	sitting (i.e., seated)
couché	lying (down)
étendu	lying (down)
penché	leaning (over)
(sus)pendu	hanging

il est allongé sur le lit	**une femme assise devant moi**
he's lying on the bed	a woman sitting in front of me

ii) In compound tenses:

• with the auxiliary **avoir**:

the past participle agrees in number and gender with the direct object only when the direct object comes before the participle, i.e. in the following cases:

— in a clause introduced by the relative pronoun **que**:

les cassettes que j'ai achetées	**la valise qu'il a perdue**
the tapes I bought	the suitcase he lost

— with a direct object pronoun:

ta carte? je l'ai reçue hier
your card? I got it yesterday

zut, mes lunettes! je les ai laissées chez moi
damn, my glasses! I've left them at home

— in a clause introduced by **combien de, quel (quelle, quels, quelles)** or **lequel (laquelle, lesquels, lesquelles)**:

combien de pays as-tu visités?
how many countries have you traveled to?

laquelle avez-vous choisie?
which one did you choose?

Note: if the direct object comes after the past participle, the participle remains in the masculine singular form:

on a rencontré des gens très sympathiques
we met some very nice people

- with the auxiliary **être**
— the past participle agrees with the subject of the verb:

quand est-elle revenue?
when did she get back?

elle était déjà partie
she'd already left

ils sont passés te voir?
did they come by to see you?

elles sont restées là
they stayed there

Note: this rule also applies when the verb is in the passive:

elle a été arrêtée
she's been arrested

— reflexive verbs

in most cases, the past participle of reflexive verbs agrees with the reflexive pronoun if the pronoun is a direct object; since the reflexive pronoun refers to the subject, the number and gender of the past participle are determined by the subject:

Jacques s'est trompé
Jacques made a mistake

Marie s'était levée tard
Marie had gotten up late

ils se sont disputés?
did they have an argument?

elles se sont vues
they saw each other

Michèle et Marie, vous vous êtes habillées?
Michèle and Marie, have you gotten dressed yet?

But: the past participle does not agree when the reflexive pronoun is an indirect object:

elles se sont écrit
they wrote *to* each other

This is the case especially where parts of the body are mentioned:

elle s'est lavé les cheveux
she washed her hair

ils se sont serré la main
they shook hands

J. THE PASSIVE

1. Formation

The passive is used when the subject does not perform the action, but is subjected to it, e.g.:

the house has been sold   he was made dispensable

Passive tenses are formed with the corresponding tense of the verb 'être' ('to be', as in English), followed by the past participle of the verb, e.g.

j'ai été invité
I was invited

The past participle must agree with its subject, e.g.:

elle a été renvoyée
she has been dismissed

ils seront déçus
they will be disappointed

elles ont été vues
they were seen

2. Avoidance of the passive

The passive is much less common in French than in English. In particular, an indirect object cannot become the subject of a sentence in French, i.e. the following sentence where 'he' is an indirect object has no equivalent in French:

> he was given a book (*i.e. a book was given to him*)

In general, French tries to avoid the passive wherever possible. This can be done in several ways:

a) *Use of the pronoun **on**:*

> **on m'a volé mon portefeuille**
> my wallet has been stolen

> **on construit une nouvelle piscine**
> a new swimming pool is being built

> **en France, on boit beaucoup de vin**
> a lot of wine is drunk in France

b) *Agent becomes subject of the verb*

If the agent, i.e. the real subject, is mentioned in English, it can become the subject of the French verb:

> **la nouvelle va les surprendre**
> they'll be surprised by *the news*

> **mon correspondant m'a invité**
> I've been invited by *my pen-pal*

> **mon cadeau te plaît?**
> are you pleased with *my present*?

c) *Use of a reflexive verb*

Reflexive forms can be created for a large number of verbs, especially in the third person:

elle s'appelle Anne	**ton absence va se remarquer**
she is called/her name is Anne	your absence will be noticed
ce plat se mange froid	**cela ne se fait pas ici**
this dish is eaten cold	that isn't done here

d) *Use of **se faire** + infinitive (when the subject is a person):*

> **il s'est fait renverser par une voiture**
> he was run over by a car

> **je me suis fait voler (tout mon argent)**
> I've been robbed (of all my money)

3. Conjugation

For a complete conjugation table of a verb in the passive, see **être aimé** (to be loved) p. 119.

K. MODAL VERBS

The modal verbs are always followed by the infinitive. They express an obligation, a probability, an intention, a possibility, or a wish, rather than a fact.

The five modal verbs are: **DEVOIR, POUVOIR, SAVOIR, VOULOIR** and **FALLOIR**.

1. Devoir (conjugation see p. 127)

Expresses: a) obligation, necessity
                b) probability
                c) intention, expectation

a) *obligation*

nous devons arriver à temps	**demain tu devras prendre le bus**
we must arrive in time	tomorrow you'll have to take the bus
nous avions dû partir	**j'ai dû avouer que j'avais tort**
we had (had) to go	I had to admit that I was wrong

In the conditional, **devoir** may be used for advice, i.e. to express what should be done (present conditional) or should have been done (past conditional):

vous devriez travailler davantage
you ought to/should work harder

tu ne devrais pas marcher sur l'herbe
you shouldn't walk on the grass

tu aurais dû tout avouer
you should have admitted everything

tu n'aurais pas dû manger ces champignons
you shouldn't have eaten those mushrooms

Note: the French infinitive is translated by a past participle in English: **manger** = eat*en*.

b) *probability*

il doit être en train de dormir
he must be sleeping (he's probably sleeping)

j'ai dû me tromper de chemin
I must have taken the wrong road

Note: in a past narrative sequence in the distant past, 'must have' is translated by a *plus-que-parfait* in French:

il dit (*passé simple*) **qu'il avait dû se tromper de chemin**
he said he must have taken the wrong road

c) *intention, expectation*

> **je dois aller chez le dentiste**
> I'm supposed to go to the dentist's
> **le train doit arriver à 19h30**
> the train is due to arrive at 7:30 p.m.

2. Pouvoir (conjugation see p. 139)

Expresses: a) ability
            b) permission
            c) possibility

a) *ability*

> **Superman peut soulever une maison**
> Superman can lift a house
> **cette voiture peut faire du 150**
> this car can do 93 mph
> **il était si faible qu'il ne pouvait pas sortir de son lit**
> he was so weak that he couldn't get out of bed

b) *permission*

> **puis-je entrer?**   **puis-je vous offrir une bière?**
> may I come in?   can/may I give you a beer?

c) *possibility*

> **cela peut arriver**
> it can happen

Note: **pouvoir** + the infinitive is usually replaced by **peut-être** and
the appropriate tense: e.g. **il s'est peut-être trompé de livres**
(he may have taken the wrong books).

In the conditional, **pouvoir** is used to express something that
could or might be (present conditional) or that could or might
have been (past conditional):

> **tu pourrais t'excuser**
> you might apologize
> **j'aurais pu vous prêter mon magnétophone**
> I could have lent you my tape-recorder

Note: with verbs of perception (e.g. **entendre** to hear, **sentir** to feel,
to smell, **voir** to see), **pouvoir** is often omitted:

> **j'entendais le bruit des vagues**
> I could hear the sound of the waves

3. **Savoir** (conjugation see p. 142)

Means: 'to know how to'
> **je sais/savais conduire une moto**
> I can/used to be able to ride a motorbike

4. **Vouloir** (conjugation see p. 148)

Expresses: a) desire
           b) wish
           c) intention

a) *desire*

> **je veux partir**   **voulez-vous danser avec moi?**
> I want to go   will you dance with me?

b) *wish*

> **je voudrais être un lapin**
> I wish I were a rabbit
>
> **je voudrais trouver un travail intéressant**
> I'd like to find an interesting job
>
> **j'aurais voulu lui donner un coup de poing**
> I would have liked to punch him

c) *intention*

> **il a voulu sauter par la fenêtre**
> he tried to jump out the window

Note: **veuillez**, the imperative of **vouloir**, is used as a somewhat exaggeratedly polite form to express a request ('would you please be so good as'):

> **veuillez ne pas déranger**
> please do not disturb

5. **Falloir** (conjugation see p. 134)

Expresses: necessity
> **il faut manger pour vivre**
> you have to eat to live
>
> **il faudrait manger plus tôt ce soir**
> we should eat earlier tonight
>
> **il aurait fallu apporter des sandwichs**
> we should have brought some sandwiches along

Note: some of the above verbs can also be used without infinitive constructions. They then take on a different meaning (e.g. **devoir** = to owe, **savoir** = to know).

L. CONJUGATION TABLES

The following verbs give the main patterns of conjugation including the conjugation of the most common irregular verbs. They are arranged in alphabetical order:

-er verb (*see p. 68*)	AIMER
-ir verb (*see p. 68*)	FINIR
-re verb (*see p. 68*)	VENDRE
Reflexive verb (*see pp. 80-3*)	SE MEFIER
Verb with auxiliary être (*see pp. 105-8*)	ARRIVER
Verb in the passive (*see pp. 150-1*)	ETRE AIME
Auxiliaries (*see pp. 103-8*)	AVOIR
	ETRE
Verb in -eler/-eter (*see pp. 97-8*)	APPELER
Verb in e + consonant + er (*see p. 100*)	ACHETER
Verb in é + consonant + er (*see pp. 101-2*)	ESPERER
Modal verbs (*see pp. 152-5*)	DEVOIR
	POUVOIR
	SAVOIR
	VOULOIR
	FALLOIR

Irregular verbs	ALLER	METTRE
	CONDUIRE	OUVRIR
	CONNAITRE	PRENDRE
	CROIRE	RECEVOIR
	DIRE	TENIR
	DORMIR	VENIR
	ECRIRE	VIVRE
	FAIRE	VOIR

ACHETER   to buy

PRESENT	IMPERFECT	FUTURE
j'achète	j'achetais	j'achèterai
tu achètes	tu achetais	tu achèteras
il achète	il achetait	il achètera
nous achetons	nous achetions	nous achèterons
vous achetez	vous achetiez	vous achèterez
ils achètent	ils achetaient	ils achèteront

PASSÉ SIMPLE	PASSÉ COMPOSÉ	PLUS-QUE-PARFAIT
j'achetai	j'ai acheté	j'avais acheté
tu achetas	tu as acheté	tu avais acheté
il acheta	il a acheté	il avait acheté
nous achetâmes	nous avons acheté	nous avions acheté
vous achetâtes	vous avez acheté	vous aviez acheté
ils achetèrent	ils ont acheté	ils avaient acheté

CONDITIONAL

PAST ANTERIOR	PRESENT	PAST
j'eus acheté etc.	j'achèterais	j'aurais acheté
	tu achèterais	tu aurais acheté
	il achèterait	il aurait acheté
	nous achèterions	nous aurions acheté
FUTURE PERFECT	vous achèteriez	vous auriez acheté
j'aurai acheté etc.	ils achèteraient	ils auraient acheté

SUBJUNCTIVE

PRESENT	IMPERFECT	PAST
j'achète	j'achetasse	j'aie acheté
tu achètes	tu achetasses	tu aies acheté
il achète	il achetât	il ait acheté
nous achetions	nous achetassions	nous ayons acheté
vous achetiez	vous achetassiez	vous ayez acheté
ils achètent	ils achetassent	ils aient acheté

IMPERATIVE	INFINITIVE	PARTICIPLE
	PRESENT	PRESENT
achète	acheter	achetant
achetons		
achetez		
	PAST	PAST
	avoir acheté	acheté

AIMER   to like, to love

PRESENT	IMPERFECT	FUTURE
j'aime	j'aimais	j'aimerai
tu aimes	tu aimais	tu aimeras
il aime	il aimait	il aimera
nous aimons	nous aimions	nous aimerons
vous aimez	vous aimiez	vous aimerez
ils aiment	ils aimaient	ils aimeront

PASSÉ SIMPLE	PASSÉ COMPOSÉ	PLUS-QUE-PARFAIT
j'aimai	j'ai aimé	j'avais aimé
tu aimas	tu as aimé	tu avais aimé
il aima	il a aimé	il avait aimé
nous aimâmes	nous avons aimé	nous avions aimé
vous aimâtes	vous avez aimé	vous aviez aimé
ils aimèrent	ils ont aimé	ils avaient aimé

	CONDITIONAL	
PAST ANTERIOR	PRESENT	PAST
j'eus aimé etc.	j'aimerais	j'aurais aimé
	tu aimerais	tu aurais aimé
	il aimerait	il aurait aimé
	nous aimerions	nous aurions aimé
FUTURE PERFECT	vous aimeriez	vous auriez aimé
j'aurai aimé etc.	ils aimeraient	ils auraient aimé

SUBJUNCTIVE

PRESENT	IMPERFECT	PAST
j'aime	j'aimasse	j'aie aimé
tu aimes	tu aimasses	tu aies aimé
il aime	il aimât	il ait aimé
nous aimions	nous aimassions	nous ayons aimé
vous aimiez	vous aimassiez	vous ayez aimé
ils aiment	ils aimassent	ils aient aimé

IMPERATIVE	INFINITIVE	PARTICIPLE
	PRESENT	PRESENT
aime	aimer	aimant
aimons		
aimez		
	PAST	PAST
	avoir aimé	aimé

ETRE AIME to be loved

PRESENT

je suis aimé(e)
tu es aimé(e)
il (elle) est aimé(e)
nous sommes aimé(e)s
vous êtes aimé(e)(s)
ils (elles) sont aimé(e)s

IMPERFECT

j'étais aimé(e)
tu étais aimé(e)
il (elle) était aimé(e)
nous étions aimé(e)s
vous étiez aimé(e)(s)
ils (elles) étaient aimé(e)s

FUTURE

je serai aimé(e)
tu seras aimé(e)
il (elle) sera aimé(e)
nous serons aimé(e)s
vous serez aimé(e)(s)
ils (elles) seront aimé(e)s

PASSÉ SIMPLE

je fus aimé(e)
tu fus aimé(e)
il (elle) fut aimé(e)
nous fûmes aimé(e)s
vous fûtes aimé(e)(s)
ils (elles) furent aimé(e)s

PASSÉ COMPOSÉ

j'ai été aimé(e)
tu as été aimé(e)
il (elle) a été aimé(e)
nous avons été aimé(e)s
vous avez été aimé(e)(s)
ils (elles) ont été aimé(e)s

PLUS-QUE-PARFAIT

j'avais été aimé(e)
tu avais été aimé(e)
il (elle) avait été aimé(e)
nous avions été aimé(e)s
vous aviez été aimé(e)(s)
ils (elles) avaient été aimé(e)s

CONDITIONAL

PAST ANTERIOR

j'eus été aimé(e) etc.

FUTURE PERFECT

j'aurai été aimé(e) etc.

PRESENT

je serais aimé(e)
tu serais aimé(e)
il (elle) serait aimé(e)
nous serions aimé(e)s
vous seriez aimé(e)(s)
ils (elles) seraient
  aimé(e)s

PAST

j'aurais été aimé(e)
tu aurais été aimé(e)
il (elle) aurait été aimé(e)
nous aurions été aimé(e)s
vous auriez été aimé(e)(s)
ils (elles) auraient été
  aimé(e)s

SUBJUNCTIVE

PRESENT

je sois aimé(e)
tu sois aimé(e)
il (elle) soit aimé(e)
nous soyons aimé(e)s
vous soyez aimé(e)(s)
ils (elles) soient aimé(e)(s)

IMPERFECT

je fusse aimé(e)
tu fusses aimé(e)
il (elle) fût aimé(e)
nous fussions aimé(e)s
vous fussiez aimé(e)(s)
ils (elles) fussent aimé(e)s

PAST

j'aie été aimé(e)
tu aies été aimé(e)
il (elle) ait été aimé(e)
nous ayons été aimé(e)s
vous ayez été aimé(e)(s)
ils (elles) aient été aimé(e)s

IMPERATIVE

sois aimé(e)
soyons aimé(e)s
soyez aimé(e)(s)

INFINITIVE

PRESENT

être aimé(e)(s)

PAST

avoir été aimé(e)(s)

PARTICIPLE

PRESENT

étant aimé(e)(s)

PAST

été aimé(e)(s)

ALLER   to go

PRESENT	IMPERFECT	FUTURE
je vais	j'allais	j'irai
tu vas	tu allais	tu iras
il va	il allait	il ira
nous allons	nous allions	nous irons
vous allez	vous alliez	vous irez
ils vont	ils allaient	ils iront

PASSÉ SIMPLE	PASSÉ COMPOSÉ	PLUS-QUE-PARFAIT
j'allai	je suis allé(e)	j'étais allé(e)
tu allas	tu es allé(e)	tu étais allé(e)
il alla	il/elle est allé(e)	il/elle était allé(e)
nous allâmes	nous sommes allé(e)s	nous étions allé(e)s
vous allâtes	vous êtes allé(e)(s)	vous étiez allé(e)(s)
ils allèrent	ils/elles sont allé(e)s	ils/elles étaient allé(e)s

	CONDITIONAL	
PAST ANTERIOR	PRESENT	PAST
je fus allé(e) etc.	j'irais	je serais allé(e)
	tu irais	tu serais allé(e)
	il irait	il/elle serait allé(e)
	nous irions	nous serions allé(e)s
FUTURE PERFECT	vous iriez	vous seriez allé(e)(s)
je serai allé(e) etc.	ils iraient	ils/elles seraient allé(e)s

SUBJUNCTIVE

PRESENT	IMPERFECT	PAST
j'aille	j'allasse	je sois allé(e)
tu ailles	tu allasses	tu sois allé(e)
il aille	il allât	il/elle soit allé(e)
nous allions	nous allassions	nous soyons allé(e)s
vous alliez	vous allassiez	vous soyez allé(e)(s)
ils aillent	ils allassent	ils/elles soient allé(e)s

IMPERATIVE	INFINITIVE	PARTICIPLE
	PRESENT	PRESENT
va	aller	allant
allons		
allez		
	PAST	PAST
	être allé(e)(s)	allé

APPELER to call

PRESENT	IMPERFECT	FUTURE
j'appelle	j'appelais	j'appellerai
tu appelles	tu appelais	tu appelleras
il appelle	il appelait	il appellera
nous appelons	nous appelions	nous appellerons
vous appelez	vous appeliez	vous appellerez
ils appellent	ils appelaient	ils appelleront

PASSÉ SIMPLE	PASSÉ COMPOSÉ	PLUS-QUE-PARFAIT
j'appelai	j'ai appelé	j'avais appelé
tu appelas	tu as appelé	tu avais appelé
il appela	il a appelé	il avait appelé
nous appelâmes	nous avons appelé	nous avions appelé
vous appelâtes	vous avez appelé	vous aviez appelé
ils appelèrent	ils ont appelé	ils avaient appelé

CONDITIONAL

PAST ANTERIOR	PRESENT	PAST
j'eus appelé etc.	j'appellerais	j'aurais appelé
	tu appellerais	tu aurais appelé
	il appellerait	il aurait appelé
	nous appellerions	nous aurions appelé
FUTURE PERFECT	vous appelleriez	vous auriez appelé
j'aurai appelé etc.	ils appelleraient	ils auraient appelé

SUBJUNCTIVE

PRESENT	IMPERFECT	PAST
j'appelle	j'appelasse	j'aie appelé
tu appelles	tu appelasses	tu aies appelé
il appelle	il appelât	il ait appelé
nous appelions	nous appelassions	nous ayons appelé
vous appeliez	vous appelassiez	vous ayez appelé
ils appellent	ils appelassent	ils aient appelé

IMPERATIVE	INFINITIVE	PARTICIPLE
	PRESENT	PRESENT
appelle	appeler	appelant
appelons		
appelez		
	PAST	PAST
	avoir appelé	appelé

121

ARRIVER   to arrive, to happen

PRESENT	IMPERFECT	FUTURE
j'arrive	j'arrivais	j'arriverai
tu arrives	tu arrivais	tu arriveras
il arrive	il arrivait	il arrivera
nous arrivons	nous arrivions	nous arriverons
vous arrivez	vous arriviez	vous arriverez
ils arrivent	ils arrivaient	ils arriveront

PASSÉ SIMPLE	PASSÉ COMPOSÉ	PLUS-QUE-PARFAIT
j'arrivai	je suis arrivé(e)	j'étais arrivé(e)
tu arrivas	tu es arrivé(e)	tu étais arrivé(e)
il arriva	il/elle est arrivé(e)	il/elle était arrivé(e)
nous arrivâmes	nous sommes arrivé(e)s	nous étions arrivé(e)s
vous arrivâtes	vous êtes arrivé(e)(s)	vous étiez arrivé(e)(s)
ils arrivèrent	ils/elles sont arrivé(e)s	ils/elles étaient arrivé(e)s

CONDITIONAL

PAST ANTERIOR	PRESENT	PAST
je fus arrivé(e) etc.	j'arriverais	je serais arrivé(e)
	tu arriverais	tu serais arrivé(e)
	il arriverait	il/elle serait arrivé(e)
	nous arriverions	nous serions arrivé(e)s
FUTURE PERFECT	vous arriveriez	vous seriez arrivé(e)(s)
je serai arrivé(e) etc.	ils arriveraient	ils/elles seraient arrivé(e)s

SUBJUNCTIVE

PRESENT	IMPERFECT	PAST
j'arrive	j'arrivasse	je sois arrivé(e)
tu arrives	tu arrivasses	tu sois arrivé(e)
il arrive	il arrivât	il/elle soit arrivé(e)
nous arrivions	nous arrivassions	nous soyons arrivé(e)s
vous arriviez	vous arrivassiez	vous soyez arrivé(e)(s)
ils arrivent	ils arrivassent	ils/elles soient arrivé(e)s

IMPERATIVE	INFINITIVE	PARTICIPLE
	PRESENT	PRESENT
arrive	arriver	arrivant
arrivons		
arrivez		
	PAST	PAST
	être arrivé(e)(s)	arrivé

122

AVOIR to have

PRESENT	IMPERFECT	FUTURE
j'ai	j'avais	j'aurai
tu as	tu avais	tu auras
il a	il avait	il aura
nous avons	nous avions	nous aurons
vous avez	vous aviez	vous aurez
ils ont	ils avaient	ils auront

PASSÉ SIMPLE	PASSÉ COMPOSÉ	PLUS-QUE-PARFAIT
j'eus	j'ai eu	j'avais eu
tu eus	tu as eu	tu avais eu
il eut	il a eu	il avait eu
nous eûmes	nous avons eu	nous avions eu
vous eûtes	vous avez eu	vous aviez eu
ils eurent	ils ont eu	ils avaient eu

	CONDITIONAL	
PAST ANTERIOR	PRESENT	PAST
j'eus eu etc.	j'aurais	j'aurais eu
	tu aurais	tu aurais eu
	il aurait	il aurait eu
	nous aurions	nous aurions eu
FUTURE PERFECT	vous auriez	vous auriez eu
j'aurai eu etc.	ils auraient	ils auraient eu

SUBJUNCTIVE

PRESENT	IMPERFECT	PAST
j'aie	j'eusse	j'aie eu
tu aies	tu eusses	tu aies eu
il ait	il eût	il ait eu
nous ayons	nous eussions	nous ayons eu
vous ayez	vous eussiez	vous ayez eu
ils aient	ils eussent	ils aient eu

IMPERATIVE	INFINITIVE	PARTICIPLE
	PRESENT	PRESENT
aie	avoir	ayant
ayons		
ayez		
	PAST	PAST
	avoir eu	eu

CONDUIRE   to lead, to drive

PRESENT	IMPERFECT	FUTURE
je conduis	je conduisais	je conduirai
tu conduis	tu conduisais	tu conduiras
il conduit	il conduisait	il conduira
nous conduisons	nous conduisions	nous conduirons
vous conduisez	vous conduisiez	vous conduirez
ils conduisent	ils conduisaient	ils conduiront

PASSÉ SIMPLE	PASSÉ COMPOSÉ	PLUS-QUE-PARFAIT
je conduisis	j'ai conduit	j'avais conduit
tu conduisis	tu as conduit	tu avais conduit
il conduisit	il a conduit	il avait conduit
nous conduisîmes	nous avons conduit	nous avions conduit
vous conduisîtes	vous avez conduit	vous aviez conduit
ils conduisirent	ils ont conduit	ils avaient conduit

	CONDITIONAL	
PAST ANTERIOR	**PRESENT**	**PAST**
j'eus conduit etc.	je conduirais	j'aurais conduit
	tu conduirais	tu aurais conduit
	il conduirait	il aurait conduit
	nous conduirions	nous aurions conduit
FUTURE PERFECT	vous conduiriez	vous auriez conduit
j'aurai conduit etc.	ils conduiraient	ils auraient conduit

SUBJUNCTIVE

PRESENT	IMPERFECT	PAST
je conduise	je conduisisse	j'aie conduit
tu conduises	tu conduisisses	tu aies conduit
il conduise	il conduisît	il ait conduit
nous conduisions	nous conduisissions	nous ayons conduit
vous conduisiez	vous conduisissiez	vous ayez conduit
ils conduisent	ils conduisissent	ils aient conduit

IMPERATIVE	*INFINITIVE*	*PARTICIPLE*
	PRESENT	**PRESENT**
conduis	conduire	conduisant
conduisons		
conduisez		
	PAST	**PAST**
	avoir conduit	conduit

CONNAITRE to know

PRESENT	IMPERFECT	FUTURE
je connais	je connaissais	je connaîtrai
tu connais	tu connaissais	tu connaîtras
il connaît	il connaissait	il connaîtra
nous connaissons	nous connaissions	nous connaîtrons
vous connaissez	vous connaissiez	vous connaîtrez
ils connaissent	ils connaissaient	ils connaîtront

PASSÉ SIMPLE	PASSÉ COMPOSÉ	PLUS-QUE-PARFAIT
je connus	j'ai connu	j'avais connu
tu connus	tu as connu	tu avais connu
il connut	il a connu	il avait connu
nous connûmes	nous avons connu	nous avions connu
vous connûtes	vous avez connu	vous aviez connu
ils connurent	ils ont connu	ils avaient connu

	CONDITIONAL	
PAST ANTERIOR	**PRESENT**	**PAST**
j'eus connu etc.	je connaîtrais	j'aurais connu
	tu connaîtrais	tu aurais connu
	il connaîtrait	il aurait connu
	nous connaîtrions	nous aurions connu
FUTURE PERFECT	vous connaîtriez	vous auriez connu
j'aurai connu etc.	ils connaîtraient	ils auraient connu

SUBJUNCTIVE

PRESENT	IMPERFECT	PAST
je connaisse	je connusse	j'aie connu
tu connaisses	tu connusses	tu aies connu
il connaisse	il connût	il ait connu
nous connaissions	nous connussions	nous ayons connu
vous connaissiez	vous connussiez	vous ayez connu
ils connaissent	ils connussent	ils aient connu

IMPERATIVE	*INFINITIVE*	*PARTICIPLE*
	PRESENT	**PRESENT**
connais	connaître	connaissant
connaissons		
connaissez		
	PAST	**PAST**
	avoir connu	connu

CROIRE   to believe

PRESENT	IMPERFECT	FUTURE
je crois	je croyais	je croirai
tu crois	tu croyais	tu croiras
il croit	il croyait	il croira
nous croyons	nous croyions	nous croirons
vous croyez	vous croyiez	vous croirez
ils croient	ils croyaient	ils croiront

PASSÉ SIMPLE	PASSE COMPOSÉ	PLUS-QUE-PARFAIT
je crus	j'ai cru	j'avais cru
tu crus	tu as cru	tu avais cru
il crut	il a cru	il avait cru
nous crûmes	nous avons cru	nous avions cru
vous crûtes	vous avez cru	vous aviez cru
ils crurent	ils ont cru	ils avaient cru

	CONDITIONAL	
PAST ANTERIOR	**PRESENT**	**PAST**
j'eus cru etc.	je croirais	j'aurais cru
	tu croirais	tu aurais cru
	il croirait	il aurait cru
	nous croirions	nous aurions cru
FUTURE PERFECT	vous croiriez	vous auriez cru
j'aurai cru etc.	ils croiraient	ils auraient cru

SUBJUNCTIVE

PRESENT	IMPERFECT	PAST
je croie	je crusse	j'aie cru
tu croies	tu crusses	tu aies cru
il croie	il crût	il ait cru
nous croyions	nous crussions	nous ayons cru
vous croyiez	vous crussiez	vous ayez cru
ils croient	ils crussent	ils aient cru

IMPERATIVE	INFINITIVE	PARTICIPLE
	PRESENT	**PRESENT**
crois	croire	croyant
croyons		
croyez		
	PAST	**PAST**
	avoir cru	cru

DEVOIR   to have to

PRESENT	IMPERFECT	FUTURE
je dois	je devais	je devrai
tu dois	tu devais	tu devras
il doit	il devait	il devra
nous devons	nous devions	nous devrons
vous devez	vous deviez	vous devrez
ils doivent	ils devaient	ils devront

PASSÉ SIMPLE	PASSÉ COMPOSÉ	PLUS-QUE-PARFAIT
je dus	j'ai dû	j'avais dû
tu dus	tu as dû	tu avais dû
il dut	il a dû	il avait dû
nous dûmes	nous avons dû	nous avions dû
vous dûtes	vous avez dû	vous aviez dû
ils durent	ils ont dû	ils avaient dû

	CONDITIONAL	
PAST ANTERIOR	PRESENT	PAST
j'eus dû etc.	je devrais	j'aurais dû
	tu devrais	tu aurais dû
	il devrait	il aurait dû
	nous devrions	nous aurions dû
FUTURE PERFECT	vous devriez	vous auriez dû
j'aurai dû.	ils devraient	ils auraient dû

SUBJUNCTIVE

PRESENT	IMPERFECT	PAST
je doive	je dusse	j'aie dû
tu doives	tu dusses	tu aies dû
il doive	il dût	il ait dû
nous devions	nous dussions	nous ayons dû
vous deviez	vous dussiez	vous ayez dû
ils doivent	ils dussent	ils aient dû

IMPERATIVE	INFINITIVE	PARTICIPLE
	PRESENT	PRESENT
dois	devoir	devant
devons		
devez		
	PAST	PAST
	avoir dû	dû (due, dus, dues)

127

DIRE to say

PRESENT	IMPERFECT	FUTURE
je dis	je disais	je dirai
tu dis	tu disais	tu diras
il dit	il disait	il dira
nous disons	nous disions	nous dirons
vous dites	vous disiez	vous direz
ils disent	ils disaient	ils diront

PASSÉ SIMPLE	PASSÉ COMPOSÉ	PLUS-QUE-PARFAIT
je dis	j'ai dit	j'avais dit
tu dis	tu as dit	tu avais dit
il dit	il a dit	il avait dit
nous dîmes	nous avons dit	nous avions dit
vous dîtes	vous avez dit	vous aviez dit
ils dirent	ils ont dit	ils avaient dit

	CONDITIONAL	
PAST ANTERIOR	PRESENT	PAST
j'eus dit etc.	je dirais	j'aurais dit
	tu dirais	tu aurais dit
	il dirait	il aurait dit
	nous dirions	nous aurions dit
FUTURE PERFECT	vous diriez	vous auriez dit
j'aurai dit etc.	ils diraient	ils auraient dit

SUBJUNCTIVE

PRESENT	IMPERFECT	PAST
je dise	je disse	j'aie dit
tu dises	tu disses	tu aies dit
il dise	il dît	il ait dit
nous disions	nous dissions	nous ayons dit
vous disiez	vous dissiez	vous ayez dit
ils disent	ils dissent	ils aient dit

IMPERATIVE	INFINITIVE	PARTICIPLE
	PRESENT	PRESENT
dis	dire	disant
disons		
dites		
	PAST	PAST
	avoir dit	dit

DORMIR   to sleep

PRESENT	IMPERFECT	FUTURE
je dors	je dormais	je dormirai
tu dors	tu dormais	tu dormiras
il dort	il dormait	il dormira
nous dormons	nous dormions	nous dormirons
vous dormez	vous dormiez	vous dormirez
ils dorment	ils dormaient	ils dormiront

PASSÉ SIMPLE	PASSÉ COMPOSÉ	PLUS-QUE-PARFAIT
je dormis	j'ai dormi	j'avais dormi
tu dormis	tu as dormi	tu avais dormi
il dormit	il a dormi	il avait dormi
nous dormîmes	nous avons dormi	nous avions dormi
vous dormîtes	vous avez dormi	vous aviez dormi
ils dormirent	ils ont dormi	ils avaient dormi

	CONDITIONAL	
PAST ANTERIOR	PRESENT	PAST
j'eus dormi etc.	je dormirais	j'aurais dormi
	tu dormirais	tu aurais dormi
	il dormirait	il aurait dormi
	nous dormirions	nous aurions dormi
FUTURE PERFECT	vous dormiriez	vous auriez dormi
j'aurai dormi etc.	ils dormiraient	ils auraient dormi

SUBJUNCTIVE

PRESENT	IMPERFECT	PAST
je dorme	je dormisse	j'aie dormi
tu dormes	tu dormisses	tu aies dormi
il dorme	il dormît	il ait dormi
nous dormions	nous dormissions	nous ayons dormi
vous dormiez	vous dormissiez	vous ayez dormi
ils dorment	ils dormissent	ils aient dormi

IMPERATIVE	INFINITIVE	PARTICIPLE
	PRESENT	PRESENT
dors	dormir	dormant
dormons		
dormez		
	PAST	PAST
	avoir dormi	dormi

129

ECRIRE to write

PRESENT	IMPERFECT	FUTURE
j'écris	j'écrivais	j'écrirai
tu écris	tu écrivais	tu écriras
il écrit	il écrivait	il écrira
nous écrivons	nous écrivions	nous écrirons
vous écrivez	vous écriviez	vous écrirez
ils écrivent	ils écrivaient	ils écriront

PASSÉ SIMPLE	PASSÉ COMPOSÉ	PLUS-QUE-PARFAIT
j'écrivis	j'ai écrit	j'avais écrit
tu écrivis	tu as écrit	tu avais écrit
il écrivit	il a écrit	il avait écrit
nous écrivîmes	nous avons écrit	nous avions écrit
vous écrivîtes	vous avez écrit	vous aviez écrit
ils écrivirent	ils ont écrit	ils avaient écrit

	CONDITIONAL	
PAST ANTERIOR	**PRESENT**	**PAST**
j'eus écrit etc.	j'écrirais	j'aurais écrit
	tu écrirais	tu aurais écrit
	il écrirait	il aurait écrit
	nous écririons	nous aurions écrit
FUTURE PERFECT	vous écririez	vous auriez écrit
j'aurai écrit etc.	ils écriraient	ils auraient écrit

SUBJUNCTIVE

PRESENT	IMPERFECT	PAST
j'écrive	j'écrivisse	j'aie écrit
tu écrives	tu écrivisses	tu aies écrit
il écrive	il écrivît	il ait écrit
nous écrivions	nous écrivissions	nous ayons écrit
vous écriviez	vous écrivissiez	vous ayez écrit
ils écrivent	ils écrivissent	ils aient écrit

IMPERATIVE	*INFINITIVE*	*PARTICIPLE*
	PRESENT	**PRESENT**
écris	écrire	écrivant
écrivons		
écrivez		
	PAST	**PAST**
	avoir écrit	écrit

ESPERER   to hope

PRESENT	IMPERFECT	FUTURE
j'espère	j'espérais	j'espérerai
tu espères	tu espérais	tu espéreras
il espère	il espérait	il espérera
nous espérons	nous espérions	nous espérerons
vous espérez	vous espériez	vous espérerez
ils espèrent	ils espéraient	ils espéreront

PASSÉ SIMPLE	PASSÉ COMPOSÉ	PLUS-QUE-PARFAIT
j'espérai	j'ai espéré	j'avais espéré
tu espéras	tu as espéré	tu avais espéré
il espéra	il a espéré	il avait espéré
nous espérâmes	nous avons espéré	nous avions espéré
vous espérâtes	vous avez espéré	vous aviez espéré
ils espérèrent	ils ont espéré	ils avaient espéré

	CONDITIONAL	
PAST ANTERIOR	PRESENT	PAST
j'eus espéré etc.	j'espérerais	j'aurais espéré
	tu espérerais	tu aurais espéré
	il espérerait	il aurait espéré
	nous espérerions	nous aurions espéré
FUTURE PERFECT	vous espéreriez	vous auriez espéré
j'aurai espéré etc.	ils espéreraient	ils auraient espéré

SUBJUNCTIVE

PRESENT	IMPERFECT	PAST
j'espère	j'espérasse	j'aie espéré
tu espères	tu espérasses	tu aies espéré
il espère	il espérât	il ait espéré
nous espérions	nous espérassions	nous ayons espéré
vous espériez	vous espérassiez	vous ayez espéré
ils espèrent	ils espérassent	ils aient espéré

IMPERATIVE	INFINITIVE	PARTICIPLE
	PRESENT	PRESENT
espère	espérer	espérant
espérons		
espérez		
	PAST	PAST
	avoir espéré	espéré

ETRE to be

PRESENT	IMPERFECT	FUTURE
je suis	j'étais	je serai
tu es	tu étais	tu seras
il est	il était	il sera
nous sommes	nous étions	nous serons
vous êtes	vous étiez	vous serez
ils sont	ils étaient	ils seront

PASSÉ SIMPLE	PASSÉ COMPOSÉ	PLUS-QUE-PARFAIT
je fus	j'ai été	j'avais été
tu fus	tu as été	tu avais été
il fut	il a été	il avait été
nous fûmes	nous avons été	nous avions été
vous fûtes	vous avez été	vous aviez été
ils furent	ils ont été	ils avaient été

	CONDITIONAL	
PAST ANTERIOR	**PRESENT**	**PAST**
j'eus été etc.	je serais	j'aurais été
	tu serais	tu aurais été
	il serait	il aurait été
	nous serions	nous aurions été
FUTURE PERFECT	vous seriez	vous auriez été
j'aurai été etc.	ils seraient	ils auraient été

SUBJUNCTIVE

PRESENT	IMPERFECT	PAST
je sois	je fusse	j'aie été
tu sois	tu fusses	tu aies été
il soit	il fût	il ait été
nous soyons	nous fussions	nous ayons été
vous soyez	vous fussiez	vous ayez été
ils soient	ils fussent	ils aient été

IMPERATIVE	*INFINITIVE*	*PARTICIPLE*
	PRESENT	**PRESENT**
sois	être	étant
soyons		
soyez		
	PAST	**PAST**
	avoir été	été

FAIRE   to do, to make

PRESENT	IMPERFECT	FUTURE
je fais	je faisais	je ferai
tu fais	tu faisais	tu feras
il fait	il faisait	il fera
nous faisons	nous faisions	nous ferons
vous faites	vous faisiez	vous ferez
ils font	ils faisaient	ils feront

PASSÉ SIMPLE	PASSÉ COMPOSÉ	PLUS-QUE-PARFAIT
je fis	j'ai fait	j'avais fait
tu fis	tu as fait	tu avais fait
il fit	il a fait	il avait fait
nous fîmes	nous avons fait	nous avions fait
vous fîtes	vous avez fait	vous aviez fait
ils firent	ils ont fait	ils avaient fait

CONDITIONAL

PAST ANTERIOR	PRESENT	PAST
j'eus fait etc.	je ferais	j'aurais fait
	tu ferais	tu aurais fait
	il ferait	il aurait fait
	nous ferions	nous aurions fait
FUTURE PERFECT	vous feriez	vous auriez fait
j'aurai fait etc.	ils feraient	ils auraient fait

SUBJUNCTIVE

PRESENT	IMPERFECT	PAST
je fasse	je fisse	j'aie fait
tu fasses	tu fisses	tu aies fait
il fasse	il fît	il ait fait
nous fassions	nous fissions	nous ayons fait
vous fassiez	vous fissiez	vous ayez fait
ils fassent	ils fissent	ils aient fait

IMPERATIVE	INFINITIVE	PARTICIPLE
	PRESENT	PRESENT
fais	faire	faisant
faisons		
faites		
	PAST	
	avoir fait	fait

133

FALLOIR to be necessary

PRESENT	IMPERFECT	FUTURE
il faut	il fallait	il faudra
PASSÉ SIMPLE	PASSÉ COMPOSÉ	PLUS-QUE-PARFAIT
il fallut	il a fallu	il avait fallu

	CONDITIONAL	
PAST ANTERIOR	PRESENT	PAST
il eut fallu		
	il faudrait	il aurait fallu
FUTURE PERFECT		
il aura fallu		

SUBJUNCTIVE		
PRESENT	IMPERFECT	PAST
il faille	il fallût	il ait fallu

IMPERATIVE	*INFINITIVE*	*PARTICIPLE*
	PRESENT	PRESENT
	falloir	
	PAST	PAST
	avoir fallu	fallu

FINIR   to finish

PRESENT	IMPERFECT	FUTURE
je finis	je finissais	je finirai
tu finis	tu finissais	tu finiras
il finit	il finissait	il finira
nous finissons	nous finissions	nous finirons
vous finissez	vous finissiez	vous finirez
ils finissent	ils finissaient	ils finiront

PASSÉ SIMPLE	PASSÉ COMPOSÉ	PLUS-QUE-PARFAIT
je finis	j'ai fini	j'avais fini
tu finis	tu as fini	tu avais fini
il finit	il a fini	il avait fini
nous finîmes	nous avons fini	nous avions fini
vous finîtes	vous avez fini	vous aviez fini
ils finirent	ils ont fini	ils avaient fini

CONDITIONAL

PAST ANTERIOR	PRESENT	PAST
j'eus fini etc.	je finirais	j'aurais fini
	tu finirais	tu aurais fini
	il finirait	il aurait fini
	nous finirions	nous aurions fini
FUTURE PERFECT	vous finiriez	vous auriez fini
j'aurai fini etc.	ils finiraient	ils auraient fini

SUBJUNCTIVE

PRESENT	IMPERFECT	PAST
je finisse	je finisse	j'aie fini
tu finisses	tu finisses	tu aies fini
il finisse	il finît	il ait fini
nous finissions	nous finissions	nous ayons fini
vous finissiez	vous finissiez	vous ayez fini
ils finissent	ils finissent	ils aient fini

IMPERATIVE	*INFINITIVE*	*PARTICIPLE*
	PRESENT	PRESENT
finis	finir	finissant
finissons		
finissez		
	PAST	PAST
	avoir fini	fini

SE MEFIER   to be suspicious

PRESENT	IMPERFECT	FUTURE
je me méfie	je me méfiais	je me méfierai
tu te méfies	tu te méfiais	tu te méfieras
il se méfie	il se méfiait	il se méfiera
nous nous méfions	nous nous méfiions	nous nous méfierons
vous vous méfiez	vous vous méfiiez	vous vous méfierez
ils se méfient	ils se méfiaient	ils se méfieront

PASSÉ SIMPLE	PASSÉ COMPOSÉ	PLUS-QUE-PARFAIT
je me méfiai	je me suis méfié(e)	je m'étais méfié(e)
tu te méfias	tu t'es méfié(e)	tu t'étais méfié(e)
il se méfia	il/elle s'est méfié(e)	il/elle s'était méfié(e)
nous nous méfiâmes	nous ns. sommes méfié(e)s	nous ns. étions méfié(e)s
vous vous méfiâtes	vous vs. êtes méfié(e)(s)	vous vs. étiez méfié(e)(s)
ils se méfièrent	ils/elles se sont méfié(e)s	ils/elles s'étaient méfié(e)s

	CONDITIONAL	
PAST ANTERIOR	**PRESENT**	**PAST**
je me fus méfié(e) etc.	je me méfierais	je me serais méfié(e)
	tu te méfierais	tu te serais méfié(e)
	il se méfierait	il/elle se serait méfié(e)
	nous nous méfierions	nous ns. serions méfié(e)s
FUTURE PERFECT	vous vous méfieriez	vous vs. seriez méfié(e)(s)
je me serai méfié(e) etc.	ils se méfieraient	ils/elles se seraient méfié(e)s

SUBJUNCTIVE

PRESENT	IMPERFECT	PAST
je me méfie	je me méfiasse	je me sois méfié(e)
tu te méfies	tu te méfiasses	tu te sois méfié(e)
il se méfie	il se méfiât	il/elle se soit méfié(e)
nous nous méfiions	nous nous méfiassions	nous ns. soyons méfié(e)s
vous vous méfiiez	vous vous méfiassiez	vous vs. soyez méfié(e)(s)
ils se méfient	ils se méfiassent	ils/elles se soient méfié(e)s

IMPERATIVE	*INFINITIVE*	*PARTICIPLE*
	PRESENT	**PRESENT**
méfie-toi	se méfier	se méfiant
méfions-nous		
méfiez-vous		
	PAST	**PAST**
	s'être méfié(e)(s)	méfié

METTRE   to put

PRESENT	IMPERFECT	FUTURE
je mets	je mettais	je mettrai
tu mets	tu mettais	tu mettras
il met	il mettait	il mettra
nous mettons	nous mettions	nous mettrons
vous mettez	vous mettiez	vous mettrez
ils mettent	ils mettaient	ils mettront

PASSÉ SIMPLE	PASSÉ COMPOSÉ	PLUS-QUE-PARFAIT
je mis	j'ai mis	j'avais mis
tu mis	tu as mis	tu avais mis
il mit	il a mis	il avait mis
nous mîmes	nous avons mis	nous avions mis
vous mîtes	vous avez mis	vous aviez mis
ils mirent	ils ont mis	ils avaient mis

	CONDITIONAL	
PAST ANTERIOR	PRESENT	PAST
j'eus mis etc.	je mettrais	j'aurais mis
	tu mettrais	tu aurais mis
	il mettrait	il aurait mis
	nous mettrions	nous aurions mis
FUTURE PERFECT	vous mettriez	vous auriez mis
j'aurai mis etc.	ils mettraient	ils auraient mis

SUBJUNCTIVE

PRESENT	IMPERFECT	PAST
je mette	je misse	j'aie mis
tu mettes	tu misses	tu aies mis
il mette	il mît	il ait mis
nous mettions	nous missions	nous ayons mis
vous mettiez	vous missiez	vous ayez mis
ils mettent	ils missent	ils aient mis

IMPERATIVE	INFINITIVE	PARTICIPLE
	PRESENT	PRESENT
mets	mettre	mettant
mettons		
mettez		
	PAST	PAST
	avoir mis	mis

137

OUVRIR to open

PRESENT	IMPERFECT	FUTURE
j'ouvre	j'ouvrais	j'ouvrirai
tu ouvres	tu ouvrais	tu ouvriras
il ouvre	il ouvrait	il ouvrira
nous ouvrons	nous ouvrions	nous ouvrirons
vous ouvrez	vous ouvriez	vous ouvrirez
ils ouvrent	ils ouvraient	ils ouvriront

PASSÉ SIMPLE	PASSÉ COMPOSÉ	PLUS-QUE-PARFAIT
j'ouvris	j'ai ouvert	j'avais ouvert
tu ouvris	tu as ouvert	tu avais ouvert
il ouvrit	il a ouvert	il avait ouvert
nous ouvrîmes	nous avons ouvert	nous avions ouvert
vous ouvrîtes	vous avez ouvert	vous aviez ouvert
ils ouvrirent	ils ont ouvert	ils avaient ouvert

	CONDITIONAL	
PAST ANTERIOR	PRESENT	PAST
j'eus ouvert etc.	j'ouvrirais	j'aurais ouvert
	tu ouvrirais	tu aurais ouvert
	il ouvrirait	il aurait ouvert
	nous ouvririons	nous aurions ouvert
FUTURE PERFECT	vous ouvririez	vous auriez ouvert
j'aurai ouvert etc.	ils ouvriraient	ils auraient ouvert

SUBJUNCTIVE

PRESENT	IMPERFECT	PAST
j'ouvre	j'ouvrisse	j'aie ouvert
tu ouvres	tu ouvrisses	tu aies ouvert
il ouvre	il ouvrît	il ait ouvert
nous ouvrions	nous ouvrissions	nous ayons ouvert
vous ouvriez	vous ouvrissiez	vous ayez ouvert
ils ouvrent	ils ouvrissent	ils aient ouvert

IMPERATIVE	INFINITIVE	PARTICIPLE
	PRESENT	PRESENT
ouvre	ouvrir	ouvrant
ouvrons		
ouvrez		
	PAST	PAST
	avoir ouvert	ouvert

POUVOIR   to be able to

PRESENT	IMPERFECT	FUTURE
je peux	je pouvais	je pourrai
(*interrog.* puis-je?)		
tu peux	tu pouvais	tu pourras
il peut	il pouvait	il pourra
nous pouvons	nous pouvions	nous pourrons
vous pouvez	vous pouviez	vous pourrez
ils peuvent	ils pouvaient	ils pourront

PASSÉ SIMPLE	PASSÉ COMPOSÉ	PLUS-QUE-PARFAIT
je pus	j'ai pu	j'avais pu
tu pus	tu as pu	tu avais pu
il put	il a pu	il avait pu
nous pûmes	nous avons pu	nous avions pu
vous pûtes	vous avez pu	vous aviez pu
ils purent	ils ont pu	ils avaient pu

	CONDITIONAL	
PAST ANTERIOR	PRESENT	PAST
j'eus pu etc.	je pourrais	j'aurais pu
	tu pourrais	tu aurais pu
	il pourrait	il aurait pu
	nous pourrions	nous aurions pu
FUTURE PERFECT	vous pourriez	vous auriez pu
j'aurai pu etc.	ils pourraient	ils auraient pu

SUBJUNCTIVE

PRESENT	IMPERFECT	PAST
je puisse	je pusse	j'aie pu
tu puisses	tu pusses	tu aies pu
il puisse	il pût	il ait pu
nous puissions	nous pussions	nous ayons pu
vous puissiez	vous pussiez	vous ayez pu
ils puissent	ils pussent	ils aient pu

IMPERATIVE	*INFINITIVE*	*PARTICIPLE*
	PRESENT	PRESENT
	pouvoir	pouvant
	PAST	PAST
	avoir pu	pu

PRENDRE to take

PRESENT	IMPERFECT	FUTURE
je prends	je prenais	je prendrai
tu prends	tu prenais	tu prendras
il prend	il prenait	il prendra
nous prenons	nous prenions	nous prendrons
vous prenez	vous preniez	vous prendrez
ils prennent	ils prenaient	ils prendront

PASSÉ SIMPLE	PASSÉ COMPOSÉ	PLUS-QUE-PARFAIT
je pris	j'ai pris	j'avais pris
tu pris	tu as pris	tu avais pris
il prit	il a pris	il avait pris
nous prîmes	nous avons pris	nous avions pris
vous prîtes	vous avez pris	vous aviez pris
ils prirent	ils ont pris	ils avaient pris

	CONDITIONAL	
PAST ANTERIOR	PRESENT	PAST
j'eus pris etc.	je prendrais	j'aurais pris
	tu prendrais	tu aurais pris
	il prendrait	il aurait pris
	nous prendrions	nous aurions pris
FUTURE PERFECT	vous prendriez	vous auriez pris
j'aurai pris etc.	ils prendraient	ils auraient pris

SUBJUNCTIVE

PRESENT	IMPERFECT	PAST
je prenne	je prisse	j'aie pris
tu prennes	tu prisses	tu aies pris
il prenne	il prît	il ait pris
nous prenions	nous prissions	nous ayons pris
vous preniez	vous prissiez	vous ayez pris
ils prennent	ils prissent	ils aient pris

IMPERATIVE	*INFINITIVE*	*PARTICIPLE*
	PRESENT	PRESENT
prends	prendre	prenant
prenons		
prenez		
	PAST	PAST
	avoir pris	pris

RECEVOIR   to receive

PRESENT	IMPERFECT	FUTURE
je reçois	je recevais	je recevrai
tu reçois	tu recevais	tu recevras
il reçoit	il recevait	il recevra
nous recevons	nous recevions	nous recevrons
vous recevez	vous receviez	vous recevrez
ils reçoivent	ils recevaient	ils recevront

PASSÉ SIMPLE	PASSÉ COMPOSÉ	PLUS-QUE-PARFAIT
je reçus	j'ai reçu	j'avais reçu
tu reçus	tu as reçu	tu avais reçu
il reçut	il a reçu	il avait reçu
nous reçûmes	nous avons reçu	nous avions reçu
vous reçûtes	vous avez reçu	vous aviez reçu
ils reçurent	ils ont reçu	ils avaient reçu

	CONDITIONAL	
PAST ANTERIOR	**PRESENT**	**PAST**
j'eus reçu etc.	je recevrais	j'aurais reçu
	tu recevrais	tu aurais reçu
	il recevrait	il aurait reçu
	nous recevrions	nous aurions reçu
FUTURE PERFECT	vous recevriez	vous auriez reçu
j'aurai reçu etc.	ils recevraient	ils auraient reçu

SUBJUNCTIVE

PRESENT	IMPERFECT	PAST
je reçoive	je reçusse	j'aie reçu
tu reçoives	tu reçusses	tu aies reçu
il reçoive	il reçût	il ait reçu
nous recevions	nous reçussions	nous ayons reçu
vous receviez	vous reçussiez	vous ayez reçu
ils reçoivent	ils reçussent	ils aient reçu

IMPERATIVE	*INFINITIVE*	*PARTICIPLE*
	PRESENT	**PRESENT**
reçois	recevoir	recevant
recevons		
recevez		
	PAST	**PAST**
	avoir reçu	reçu

SAVOIR to know

PRESENT	IMPERFECT	FUTURE
je sais	je savais	je saurai
tu sais	tu savais	tu sauras
il sait	il savait	il saura
nous savons	nous savions	nous saurons
vous savez	vous saviez	vous saurez
ils savent	ils savaient	ils sauront

PASSÉ SIMPLE	PASSÉ COMPOSÉ	PLUS-QUE-PARFAIT
je sus	j'ai su	j'avais su
tu sus	tu as su	tu avais su
il sut	il a su	il avait su
nous sûmes	nous avons su	nous avions su
vous sûtes	vous avez su	vous aviez su
ils surent	ils ont su	ils avaient su

	CONDITIONAL	
PAST ANTERIOR	**PRESENT**	**PAST**
j'eus su etc.	je saurais	j'aurais su
	tu saurais	tu aurais su
	il saurait	il aurait su
	nous saurions	nous aurions su
FUTURE PERFECT	vous sauriez	vous auriez su
j'aurai su etc.	ils sauraient	ils auraient su

SUBJUNCTIVE

PRESENT	IMPERFECT	PAST
je sache	je susse	j'aie su
tu saches	tu susses	tu aies su
il sache	il sût	il ait su
nous sachions	nous sussions	nous ayons su
vous sachiez	vous sussiez	vous ayez su
ils sachent	ils sussent	ils aient su

IMPERATIVE	INFINITIVE	PARTICIPLE
	PRESENT	**PRESENT**
sache	savoir	sachant
sachons		
sachez		
	PAST	**PAST**
	avoir su	su

TENIR to hold

PRESENT	IMPERFECT	FUTURE
je tiens	je tenais	je tiendrai
tu tiens	tu tenais	tu tiendras
il tient	il tenait	il tiendra
nous tenons	nous tenions	nous tiendrons
vous tenez	vous teniez	vous tiendrez
ils tiennent	ils tenaient	ils tiendront

PASSÉ SIMPLE	PASSÉ COMPOSÉ	PLUS-QUE-PARFAIT
je tins	j'ai tenu	j'avais tenu
tu tins	tu as tenu	tu avais tenu
il tint	il a tenu	il avait tenu
nous tînmes	nous avons tenu	nous avions tenu
vous tîntes	vous avez tenu	vous aviez tenu
ils tinrent	ils ont tenu	ils avaient tenu

	CONDITIONAL	
PAST ANTERIOR	**PRESENT**	**PAST**
j'eus tenu etc.	je tiendrais	j'aurais tenu
	tu tiendrais	tu aurais tenu
	il tiendrait	il aurait tenu
	nous tiendrions	nous aurions tenu
FUTURE PERFECT	vous tiendriez	vous auriez tenu
j'aurai tenu etc.	ils tiendraient	ils auraient tenu

SUBJUNCTIVE

PRESENT	IMPERFECT	PAST
je tienne	je tinsse	j'aie tenu
tu tiennes	tu tinsses	tu aies tenu
il tienne	il tînt	il ait tenu
nous tenions	nous tinssions	nous ayons tenu
vous teniez	vous tinssiez	vous ayez tenu
ils tiennent	ils tinssent	ils aient tenu

IMPERATIVE	*INFINITIVE*	*PARTICIPLE*
	PRESENT	**PRESENT**
tiens	tenir	tenant
tenons		
tenez		
	PAST	**PAST**
	avoir tenu	tenu

VENDRE to sell

PRESENT	IMPERFECT	FUTURE
je vends	je vendais	je vendrai
tu vends	tu vendais	tu vendras
il vend	il vendait	il vendra
nous vendons	nous vendions	nous vendrons
vous vendez	vous vendiez	vous vendrez
ils vendent	ils vendaient	ils vendront

PASSÉ SIMPLE	PASSÉ COMPOSÉ	PLUS-QUE-PARFAIT
je vendis	j'ai vendu	j'avais vendu
tu vendis	tu as vendu	tu avais vendu
il vendit	il a vendu	il avait vendu
nous vendîmes	nous avons vendu	nous avions vendu
vous vendîtes	vous avez vendu	vous aviez vendu
ils vendirent	ils ont vendu	ils avaient vendu

	CONDITIONAL	
PAST ANTERIOR	**PRESENT**	**PAST**
j'eus vendu etc.	je vendrais	j'aurais vendu
	tu vendrais	tu aurais vendu
	il vendrait	il aurait vendu
	nous vendrions	nous aurions vendu
FUTURE PERFECT	vous vendriez	vous auriez vendu
j'aurai vendu etc.	ils vendraient	ils auraient vendu

SUBJUNCTIVE

PRESENT	IMPERFECT	PAST
je vende	je vendisse	j'aie vendu
tu vendes	tu vendisses	tu aies vendu
il vende	il vendît	il ait vendu
nous vendions	nous vendissions	nous ayons vendu
vous vendiez	vous vendissiez	vous ayez vendu
ils vendent	ils vendissent	ils aient vendu

IMPERATIVE	*INFINITIVE*	*PARTICIPLE*
	PRESENT	**PRESENT**
vends	vendre	vendant
vendons		
vendez		
	PAST	**PAST**
	avoir vendu	vendu

VENIR to come

PRESENT	IMPERFECT	FUTURE
je viens	je venais	je viendrai
tu viens	tu venais	tu viendras
il vient	il venait	il viendra
nous venons	nous venions	nous viendrons
vous venez	vous veniez	vous viendrez
ils viennent	ils venaient	ils viendront

PASSÉ SIMPLE	PASSÉ COMPOSÉ	PLUS-QUE-PARFAIT
je vins	je suis venu(e)	j'étais venu(e)
tu vins	tu es venu(e)	tu étais venu(e)
il vint	il/elle est venu(e)	il/elle était venu(e)
nous vînmes	nous sommes venu(e)s	nous étions venu(e)s
vous vîntes	vous êtes venu(e)(s)	vous étiez venu(e)(s)
ils vinrent	ils/elles sont venu(e)s	ils/elles étaient venu(e)s

CONDITIONAL

PAST ANTERIOR	PRESENT	PAST
je fus venu(e) etc.	je viendrais	je serais venu(e)
	tu viendrais	tu serais venu(e)
	il viendrait	il/elle serait venu(e)
	nous viendrions	nous serions venu(e)s
FUTURE PERFECT	vous viendriez	vous seriez venu(e)(s)
je serai venu(e) etc.	ils viendraient	ils/elles seraient venu(e)s

SUBJUNCTIVE

PRESENT	IMPERFECT	PAST
je vienne	je vinsse	je sois venu(e)
tu viennes	tu vinsses	tu sois venu(e)
il vienne	il vînt	il/elle soit venu(e)
nous venions	nous vinssions	nous soyons venu(e)s
vous veniez	vous vinssiez	vous soyez venu(e)(s)
ils viennent	ils vinssent	ils/elles soient venu(e)s

IMPERATIVE	INFINITIVE	PARTICIPLE
	PRESENT	PRESENT
viens	venir	venant
venons		
venez		
	PAST	PAST
	être venu(e)(s)	venu

VIVRE   to live

PRESENT	IMPERFECT	FUTURE
je vis	je vivais	je vivrai
tu vis	tu vivais	tu vivras
il vit	il vivait	il vivra
nous vivons	nous vivions	nous vivrons
vous vivez	vous viviez	vous vivrez
ils vivent	ils vivaient	ils vivront

PASSÉ SIMPLE	PASSÉ COMPOSÉ	PLUS-QUE-PARFAIT
je vécus	j'ai vécu	j'avais vécu
tu vécus	tu as vécu	tu avais vécu
il vécut	il a vécu	il avait vécu
nous vécûmes	nous avons vécu	nous avions vécu
vous vécûtes	vous avez vécu	vous aviez vécu
ils vécurent	ils ont vécu	ils avaient vécu

	CONDITIONAL	
PAST ANTERIOR	**PRESENT**	**PAST**
j'eus vécu etc.	je vivrais	j'aurais vécu
	tu vivrais	tu aurais vécu
	il vivrait	il aurait vécu
	nous vivrions	nous aurions vécu
FUTURE PERFECT	vous vivriez	vous auriez vécu
j'aurai vécu etc.	ils vivraient	ils auraient vécu

SUBJUNCTIVE

PRESENT	IMPERFECT	PAST
je vive	je vécusse	j'aie vécu
tu vives	tu vécusses	tu aies vécu
il vive	il vécût	il ait vécu
nous vivions	nous vécussions	nous ayons vécu
vous viviez	vous vécussiez	vous ayez vécu
ils vivent	ils vécussent	ils aient vécu

IMPERATIVE	*INFINITIVE*	*PARTICIPLE*
	PRESENT	**PRESENT**
vis	vivre	vivant
vivons		
vivez		
	PAST	**PAST**
	avoir vécu	vécu

VOIR to see

PRESENT	IMPERFECT	FUTURE
je vois	je voyais	je verrai
tu vois	tu voyais	tu verras
il voit	il voyait	il verra
nous voyons	nous voyions	nous verrons
vous voyez	vous voyiez	vous verrez
ils voient	ils voyaient	ils verront

PASSÉ SIMPLE	PASSÉ COMPOSÉ	PLUS-QUE-PARFAIT
je vis	j'ai vu	j'avais vu
tu vis	tu as vu	tu avais vu
il vit	il a vu	il avait vu
nous vîmes	nous avons vu	nous avions vu
vous vîtes	vous avez vu	vous aviez vu
ils virent	ils ont vu	ils avaient vu

	CONDITIONAL	
PAST ANTERIOR	PRESENT	PAST
j'eus vu etc.	je verrais	j'aurais vu
	tu verrais	tu aurais vu
	il verrait	il aurait vu
	nous verrions	nous aurions vu
FUTURE PERFECT	vous verriez	vous auriez vu
j'aurai vu etc.	ils verraient	ils auraient vu

SUBJUNCTIVE

PRESENT	IMPERFECT	PAST
je voie	je visse	j'aie vu
tu voies	tu visses	tu aies vu
il voie	il vît	il ait vu
nous voyions	nous vissions	nous ayons vu
vous voyiez	vous vissiez	vous ayez vu
ils voient	ils vissent	ils aient vu

IMPERATIVE	INFINITIVE	PARTICIPLE
	PRESENT	PRESENT
vois	voir	voyant
voyons		
voyez		
	PAST	PAST
	avoir vu	vu

VOULOIR to want

PRESENT	IMPERFECT	FUTURE
je veux	je voulais	je voudrai
tu veux	tu voulais	tu voudras
il veut	il voulait	il voudra
nous voulons	nous voulions	nous voudrons
vous voulez	vous vouliez	vous voudrez
ils veulent	ils voulaient	ils voudront

PASSÉ SIMPLE	PASSÉ COMPOSÉ	PLUS-QUE-PARFAIT
je voulus	j'ai voulu	j'avais voulu
tu voulus	tu as voulu	tu avais voulu
il voulut	il a voulu	il avait voulu
nous voulûmes	nous avons voulu	nous avions voulu
vous voulûtes	vous avez voulu	vous aviez voulu
ils voulurent	ils ont voulu	ils avaient voulu

	CONDITIONAL	
PAST ANTERIOR	PRESENT	PAST
j'eus voulu etc.	je voudrais	j'aurais voulu
	tu voudrais	tu aurais voulu
	il voudrait	il aurait voulu
	nous voudrions	nous aurions voulu
FUTURE PERFECT	vous voudriez	vous auriez voulu
j'aurai voulu etc.	ils voudraient	ils auraient voulu

SUBJUNCTIVE

PRESENT	IMPERFECT	PAST
je veuille	je voulusse	j'aie voulu
tu veuilles	tu voulusses	tu aies voulu
il veuille	il voulût	il ait voulu
nous voulions	nous voulussions	nous ayons voulu
vous vouliez	vous voulussiez	vous ayez voulu
ils veuillent	ils voulussent	ils aient voulu

IMPERATIVE	INFINITIVE	PARTICIPLE
	PRESENT	PRESENT
veuille	vouloir	voulant
veuillons		
veuillez		
	PAST	PAST
	avoir voulu	voulu

M. VERB CONSTRUCTIONS

There are two main types of verb constructions: verbs can be followed:

1. by another verb in the infinitive
2. by an object (a noun or a pronoun)

1. Verbs followed by an infinitive

There are three main constructions when a verb is followed by an infinitive:

    a) verb + infinitive (without any linking preposition)
    b) verb + **à** + infinitive
    c) verb + **de** + infinitive

For examples of these three types of constructions, see pp. 101–4 and 106–7.

a) *Verbs followed by an infinitive without a preposition*

These include verbs of wishing and desiring, of movement, and of perception:

adorer to love	**aimer** to like/love	**aimer mieux** to prefer
aller to go (and)	**compter** to intend to	**descendre** to go down (and)
désirer to wish	**détester** to hate	**devoir** to have to
écouter to listen to	**entendre** to hear	**entrer** to go in (and)
envoyer to send	**espérer** to hope to	**faire** to make
falloir to be necessary	**laisser** to let	**monter** to go up (and)
oser to dare	**pouvoir** to be able to	**préférer** to prefer to
regarder to watch	**rentrer** to go in/back (and)	**savoir** to know how to
sembler to seem to	**sentir** to feel	**sortir** to go out (and)
souhaiter to wish to	**valoir mieux** to be better to	**venir** to come (and)
voir to see	**vouloir** to want to	

b) *Verbs followed by* **à** + *infinitive*

aider à	to help (to do)
s'amuser à	to enjoy (doing)
apprendre à	to learn (to do)
s'apprêter à	to get ready (to do)
arriver à	to manage (to do)/succeed (in doing)
s'attendre à	to expect (to do)
autoriser à	to allow (to do)
chercher à	to try (doing/to do)
commencer à	to begin/start (doing/to do)
consentir à	to agree (to do)
consister à	to consist in (doing)
continuer à	to continue (doing/to do)
se décider à	to make up one's mind (to do)
encourager à	to encourage (to do)
enseigner à	to teach how (to do)
forcer à	to force (to do)
s'habituer à	to get used (to doing)
hésiter à	to hesitate (to do)
inciter à	to prompt (to do)
s'intéresser à	to be interested in (doing)
inviter à	to invite (to do)
se mettre à	to begin/start (doing/to do)
obliger à	to force (to do)
parvenir à	to manage (to do)/succeed (in doing)
passer son temps à	to spend one's time (doing)
perdre son temps à	to waste one's time (doing)
persister à	to persist in (doing)
pousser à	to urge (to do)
se préparer à	to get ready (to do)
renoncer à	to give up (doing)
rester à	to be left (to do)
réussir à	to manage (to do)/succeed (in doing)
servir à	to be used for (doing)
songer à	to think of (doing)
tarder à	to delay/be late in (doing)
tenir à	to insist (on doing)

c) *Verbs followed by* **de** + *infinitive*:

accepter de	to agree (to do)
accuser de	to accuse of (doing)
achever de	to finish (doing)
(s')arrêter de	to stop (doing)
avoir besoin de	to need (to do)
avoir envie de	to feel like (doing)
avoir peur de	to be afraid (to do)
cesser de	to stop (doing)
se charger de	to take it upon oneself (to do)

commander de	to order (to do)
conseiller de	to advise (to do)
se contenter de	to be satisfied (to do)
craindre de	to be afraid (to do)
décider de	to decide (to do)
déconseiller de	to advise against (doing)
défendre de	to forbid (to do)
demander de	to ask (to do)
se dépêcher de	to hurry (to do)
dire de	to tell (to do)
dissuader de	to dissuade from (doing)
s'efforcer de	to make an effort (to do)
empêcher de	to prevent (from doing)
s'empresser de	to hurry (to do)
entreprendre de	to undertake (to do)
essayer de	to try (to do/doing)
s'étonner de	to be surprised (at doing)
éviter de	to avoid (doing)
s'excuser de	to apologize for (doing)
faire semblant de	to pretend (to do)
feindre de	to pretend (to do)
finir de	to finish (doing)
se garder de	to be careful not to (do)
se hâter de	to hurry (to do)
interdire de	to forbid (to do)
jurer de	to swear (to do)
manquer de	'to nearly' (do)
menacer de	to threaten (to do)
mériter de	to deserve (to do)
négliger de	to fail (to do)
s'occuper de	to take it upon oneself (to do)
offrir de	to offer (to do)
omettre de	to neglect (to do)
ordonner de	to order (to do)
oublier de	to forget (to do)
permettre de	to allow (to do)
persuader de	to persuade (to do)
prier de	to ask/beg (to do)
promettre de	to promise (to do)
proposer de	to offer (to do)
recommander de	to recommend (doing)
refuser de	to refuse (to do)
regretter de	to be sorry (to do)
remercier de	to thank for (doing)
résoudre de	to resolve (to do)
risquer de	to risk (doing)
se souvenir de	to remember (doing)
suggérer de	to suggest (doing)

supplier de	to beg (to do)
tâcher de	to try (to do/doing)
tenter de	to try (to do/doing)
venir de	to have just (done)

2. Verbs followed by an object

In general, verbs that take a direct object in French also take a direct object in English, and verbs followed by a prepositional phrase in French (i.e. verb + preposition + object) are followed likewise in English.

There are however some exceptions:

a) *Verbs followed by a prepositional phrase in English but not in French (the English preposition is not translated):*

attendre	to wait for
chercher	to look for
demander	to ask for
écouter	to listen to
espérer	to hope for
payer	to pay for
regarder	to look at
reprocher	to blame for

on a demandé l'addition	**j'attendais l'autobus**
we asked for the check	I was waiting for the bus
je cherche mon frère	**tu écoutes la radio?**
I'm looking for my brother	are you listening to the radio?

b) *Verbs that take a direct object in English, but a prepositional phrase with à in French:*

convenir à	to suit
se fier à	to trust
jouer à	to play (*game, sport*)
jouer de	to play (*musical instrument*)
obéir à	to obey
désobéir à	to disobey
pardonner à	to forgive
renoncer à	to give up
répondre à	to answer
résister à	to resist
ressembler à	to resemble (to look like)
téléphoner à	to phone

tu peux te fier à moi	**tu joues souvent au tennis?**
you can trust me	do you play tennis often?
il joue bien de la guitare	**tu as répondu à sa lettre?**
he plays the guitar well	did you answer his letter?

| **téléphonons au médecin**
let's phone the doctor | **obéis à ton père!**
obey your father! |

c) *Verbs that take a direct object in English, but a prepositional phrase with **de** in French:*

s'apercevoir de	to notice
s'approcher de	to come near
avoir besoin de	to need
changer de	to change
douter de	to doubt
se douter de	to suspect
s'emparer de	to seize, to grab
jouir de	to enjoy
manquer de	to lack, to miss
se méfier de	to mistrust, to distrust
se servir de	to use
se souvenir de	to remember
se tromper de ...	to get the wrong ...

je dois changer de train? do I have to change trains?	**il ne s'est aperçu de rien** he didn't notice anything
méfiez-vous de lui don't trust him	**je me servirai de ton vélo** I'll use your bike
tu te souviens de Jean? do you remember Jean?	**il s'est trompé de numéro** he got the wrong number

d) *Some verbs take **à** or **de** before an object, whereas their English equivalent uses a different preposition:*

i) Verb + **à** + object:

croire à	to believe in
s'intéresser à	to be interested in
penser à	to think of/about
songer à	to think of
rêver à	to dream of/about
servir à	to be used for

je m'intéresse au football et à la course automobile
I'm interested in soccer and in auto racing

à quoi penses-tu? what are you thinking about?	**ça sert à quoi?** what is this used for?

ii) Verb + **de** + object:

dépendre de	to depend on
être fâché de	to be annoyed/angry at
féliciter de	to congratulate on
parler de	to speak of/about
remercier de	to thank for
rire de	to laugh at
traiter de	to deal with, to be about
vivre de	to live on/off of

153

> **cela dépendra du temps**   **il m'a parlé de toi**
> it'll depend on the weather   he told me about you
>
> **tu l'as remercié du cadeau qu'il t'a fait?**
> did you thank him for the present he gave you?

3. Verbs followed by one direct object and one indirect object

a) In general, these are verbs of giving or lending, and their English equivalents are constructed in the same way, e.g.:

> **donner quelque chose à quelqu'un**
> to give something to someone
>
> **il a vendu son ordinateur à son voisin**
> he sold his computer to his neighbor

Note: After such verbs, the preposition 'to' is often omitted in English, but à cannot be omitted in French. Special care must be taken when object pronouns are used with these verbs (see p. 73.)

b) With verbs expressing 'taking away', à is translated by 'from' (**qn** stands for 'quelqu'un' and **sb** for 'somebody'):

acheter à qn	to buy from sb
cacher à qn	to hide from sb
demander à qn	to ask sb for
emprunter à qn	to borrow from sb
enlever à qn	to take away from sb
ôter à qn	to take away from sb
prendre à qn	to take from sb
voler à qn	to steal from sb

> **à qui as-tu emprunté cela?**   **il l'a volé à son frère**
> who did you borrow that from?   he stole it from his brother

4. Verb + indirect object + de + infinitive

Some verbs that take a direct object in English are followed by à + object + de + infinitive in French (**qn** stands for 'quelqu'un' and **sb** for 'somebody'):

commander à qn de faire	to order sb to do
conseiller à qn de faire	to advise sb to do
défendre à qn de faire	to forbid sb to do
demander à qn de faire	to ask sb to do
dire à qn de faire	to tell sb to do
ordonner à qn de faire	to order sb to do
permettre à qn de faire	to allow sb to do
promettre à qn de faire	to promise sb to do
proposer à qn de faire	to offer to do for sb, to suggest to sb to do

je lui ai conseillé de ne pas essayer
I advised him not to try

demande à ton fils de t'aider
ask your son to help you

j'ai promis à mes parents de ne jamais recommencer
I promised my parents never to do it again

8. PREPOSITIONS

Prepositions in both French and English can have many different meanings, and this presents considerable difficulties for the student. The following guide to the most common prepositions sets out the generally accepted meanings on the left, with a description of their use in parentheses, and an example. The main meanings are given first. Prepositions are listed in alphabetical order.

à

at	(place)	**au troisième arrêt**	at the third stop
	(date)	**à Noël**	at Christmas
	(time)	**à trois heures**	at three o'clock
	(idiom)	**au hasard, au travail**	at random, at work
in	(place)	**à Montmartre**	in Montmartre
		à Washington	in Washington
		au supermarché	in the supermarket
		à la campagne	in the country
		au lit	in bed
		au loin	in the distance
	(manner)	**à la française**	in the French way
		à ma façon	(in) my way
to	(place)	**aller au théâtre**	to go to the theater
		aller à la Nouvelle-Orléans	to go to New Orleans
	(+ infinitive)	**c'est facile à faire**	it's easy to do (*see p. 104*)

away from	(distance)	**à 3 km d'ici** three kilometers from here
by	(means)	**aller à bicyclette/à vélo** to go by bike **je l'ai reconnu à ses habits** I recognized him by his clothes
	(manner)	**fait à la main** made by hand, handmade
	(rate)	**à la centaine** by the hundred **100 km à l'heure** 60 mph
for / up to	(+ pronoun)	**c'est à vous de jouer** it's your turn/move **c'est à nous de le lui dire** it's up to us to tell it to him
	(purpose)	**une tasse à café** a coffee cup
his / her / my etc.	(possessive)	**son sac à elle** *her* bag(*emphatic*)
on	(means)	**aller à cheval/à pied** to go on horseback/on foot
	(place)	**à la page 12** on page 12 **à droite/à gauche** on/to the right/left
	(time)	**à cette occasion** on this occasion
with	(descriptive)	**une maison à cinq pièces** a house with five rooms **un homme aux cheveux blonds** a man with blond hair **l'homme à la valise** the man with the suitcase
	(idiom)	**à bras ouverts** with open arms

*For the use of the preposition **à** with the infinitive see verb constructions p. 150.*

après

after   (time)   **après votre arrivée**
after your arrival

         (sequence)   **24 ans après la mort
du président**
24 years after the death
of the president

après avoir/être *(see p. 107)*

---

auprès de

near   **assieds-toi auprès de moi**
sit down beside me

compared to   **ce n'est rien auprès
de ce que tu as fait**
it's nothing compared
to what you've done

---

avant

before   (time)   **avant cet après-midi**
before this afternoon
avant ce soir
before tonight
avant de s'asseoir
before sitting down

         (preference)   **la famille avant tout**
the family first and foremost

---

avec

with   (association)   **aller avec lui**
to go with him

         (means)   **il a tondu le gazon
avec une tondeuse**
he mowed the lawn
with a lawnmower

chez

at	(place)	**chez moi/toi** at/to my/your house **chez mon oncle** at my uncle's **chez le pharmacien** at the drugstore
among		**chez les Canadiens** among the Canadians
about		**ce qui m'énerve chez toi,** 　**c'est ...** what annoys me about you is ...
in		**chez Shakespeare** in Shakespeare's work

contre

against	(place)	**contre le mur** against the wall
with	(after verb)	**je suis fâché contre elle** I'm angry with/at her
for		**échanger des gants contre** 　**un foulard** to exchange gloves for a scarf

dans

in	(position)	**dans ma serviette** in my briefcase
	(time)	**je pars dans deux jours** I'm leaving in two days
	(idiom)	**dans l'attente de vous voir** looking forward to seeing you
from	(idiom)	**prendre quelque chose** 　**dans l'armoire** to take something from the closet
on	(idiom)	**dans le train** on the train
out of	(idiom)	**boire dans un verre** to drink out of/from a glass

de

from	(place)	**je suis venu du Texas** I have come from Texas
	(date)	**du 5 février au 10 mars** from February 5th to March 10th **d'un week-end à l'autre** from one weekend to the next
of	(adjectival)	**un cri de triomphe** a shout of triumph
	(contents)	**une tasse de café** a cup of coffee
	(cause)	**mourir de faim** to starve to death
	(measurement)	**long de 3 mètres** 3 meters long
	(time)	**ma montre retarde de 10 minutes** my watch is 10 minutes slow
	(price)	**le montant est de 200 francs** the total is 200 francs
	(possessive)	**le tatouage de ma sœur** my sister's tattoo
	(adjectival)	**les vacances de Pâques** the Easter vacation
	(after 'quelque chose')	**quelque chose de bon** something good
	(after 'rien')	**rien de nouveau** nothing new
	(after 'personne')	**personne d'autre** nobody else
	(quantity)	**beaucoup de, peu de** many, few/not much/not many
by	(idiom)	**je le connais de vue** I know him by sight
in	(manner)	**de cette façon** in this way
	(after superlatives)	**la plus haute montagne du Montana** the highest mountain in Montana
on	(position)	**de ce côté-là** on that side
than	(comparative)	**moins de 5 francs** less than 5 francs

		plus de trois more than three
to	(after adjectives)	**ravi de vous voir** delighted to see you **il est facile de le faire** it's easy to do it
	(after verbs)	**s'efforcer de** to make an effort to
with	(cause)	**tomber de fatigue** to drop with/from exhaustion

depuis

for	(time)	**j'étudie le français depuis 3 ans** I have been studying French for 3 years **j'étudiais le français depuis 3 ans** I had been studying French for 3 years **je n'ai pas vu de lapin depuis des années** I haven't seen a rabbit for years
from	(place)	**depuis ma fenêtre, je vois le lac** from my window I can see the lake
	(time)	**depuis le matin jusqu'au soir** from morning till evening
since		**depuis dimanche** since Sunday

derrière

behind	(place)	**derrière la maison** behind the house

dès

from	(time)	**dès six heures** from six o'clock on **dès 1934** as far back as 1934 **dès le début** from the beginning **dès maintenant** from now on
	(place)	**dès Miami** from (the moment of leaving) Miami

161

devant

before / in front of	(place)	**devant l'école** in front of the school

en

in	(place)	**être en ville** to be in town **en Californie** in California
	(color)	**un mur peint en jaune** a wall painted yellow
	(material)	**une montre en or** a gold watch
by	(means)	**en auto/en avion** by car/by plane
	(dates etc.)	**en quelle année?** in what year? **en 1997** in 1997 **en été, en juillet** in the summer, in July
	(dress)	**en bikini** in a bikini
	(language)	**en chinois** in Chinese
	(time)	**j'ai fait mes devoirs en 20 minutes** I did my homework in 20 minutes
like, as		**il s'est habillé en femme** he dressed like a woman
on	(idiom)	**en vacances** on vacation **en moyenne** on an average
	(+ present participle)	**en faisant** on/while/by doing

Note: **en** *is generally not used with the definite article except in certain expressions:* **en l'an 2000** *(in the year 2000),* **en l'honneur de** *(in honor of), and* **en la présence de** *(in the presence of).*

en tant que

as/in (my) capacity as	**en tant que professeur** as a teacher

entre

among		**être entre amis** to be among friends
between	(place)	**entre Toronto et Montréal** between Toronto and Montreal
	(time)	**entre 6 et 10 heures** between 6 and 10
	(idiom)	**entre toi et moi** just between you and me
in	(punctuation)	**entre guillemets** in quotes **entre parenthèses** in parentheses

d'entre

of/from among	**certains d'entre eux** some of them

envers

to/towards	**être bien disposé envers quelqu'un** to be well-disposed toward someone

hors de

out of	**hors de danger** out of danger

jusque

up to / as far as	(place)	**jusqu'à la frontière espagnole** as far as the Spanish border
	(time)	**jusqu'ici/jusque-là** up to now/until then
till / until		**jusqu'à demain** until tomorrow

malgré

in spite of / despite	**malgré la chaleur** in spite of the heat

par

by	(agent)	**la lettre a été envoyée par mon ami** the letter was sent by my friend
	(means of transport)	**par le train** by train
	(distributive)	**trois fois par semaine** three times a week
by		**deux par deux** two by two
	(place)	**par ici/là** this/that way
in / on	(weather)	**par un temps pareil** in such weather **par un beau jour d'hiver** on a beautiful winter's day
through / out of	(place)	**regarder par la fenêtre** to look out the window **jeter du pain par la fenêtre** to throw bread out the window
to / on		**tomber par terre** to fall to the ground **étendu par terre** lying on the ground
	(+ infinitive)	**commencer/finir par faire** to begin by/end up doing

parmi

among   **parmi ses ennemis**
                               among his enemies

pendant

for	(time)	**il l'avait fait pendant 5 années**
		he had done it for 5 years
during		**pendant l'été**
		during the summer

pour

for		**ce livre est pour vous**
		this book is for you
		mourir pour la patrie
		to die for one's country
	(purpose)	**c'est pour cela que je suis venu**
		that's why I have come
	(emphatic)	**pour moi, je crois que**
		personally, I think that
	(time)	**j'en ai pour une heure**
		it'll take me an hour
		je serai là pour 2 semaines
		I'll be here for 2 weeks

(**pour** stresses intention and future time: see **depuis** and **pendant**, pp. 161 and above)

	(idiom)	**c'est bon pour la santé**
		it's good for the health
to	(+ infinitive)	**il était trop paresseux pour réussir aux examens**
		he was too lazy to pass the exams

près de

near	(place)	**près du marché**
		near the market
nearly	(time)	**il est près de minuit**
		it's nearly/almost midnight
	(quantity)	**près de cinquante**
		nearly fifty

quant à

as for	**quant à moi** as for me

sans

without	(+ noun)	**sans espoir** without hope/hopeless
	(+ pronoun)	**je n'irai pas sans vous** I won't go without you
	(+ infinitive)	**sans parler** without speaking **sans s'arrêter** without stopping

sauf

except for	**ils sont tous partis, sauf Carmen** everyone left except (for) Carmen
barring	**sauf accidents/sauf imprévu** barring accidents/the unexpected

selon

according to	**selon le président** according to the president **selon moi** in my opinion

sous

under	(physical)	**sous la table** under the table
	(historical)	**sous le régime de Vichy** under the Vichy regime
in	(weather)	**sous la pluie** in the rain
	(idiom)	**sous peu** shortly/before long **sous la main** at hand

sous tous les rapports
in every respect
sous mes yeux
before my eyes

sur

on / upon	(place)	**le bol est sur la table** the bowl is on the table
off		**prendre sur le rayon** to take off the shelf
out of	(proportion)	**neuf sur dix** nine out of ten
		une semaine sur trois one week in three
over	(place)	**le ponts sur la Seine** the bridges over the Seine
about	(idiom)	**une histoire sur ...** a story about ...
at		**sur ces paroles** at these words
		sur ce, il est sorti at this/at which point he went out
by		**quatre mètres sur cinq** four meters by five
in		**sur un ton amer** in a bitter tone (of voice)
over		**l'emporter sur quelqu'un** to win out over someone

vers

toward(s)	(place)	**vers le nord** towards the north
	(time)	**vers la fin du match** toward the end of the match
about	(time)	**vers 10 heures** about 10 o'clock

voici/voilà

here	(is)	**le voici qui vient** here he comes
there	(is)	**voilà où elle demeure** that's were she lives

9. CONJUNCTIONS

Conjunctions are words or expressions that link words, phrases, or clauses. They fall into two categories:

A. coordinating
B. subordinating

A. COORDINATING CONJUNCTIONS

1. Definition

These link two similar words or groups of words (e.g., nouns, pronouns, adjectives, adverbs, prepositions, phrases. or clauses). The principal coordinating conjunctions (or adverbs used as conjunctions) are:

et	**mais**	**ou**
and	but	or
ou bien	**soit**	**ni**
or (else)	either	neither
alors	**aussi**	**donc**
then	therefore, so	then, therefore
puis	**car**	**or**
then (*next*)	for (*because*)	now, now then
cependant	**néanmoins**	**pourtant**
however	nevertheless	yet, however
toutefois		
however		

il est malade, mais il ne veut pas aller au lit
he's sick but he doesn't want to go to bed

il faisait beau, alors il est allé se promener
it was nice out so he went for a walk

2. Repetition

a) Some coordinating conjunctions are repeated:

soit ... soit	either ... or

prenez soit l'un soit l'autre
take one or the other

ni ... ni	neither ... nor

le vieillard n'avait ni amis ni argent
the old man had neither friends nor money

b) **et** and **ou** can be repeated in texts of a literary nature:

et ... et	both ... and
ou ... ou	either ... or

3. aussi

aussi means 'therefore' when placed before the verb. The subject pronoun is placed after the verb (see p. 182).

il pleuvait, aussi Pascal n'est-il pas sorti
it was raining, so Pascal didn't go out

When **aussi** follows the verb it means 'also':

j'ai aussi mis mon imperméable
I also put my raincoat on

B. SUBORDINATING CONJUNCTIONS

These join a subordinate clause to another clause, usually a main clause. The principal subordinating conjunctions are:

comme	as, since	**parce que**	because
puisque	since	**ainsi que**	(just) as
à mesure que	as	**tant que**	as/so long as
avant que	before	**après que**	after
jusqu'à ce que	until	**depuis que**	since
pendant que	while	**tandis que**	whereas, while
si	if	**à moins que**	unless
pourvu que	provided that	**quoique**	although
bien que	although	**quand**	when
lorsque	when	**dès que**	as soon as
aussitôt que	as soon as	**pour que**	in order that
afin que	so that	**de sorte que**	so that, in such a way that
de façon que	so that, in such a way that	**de peur que (+ ne)**	for fear that, lest

Note: Some subordinating conjunctions require the subjunctive (see pp. 95-6).

C. QUE

que can be coordinating or subordinating:

1. **coordinating**, in comparisons
(see pp. 31–3 and 38–9)

> **il est plus fort que moi**
> he's stronger than I am

2. **subordinating**

a) *meaning 'that'*:

> **elle dit qu'elle l'a vu**   **je pense que tu as raison**
> she says that she saw him   I think you're right

> **il faut que tu viennes**
> you have to come

b) *replacing another conjunction*:

When a conjunction introduces more than one verb, **que** may replace the second subordinating conjunction to avoid repetition:

> **comme il était tard, et que j'étais fatigué, je suis rentré**
> since it was late and I was tired, I went home

Note: the mood after que is the same as that taken by the conjunction it replaces, except in the case of **si**, in which **que** requires the subjunctive:

> **s'il fait beau et que tu sois libre, nous irons à la piscine**
> if it's nice out and if you're free, we'll go to the pool

10. NUMBERS AND QUANTITY

A. CARDINAL NUMBERS

0	**zéro**	40	**quarante**
1	**un (une)**	50	**cinquante**
2	**deux**	60	**soixante**
3	**trois**	70	**soixante-dix**
4	**quatre**	71	**soixante et onze**
5	**cinq**	72	**soixante-douze**
6	**six**	80	**quatre-vingt(s)**
7	**sept**	90	**quatre-vingt-dix**
8	**huit**	99	**quatre-vingt-dix**
9	**neuf**		**neuf**
10	**dix**	100	**cent**
11	**onze**	101	**cent un(e)**
12	**douze**	102	**cent deux**
13	**treize**	121	**cent vingt et un(e)**
14	**quatorze**	122	**cent vingt-deux**
15	**quinze**	200	**deux cents**
16	**seize**	201	**deux cent un(e)**
17	**dix-sept**	1,000	**mille**
18	**dix-huit**	1,988	**mille neuf cent quatre-vingt-huit**
19	**dix-neuf**	2,000	**deux mille**
20	**vingt**	10,000	**dix mille**
21	**vingt et un(e)**	1,000,000	**un million**
30	**trente**	2,000,000	**deux millions**

Note:

a) **un** is the only cardinal number that agrees with the noun in gender:

    un kilo   **une pomme**
    a kilo   an apple

b) hyphens are used in compound numbers between 17 and 99 except where **et** is used (this also applies to compound numbers after 100: **cent vingt-trois** 123).

c) **cent** and **mille** are not preceded by **un** as in English (one hundred).

d) vingt and **cent** multiplied by a number take an **s** when they are not followed by another number.

e) mille is invariable.

f) un million is a noun, and is variable.

B. ORDINAL NUMBERS

		abbreviation
1st	**premier/première**	**1ᵉʳ/1ᵉʳᵉ**
2nd	**deuxième/second**	**2ᵉ**
3rd	**troisième**	**3ᵉ**
4th	**quatrième**	**4ᵉ**
5th	**cinquième**	**5ᵉ**
6th	**sixième**	**6ᵉ**
7th	**septième**	**7ᵉ**
8th	**huitième**	**8ᵉ**
9th	**neuvième**	**9ᵉ**
10th	**dixième**	**10ᵉ**
11th	**onzième**	**11ᵉ**
12th	**douzième**	**12ᵉ**
13th	**treizième**	**13ᵉ**
14th	**quatorzième**	**14ᵉ**
15th	**quinzième**	**15ᵉ**
16th	**seizième**	**16ᵉ**
17th	**dix-septième**	**17ᵉ**
18th	**dix-huitième**	**18ᵉ**
19th	**dix-neuvième**	**19ᵉ**
20th	**vingtième**	**20ᵉ**
21st	**vingt et unième**	**21ᵉ**
22nd	**vingt-deuxième**	**22ᵉ**
30th	**trentième**	**30ᵉ**
100th	**centième**	**100ᵉ**
101st	**cent unième**	**101ᵉ**
200th	**deux centième**	**200ᵉ**
1,000th	**millième**	**1000ᵉ**
10,000th	**dix millième**	**10 000ᵉ**
1,000,000th	**millionième**	**1 000 000ᵉ**

Note:

a) ordinal numbers are formed by adding **-ième** to cardinal numbers, except for **premier** and **second**; **cinq, neuf**, and numbers ending in **e**, undergo slight changes: **cinquième, neuvième, onzième, douzième** etc.

b) ordinal numbers agree with the noun in gender and number:

le premier président   **la première fleur du printemps**
the first president   the first flower of spring

c) there is usually no elision with **huitième** and **onzième**:

le huitième jour	**du onzième candidat**
the eighth day	of the eleventh candidate

d) cardinal numbers are used for monarchs, except for 'first':

Louis quatorze	**Charles premier**
Louis XIV	Charles I

C. FRACTIONS AND ARITHMETICAL EXPRESSIONS

1. Fractions

Fractions are expressed as in English: cardinal followed by ordinal:

deux cinquièmes
two fifths

But: ¼ **un quart** ½ **un demi, une demie; la moitié**
⅓ **un tiers** ¾ **trois quarts**

2. Decimals

The English decimal point is expressed by a comma in French:
un virgule huit (1,8)
one point eight (1.8)

3. Approximate numbers

une huitaine	**une dizaine**
about eight	about ten
une trentaine	**une centaine**
some thirty	about a hundred

But: **un millier**
about a thousand

Note: **de** *is used when the approximate number is followed by a noun:*
une vingtaine d'enfants
about twenty children

4. Arithmetic

Addition:	**deux plus quatre**	$2 + 4$
Subtraction:	**cinq moins deux**	$5 - 2$
Multiplication:	**trois fois cinq**	3×5
Division:	**six divisé par deux**	$6 \div 2$
Square:	**deux au carré**	2^2

D. MEASUREMENTS AND PRICES

1. Measurements

a) *Dimensions*

la salle de classe est longue de 12 mètres
la salle de classe a/fait 12 mètres de longueur/de long
the classroom is twelve meters long

Similarly:

profond(e)/de profondeur/de profond	deep
épais(se)/d'épaisseur	thick
haut(e)/de hauteur/de haut	high

ma chambre fait quatre mètres sur trois
my bedroom is about four by three meters

b) *Distance*

à quelle distance sommes-nous du jardin zoologique?
how far are we from the zoo?

nous sommes à deux kilomètres de la prison
we are two kilometers from the prison

combien y a-t-il d'ici au Havre?
how far is it to Le Havre?

2. Price

ce chandail m'a coûté deux cents francs
this sweater cost me 200 francs

j'ai payé ce chandail deux cents francs
I paid 200 francs for this sweater

des pommes à dix francs le kilo
apples at 10 francs a kilo

du vin blanc à douze francs la bouteille
white wine at 12 francs a bottle

cela fait/revient à quarante-deux francs
that comes to 42 francs

ils coûtent vingt-cinq francs pièce
they cost 25 francs each/apiece

E. EXPRESSIONS OF QUANTITY

Quantity may be expressed by an adverb of quantity (e.g. 'a lot', 'too much') or by a noun that names the actual quantity involved (e.g. 'a bottle', 'a dozen').

1. Expression of quantity + 'de' + noun

Before a noun, adverbs and other expressions of quantity are followed by **de** (**d'** before a vowel or a silent **h**) and never by **du, de la**, or **des**, except for **bien du/de la/des** and **la plupart des** (or **la plupart du**, in the expression **la plupart du temps**):

assez de
enough

autant de
as much/many

beaucoup de
a lot of, much, many

combien de
how much/many

moins de
less, fewer

plus de
more

peu de
little, few

un peu de
a little

tant de
so much/many

tellement de
so much/many

trop de
too much/many

la plupart du/des
most (*see above*)

bien du/de la/des
many, a lot of

j'ai beaucoup d'amis
I have a lot of friends

il y a assez de fromage?
is there enough cheese?

il y a combien de pièces?
how many rooms are there?

**je n'ai pas beaucoup
   de temps**
I don't have much time

**mange plus de
   légumes!**
eat more vegetables!

tu as combien d'argent?
how much money do you have?

peu de gens le savent
not many people know that

il y avait peu de choix
there was little/not much choice

il y a tant d'années
so many years ago

tu veux un peu de pain?
would you like a little bread?

il y a trop de voitures
there are too many cars

j'ai trop de travail
I have too much work

la plupart des Français
most French people

bien des gens
a good many people

2. Noun expressing quantity + 'de' + noun

une boîte de
a box/can/jar of

une bouteille de
a bottle of

une bouchée de
a mouthful of (*food*)

une cuillerée de
a spoonful of

une douzaine de a dozen	**une gorgée de** a mouthful/gulp of (*drink*)
un kilo de a kilo of	**un litre de** a liter of
une livre de a pound of	**un morceau de** a piece of
un paquet de a pack of	**une paire de** a pair of
une part de a share/helping of	**une tasse de** a cup of
une tranche de a slice of	**un verre de** a glass of

je voudrais une boîte de thon et une bouteille de jus de pomme
I'd like a can of tuna fish and a bottle of apple juice

il a mangé une douzaine d'œufs et six morceaux de poulet
he ate a dozen eggs and six pieces of chicken

3. Expressions of quantity used without a noun

When an expression of quantity is not followed by a noun, **de** is replaced by the pronoun **en** (see p. 56):

il y avait beaucoup de neige; il y en avait beaucoup
there was a lot of snow; there was a lot (of it)

elle a mangé trop de chocolats; elle en a trop mangé
she ate too many chocolates; she ate too many (of them)

11. EXPRESSIONS OF TIME

A. THE TIME

quelle heure est-il?   what time is it?

a) *full hours*

il est midi/minuit
it's 12 noon/midnight

il est une heure
it's 1 o'clock

b) *half-hours*

il est minuit et demi(e)
it's 12:30 a.m.

il est midi et demi(e)
it's 12:30 p.m.

il est une heure et demie
it's 1:30

c) *quarter-hours*

**il est deux heures
    un/et quart**
it's (a) quarter past/after two

**il est deux heures
    moins le/un quart**
it's (a) quarter to/of two

d) *minutes*

**il est quatre heures
    vingt-trois**
it's 23 minutes past four
it's four twenty-three

**il est cinq heures
    moins vingt**
it's twenty to five
it's four forty

Note: **minutes** is usually omitted; **heures** is never omitted.

e) *a.m. and p.m.*

du matin
a.m.

de l'après-midi/du soir
p.m.

**il est sept heures dix
    du soir**
it's 7:10 p.m.

**il est sept heures moins
    dix du matin**
it's 6:50 a.m.

The 24-hour clock is commonly used:

dix heures trente
10:30 a.m.

quatorze heures trente-cinq
2:35 p.m.

dix-neuf heures dix
7:10 p.m.

Note: times are often abbreviated as follows:

dix-neuf heures dix   19h10

B. THE DATE

1. Names of months, days, and seasons

a) *Months (les mois)*

janvier	January
février	February
mars	March
avril	April
mai	May
juin	June
juillet	July
août	August
septembre	September
octobre	October
novembre	November
décembre	December

b) *Days of the week (les jours de la semaine)*

lundi	Monday
mardi	Tuesday
mercredi	Wednesday
jeudi	Thursday
vendredi	Friday
samedi	Saturday
dimanche	Sunday

c) *Seasons (les saisons)*

le printemps (spring)	**l'été** (summer)
l'automne (autumn/fall)	**l'hiver** (winter)

For prepositions used with the seasons see p. 17.

Note: in French the months and days are masculine and do not have a capital letter, unless they begin a sentence.

2. Dates

a) cardinals (e.g. **deux, trois**) are used for the dates of the month except the first:

le quartorze juillet   **le deux novembre**
the fourteenth of July   November second

But: **le premier février**
the first of February

The definite article is used as in English; French does not use prepositions ('on' and 'of' in English):

je vous ai écrit le trois mars
I wrote you on the third of March

b) **mil** (a thousand) is used instead of **mille** in dates from 1001 on:

> **mil neuf cent quatre-vingt-sept**
> nineteen (hundred and) eighty-seven

3. Année, journée, matinée, soirée

Année, journée, matinée, soirée (the feminine forms of **an, jour, matin,** and **soir**) are usually found in the following cases:

a) *when duration is implied* (e.g. the whole day):

pendant une année	for a (whole) year
toute la journée	all day long
dans la matinée	in the (course of the) morning
passer une soirée	to spend an evening
l'année scolaire/	the school/academic year
universitaire	

b) *with an ordinal number* (e.g. **première**) *or an indefinite expression:*

la deuxième année	the second year
dans sa vingtième année	in his twentieth year
plusieurs/quelques années	several/a few years
de nombreuses/bien	many years
des années	
environ une année	about a year

c) *with an adjective:*

de bonnes/mauvaises années	good/bad years

C. IDIOMATIC EXPRESSIONS

à cinq heures	at 5 o'clock
à onze heures environ	about/around 11 o'clock
vers minuit	about/around midnight
vers (les) dix heures	about/around 10 o'clock
il est six heures passées	it's past/after 6 o'clock
à quatre heures précises/pile	at exactly 4 o'clock/ 4 o'clock on the dot
il est neuf heures sonnées	it has struck nine
sur le coup de trois heures	on the stroke of three
à partir de neuf heures	from 9 o'clock on
peu avant sept heures	shortly/a little before seven
peu après sept heures	shortly/a little after seven
tôt ou tard	sooner or later
au plus tôt	at the earliest
au plus tard	at the latest
il est tard	it is late
il est en retard	he is late
il se lève tard	he gets up late
il est arrivé en retard	he arrived late

le train a vingt minutes de retard	the train is twenty minutes late
ma montre retarde de six minutes	my watch is six minutes slow
ma montre avance de six minutes	my watch is six minutes fast
ce soir	tonight
demain soir	tomorrow night
hier soir	yesterday evening, last night
demain matin	tomorrow morning
demain en huit	a week from tomorrow
le lendemain	the next day
le lendemain matin	the next morning
hier matin	yesterday morning
la semaine dernière	last week
la semaine prochaine	next week
lundi	(on) Monday
le lundi	(on) Mondays
il y a trois semaines	three weeks ago
une demi-heure	a half-hour, half an hour
un quart d'heure	a quarter of an hour
trois quarts d'heure	three quarters of an hour
passer son temps (à faire)	to spend one's time (doing)
perdre son temps	to waste one's time
de temps en temps	from time to time
tous les samedis	every Saturday
tous les samedis soirs	every Saturday evening/night
le combien sommes-nous aujourd'hui?	what's the date today?
nous sommes/c'est le trois avril	it is the third of April
le vendredi treize juillet	Friday, the thirteenth of July
en février/au mois de février	in February/in the month of February
en 1970	in 1970
dans les années soixante	in the sixties
au dix-septième siècle	in the seventeenth century
le jour de l'An	New Year's Day
avoir treize ans	to be thirteen (years old)
être âgé de quatorze ans	to be fourteen (years old)
elle fête ses vingt ans	she's celebrating her twentieth birthday
un plan quinquennal	a five-year plan
une année bissextile	a leap year
une année civile	a calendar year
une année-lumière	a light year

12. THE SENTENCE

A. WORD ORDER

Word order is usually the same in French as in English, except in the following cases:

1. Adjectives

Most French adjectives follow the noun (see pp. 29–31):

de l'argent *italien*
(some) *Italian* money

j'ai les yeux *bleus*
I have *blue* eyes

2. Adverbs

In simple tenses, adverbs usually follow the verb (see pp. 37–8):

j'y vais *rarement*
I *seldom* go there

il fera *bientôt* nuit
it will *soon* be dark

3. Object pronouns

Object pronouns usually come before the verb (see p. 53):

je *t'*attendrai
I'll wait *for you*

il *la* lui a vendue
he sold *it* to him

4. Noun phrases

Noun phrases are formed differently in French (see pp. 196–7):

une chemise en coton
a cotton shirt

le père de mon copain
my friend's father

5. Exclamations

The word order is not affected after **que** or **comme** (unlike after 'how' in English):

que tu es bête!
you are silly!
(how silly you are!)

qu'il fait froid!
it's so cold!

comme il chante mal!
he sings so badly!

comme c'est beau!
that's so beautiful!

6. DONT

dont must be followed by the subject of the clause it introduces; compare:

> **l'agence d'emploi dont *j*'ai perdu la lettre**
> the employment agency whose letter I lost

> **l'agence d'emploi dont *la lettre* est arrivée hier**
> the employment agency whose letter arrived yesterday

7. Inversion

In certain cases, the subject of a French clause is placed after the verb, making the word order the same as that of an interrogative sentence (see p. 186). This occurs:

a) *after the following*, but only when they start a clause:

à peine	**aussi**	**peut-être**
hardly, scarcely	therefore	maybe, perhaps

> **à peine Alain était-il sorti qu'il a commencé à pleuvoir**
> Alain had hardly gone out when it started to rain

> **il y avait une grève du métro, aussi a-t-il pris un taxi**
> there was a subway strike, so he took a cab

> **peut-être vont-ils téléphoner plus tard**
> maybe they'll phone later

But: **Alain était à peine sorti qu'il a commencé à pleuvoir**

ils vont peut-être téléphoner plus tard

b) *when a verb of saying follows direct speech*:

> **"si tu veux", a répondu Marie**
> "if you want", Marie replied

> **"attention!" a-t-elle crié**
> "watch out!", she shouted

> **"j'espère que non", dit-il**
> "I hope not", he said

> **"répondez!" ordonna-t-il**
> "answer!", he ordered

B. NEGATIVE EXPRESSIONS

1. Main negative words

a)	**ne ... pas**	not
	ne ... point	not at all (*literary*)
	ne ... plus	no more/longer, not ... any more
	ne ... jamais	never
	ne ... rien	nothing, not ... anything
	ne ... guère	hardly
b)	**ne ... personne**	nobody, no one, not ... anyone
	ne ... que	only

ne ... ni (**ni ... ni**)	neither ... nor
ne ... aucun(e)	no, not any, none
ne ... nul(le)	no
ne ... nulle part	nowhere, not ... anywhere

Note:

i) **ne** becomes **n'** before a vowel or a silent **h**

ii) **aucun** and **nul**, like other adjectives and pronouns, agree with the word they refer to; they are only used in the singular.

2. Position of negative expressions

a) *with simple tenses and with the imperative*

negative words enclose the verb: **ne** comes before the verb, and the second part of the negative expression comes after the verb:

je ne la connais pas I don't know her	**n'insistez pas!** don't insist!
je n'ai plus d'argent I don't have any money left	**tu ne le sauras jamais** you'll never know
ne dis rien don't say anything	**il n'y a personne** no one's here
je n'avais que dix francs I had only ten francs	**il n'est nulle part** it isn't anywhere
tu n'as aucun sens **de l'humour** you have no sense of humor	**ce n'est ni noir ni bleu** it's neither black nor blue

b) *with compound tenses*

with **ne ... pas** and the other expressions in list **1a**, the word order is: **ne** + auxiliary + **pas** + past participle:

il n'est pas revenu he didn't come back	**je n'ai plus essayé** I didn't try any more
je n'avais jamais vu Paris I had never seen Paris	**on n'a rien fait** we haven't done anything

with **ne ... personne** and the other expressions in list **1b**, the word order is: **ne** + auxiliary + past participle + **personne/que/ni** etc.:

il ne l'a dit à personne he didn't tell anyone	**tu n'en as acheté qu'un?** did you buy only one?
je n'en ai aimé aucun I didn't like any of them	**il n'est allé nulle part** he hasn't gone anywhere

c) *with the infinitive*

i) **ne . . . pas** and the other expressions in list **1a** are placed together before the verb:

je préfère ne pas y aller	**essaie de ne rien perdre**
I'd rather not go there	try not to lose anything

ii) **ne . . . personne** and the other expressions in list **1b** enclose the infinitive:

il a été surpris de ne voir personne
he was surprised not to see anybody

j'ai décidé de n'en acheter aucun
I decided not to buy any of them

d) *at the beginning of a sentence*

when **personne, rien, aucun**, and **ni . . . ni** begin a sentence, they are followed by **ne:**

personne ne le sait	**rien n'a changé**
nobody knows it	nothing has changed
ni Paul ni Simone **ne sont venus**	**aucun secours n'est arrivé**
neither Paul nor Simone came	no help arrived

3. Combination of negative expressions

Negative expressions can be combined:

ne . . . plus jamais	**ne . . . jamais rien**
ne . . . plus rien	**ne . . . jamais personne**
ne . . . plus personne	**ne . . . jamais ni . . . ni**
ne . . . plus ni . . . ni	**ne . . . jamais que**
ne . . . plus que	
on ne l'a plus jamais revu	**il n'y a plus rien**
we never saw him again	there isn't anything left
plus personne ne viendra	**tu ne dis jamais rien**
no one will come any more	you never say anything
je ne bois jamais que de l'eau	**je ne vois jamais personne**
I never drink anything but water	I never see anybody

Note: with **plus** and **jamais** both orders are possible: *e.g.* **on ne l'a jamais plus revu**

4. Negative expressions without a verb

a) *PAS*

pas (not) is the most common of all negatives; it is frequently used without a verb:

tu l'aimes?—pas beaucoup	**ah non, pas lui!**
do you like it?—not much	oh no, not him!

non merci, pas pour moi
no thanks, not for me

un roman pas très long
not a very long novel

lui, il viendra, mais pas moi
he will come, but I won't

j'aime ça; pas toi?
I like that; don't you?

b) *NE*

ne is not used when there is no verb:

qui a crié?—personne
who shouted?—nobody

jamais de la vie!
not on your life!

rien! je ne veux rien!
nothing! I want nothing!

rien du tout
nothing at all

c) *NON*

non (no) is always used without a verb:

tu aimes la natation?—non, pas du tout
do you like swimming—no, not at all

tu viens, oui ou non?
are you coming, yes or no?

je crois que non
I don't think so

Note: **non plus** = 'neither':

je ne le crois pas—(ni) moi non plus
I don't believe him—neither do I

je n'ai rien mangé—nous non plus
I haven't eaten anything—neither have we

C. DIRECT AND INDIRECT QUESTIONS

1. Direct questions

There are three ways of forming direct questions in French:

    a) subject + verb (+ interrogative word)
    b) (interrogative word) + **est-ce que** + subject + verb
    c) (interrogative word) + verb + subject = inversion

a) *subject + verb (+ interrogative word)*

The word order remains the same as in statements (subject + verb) but the intonation changes: the voice is raised at the end of the sentence. This is by far the most common question form in conversational French:

tu l'as acheté où?
where did you buy it?

je peux téléphoner d'ici?
can I phone from here?

vous prendrez quel train?
which train will you take?

tu lui fais confiance?
do you trust him?

c'était comment?	**la gare est près d'ici?**
what was it like?	is the station near here?
le train part à quelle heure?	**cette robe me va?**
what time does the train leave?	does this dress suit me?

b) *(interrogative word)* + ***est-ce que*** + subject + verb

This question form is also very common in conversation:

qu'est-ce que tu as?	**est-ce qu'il est là?**
what's the matter with you?	is he in?

est-ce que ton ami s'est amusé?
did your friend have a good time?

où est-ce que vous avez mal?
where does it hurt?

c) *inversion*

This question form is the most formal of the three, and the least commonly used in conversation.

  i) if the subject is a pronoun, word order is as follows:
  (interrogative word) + verb + hyphen + subject

où allez-vous?	**voulez-vous commander?**
where are you going?	do you wish to order?
quand est-il arrivé?	**avez-vous bien dormi?**
when did he arrive?	did you sleep well?

  ii) if the subject is a noun, a pronoun referring to the noun is inserted after the verb, and linked to it with a hyphen:
  (interrogative word) + noun subject + verb + hyphen + pronoun

où ton père travaillait-il?	**Nicole en veut-elle?**
where did your father work?	does Nicole want any?

  iii) **-t-** is inserted before **il**, **elle**, and **on** when the verb ends in a vowel:

comment va-t-il voyager?	**aime-t-elle le café?**
how will he travel?	does she like coffee?
pourquoi a-t il refusé?	**Marie viendra-t-elle?**
why did he refuse?	will Marie be coming?

Note: when an interrogative word (except **pourquoi**) is used, modern French will often just invert verb and noun subject, without adding a pronoun; no hyphen is then necessary:

où travaille ton père?	**pourquoi est-ce que**
where does your father work?	**le bébé pleure?**
	why is the baby crying?

2. Indirect questions

a) *Definition*

Indirect questions follow a verb and are introduced by an interrogative word, e.g.:

    ask him when he will arrive   I don't know why he did it

b) *Word order*

  i) The word order is usually the same as in statements: interrogative word + subject + verb:

    je ne sais pas s'il voudra   **dis-moi où tu l'as mis**
    I don't know if he'll want to   tell me where you put it

    il n'a pas dit quand il appellerait
    he didn't say when he would phone

  ii) If the subject is a noun, verb and subject are sometimes inverted:

    demande-leur où est le camping
    ask them where the campsite is

But: **je ne comprends pas comment l'accident s'est produit**
    I don't understand how the accident happened

    il ne savait pas pourquoi les magasins étaient fermés
    he didn't know why the stores were closed

3. Translation of English question tags

a) Examples of question tags are: isn't it? aren't you? doesn't he? won't they? haven't you? is it? did you? etc.

b) French doesn't use question tags as often as English. Some of them can however be translated in the following ways:

  i) **n'est-ce pas?**

n'est-ce pas? is used at the end of a sentence when agreement with a statement is expected:

    c'était très intéressant, n'est-ce pas?
    it was very interesting, wasn't it?

    tu voudrais trouver un emploi stable, n'est-ce pas?
    you would like to find a steady job, wouldn't you?

    vous n'arriverez pas trop tard, n'est-ce pas?
    you won't be arriving too late, right?

  ii) **hein?** and **non?**

In conversation **hein?** and **non?** are often used after affirmative statements instead of **n'est-ce pas:**

    il fait beau, hein?   **il est amusant, non?**
    it's nice weather, isn't it?   he's funny, isn't he?

D. ANSWERS ('YES' AND 'NO')

1. OUI, SI, and NON

a) **oui** and **si** mean 'yes' and are equivalent to longer positive answers such as: 'yes, it is', 'yes, I will', 'yes, he has' etc.:

> **tu m'écriras?—oui, bien sûr!**
> will you write me?—(yes,) of course I will!

b) **non** means 'no' and is equivalent to longer negative answers such as: 'no, it isn't', 'no, I didn't' etc.:

> **c'était bien?—non, on s'est ennuyé(s)**
> was it o.k.?—no, it wasn't; we were bored

2. OUI or SI?

oui and **si** both mean 'yes', but **oui** is used to answer an affirmative question, and **si** to contradict a negative question:

> **cette place est libre?—oui**
> is this seat free?—yes (it is)
>
> **tu n'aimes pas lire?—si, bien sûr!**
> don't you like reading?—yes, of course (I do)!

13. TRANSLATION PROBLEMS

A. GENERAL TRANSLATION PROBLEMS

1. French words not translated in English

Some French words are not translated in English, especially:

a) *Articles*

Definite and indefinite articles are not always translated (see pp. 10–12):

> **dans *la* société moderne, *les* prix sont élevés**
> in modern society, prices are high

> **ah non! encore *du* riz! je déteste *le* riz!**
> oh no! rice again! I hate rice!

b) *que*

que meaning 'that' as a conjunction (see p. 170) or 'that'/'which'/'whom' as a relative pronoun object (see p. 63) cannot be omitted in French:

> **j'espère *que* tu vas mieux** **elle pense *que* c'est vrai**
> I hope you're better she thinks it's true

> **celui *que* j'ai vu** **c'est un pays *que* j'aime**
> the one I saw it's a country I love

c) *Prepositions*

Some French verbs are followed by a preposition (+ indirect object) while their English equivalents take a direct object (without preposition) (see pp. 152–4):

> **elle a téléphoné *au* médecin** **tu l'as dit *à* ton père?**
> she phoned the doctor did you tell your father?

d) *le*

When **le** (it) is used in an impersonal sense (see pp. 52–3), it is either not translated or is translated as **so.**

> **oui, je *le* sais** **dis-*le*-lui**
> yes, I know tell him (so)

2. English words not translated in French

Some English words are not translated in French, for example:

a) *Prepositions*

i) with verbs that take an indirect object in English, but a direct object in French (see p. 152):

tu l'as payé combien?	**écoutez cette chanson**
how much did you pay *for* it?	listen *to* this song

ii) in certain expressions (see pp. 179–80):

je viendrai te voir lundi soir
I'll come see you (*on*) Monday night

b) *'can'*

'can' + verb of hearing or seeing (see p. 114):

je ne vois rien!	**tu entends la musique?**
I can't see anything	can you hear the music?

3. Other differences

a) *English phrasal verbs*

Phrasal verbs are verbs that, when followed by a preposition, take on a different meaning, e.g. 'to give up', 'to walk out'. They do not exist in French and are translated by simple verbs or by expressions:

to give up	to run away	to run across (*i.e. literally*)
abandonner	**s'enfuir**	**traverser en courant**

b) *English possessive adjectives*

English possessive adjectives (my, your, etc.) are translated by the French definite article (**le/la/les**) when parts of the body are mentioned (see p. 61):

brush *your* teeth	he hurt *his* foot
brosse-toi *les* **dents**	**il s'est fait mal** *au* **pied**

c) *'from'*

'from' is translated by **à** with verbs of 'taking away' (see p. 154):

he hid it *from* his parents	borrow some *from* your dad
il l'a caché *à* **ses parents**	**empruntes-en** *à* **ton père**

B. SPECIFIC TRANSLATION PROBLEMS

1. Words in -ing

The English verb form ending in **-ing** is translated in a number of ways in French:

a) *by the appropriate French tense* (see pp. 86–7):

he's speaking (present tense)	**il parle**
he was speaking (imperfect)	**il parlait**
he will be speaking (future)	**il parlera**
he has been speaking (*passé composé*)	**il a parlé**
he had been speaking (*plus-que-parfait*)	**il avait parlé**
he would be speaking (conditional)	**il parlerait**

b) *by a French present participle* (see pp. 108–9)

i) as an adjective:

un livre amusant   **c'est effrayant**
an amusing book   it's frightening

ii) as a verb, with **en** (while/on/by doing something; see pp. 108–9):

"ça ne fait rien", dit-il en souriant
"it doesn't matter", said he, smiling

j'ai vu mes copains en sortant du lycée
I saw my friends while (I was) coming out of school

But: **en** + present participle cannot be used when the two verbs have different subjects, e.g.:

I saw my brother coming out of school
j'ai vu mon frère sortir du lycée/qui sortait du lycée

c) *by a present infinitive* (see pp. 101–7):

i) after a preposition:

au lieu de rire   **avant de traverser**
instead of laughing   before crossing

ii) after verbs of perception:

je l'ai entendu appeler   **je l'ai vue entrer**
I heard him calling   I saw her going in

iii) after verbs of liking and disliking:

j'adore faire du camping   **tu aimes lire?**
I love camping   do you like reading?

iv) after verbs followed by **à** or **de**:

tu passes tout ton temps à ne rien faire
you spend all your time doing nothing

il a commencé à neiger   **continuez à travailler**
it started snowing   keep working

tu as envie de sortir?   **il doit finir de manger**
do you feel like going out?   he has to finish eating

    v) when an English verb in **-ing** is the subject of another verb:

attendre serait inutile   **écrire est une corvée!**
waiting would be pointless   writing is a real chore!

    vi) when an English verb in **-ing** follows 'is' or 'was' etc.:

mon passe-temps favori, c'est d'aller à la discothèque
my favorite pastime is going to the disco

d) *by a past infinitive* (see p. 107)

    i) after **après** (after):

j'ai pris une douche après avoir nettoyé ma chambre
I took a shower after cleaning my room

    ii) after certain verbs:

regretter	**remercier de**	**se souvenir de**
to regret	to thank for	to remember

e) *by a noun*

particularly when referring to sports, activities, hobbies, etc.:

le ski	**la natation**	**l'équitation**
skiing	swimming	horse-riding
la voile	**le patinage**	**le canoë**
sailing	skating	canoeing
la lecture	**la planche à voile**	**la cuisine**
reading	wind-surfing	cooking
la boxe	**la lutte**	**la marche à pied**
boxing	wrestling	walking/hiking

2. It is (it's)

'it is' ('it's') can be translated in three ways in French:

     a) il/elle + être
     b) ce + être
     c) il + être

a) *il or elle* (see pp. 51–2)

il or **elle** are used with the verb **être** to translate 'it is', 'it was' etc. (+ adjective) when referring to a particular masculine or feminine noun (a thing, a place, etc.):

merci de/pour ta carte: elle était très amusante
thanks for your card; it was very funny

regarde ce blouson: il n'est vraiment pas cher
look at that jacket; it really isn't expensive

b) *ce* (see pp. 42–3)

ce (c' before a vowel) is used with the verb **être** to translate 'it is', 'it was' etc. in two cases:

i) if **être** is followed by a word that is not an adjective on its own, i.e. by a noun, a pronoun, an expression of place etc.:

c'était sa voix	**c'est une grande maison**
it was his voice	it's a big house
c'est moi! c'est Claude!	**c'est le tien?**
it's me! it's Claude!	is it yours?
c'est en France que tu vas?	**c'est pour lundi**
is it France you're going to?	it's for Monday

ii) if **être** is followed by an adjective that refers to something previously mentioned, an idea, an event, a fact, but not to a specific noun:

l'homme n'ira jamais sur Saturne; ce n'est pas possible
man will never go to Saturn; it's not possible

j'ai passé mes vacances en Italie; c'était formidable!
I spent my vacation in Italy; it was terrific!

oh, je m'excuse!—ce n'est pas grave
oh, I'm sorry!—it's all right

c) *il* (see p. 83–6)

il is used to translate 'it is', 'it was' etc. in three cases:

i) with **être** followed by an adjective + **de** or **que** (i.e. referring to something that follows, but not to a specific noun):

il est impossible de connaître l'avenir
it's impossible to know the future

il est évident que tu ne me crois pas
it's obvious you don't believe me

ii) to describe the weather (see p. 83):

il y a du vent	**il faisait très froid**
it's windy	it was very cold

iii) with **être** to tell the time and in phrases relating to the time of day, or in such expressions as **il est temps de** (it's time to):

il est deux heures du matin	**ah bon! il est tard!**
it's two a.m.	really! it's late!
il est temps de partir	
it's time to go	

Note: with other expressions of time, **c'est** is used:

c'est lundi ou mardi?	**c'était l'été**
is it Monday or Tuesday?	it was summer

3. To be

Although 'to be' is usually translated by **être,** it can also be translated in the following ways:

a) *avoir*

i) **avoir** is used instead of **être** in many set expressions:

avoir faim/soif	to be hungry/thirsty
avoir chaud/froid	to be warm/cold
avoir peur/honte	to be afraid/ashamed
avoir tort/raison	to be right/wrong

ii) **avoir** is also used for age:

quel âge as-tu?	**j'ai vingt-cinq ans**
how old are you?	I'm twenty-five

b) *aller*

aller is used for describing health:

je vais mieux	**tout le monde va bien**
I'm feeling better	everyone's fine

c) *faire*

faire is used in many expressions to describe the weather (see p. 84):

il fait beau	**il fera chaud**
it's nice out	it will be hot

Note: **il y a** can also be used to describe the weather, but only before **du/de la/des:**

il y a du vent/des nuages/de la tempête
it's windy/cloudy/stormy

d) *untranslated*

'to be' is not translated when it is the first part of an English progressive tense; instead, the appropriate tense is used in French (see p. 86):

I'm taking a bath	he was driving slowly
je prends un bain	**il conduisait lentement**

4. Any

'any' can be translated in three different ways:

a) *du/de la/de l'/des,* or *de* (see pp. 13–4)

the partitive article is used with a noun in negative and interrogative sentences:

il ne mange jamais de viande	**tu veux du pain?**
he never eats (any) meat	do you want some bread?

b) *en* (see p. 56)

en is used to translate 'any' without a noun in negative and inter-rogative sentences:

je n'en ai pas	**il en reste?**
I don't have any	is there any left?

c) *n'importe quel(le)/quel(le)s* or *tout(e)/tou(te)s*

these are used to translate 'any' (and 'every') when they mean 'no matter which':

il pourrait arriver à n'importe quel moment
he could be arriving any time

prends n'importe quelle couleur, je les aime toutes
take any color, I like them all

5. Anyone, anything, anywhere

Like 'any', these can be translated in different ways:

a) *in interrogative sentences:*

il y a quelqu'un?	**tu l'as vu quelque part?**
is anyone in?	did you see it anywhere?
il a dit quelque chose?	
did he say anything?	

b) *in negative sentences:*

il n'y a personne	**je ne le vois nulle part**
there isn't anyone	I can't see it anywhere
je n'ai rien fait	
I didn't do anything	

c) *in the sense of 'any' (and 'every'), 'no matter which':*

n'importe qui peut le faire	**il croit n'importe quoi**
anyone can do that	he believes anything
j'irai n'importe où	**n'importe quand**
I'll go anywhere	anytime

6. You, your, yours, yourself

French has two separate sets of words to translate 'you', 'your', 'yours', 'yourself':

a) **tu, te(t'), toi, ton/ta/tes, le tien** etc.
b) **vous, votre/vos, le vôtre** etc.

For their respective meanings and uses, see pp. 51–53, 58, 60–2.

a) *tu etc.*

tu, te, ton etc. correspond to the **tu** form of the verb (second person singular) and are used when speaking to one person you know well (a friend, a relative) or to someone younger. They represent the familiar form of address:

> *tu* **viens au concert avec** *ton* **copain, Annie? alors,**
> **je** *t'***achète deux places; une pour** *toi* **et une pour lui**
> are *you* coming to the concert with *your* boyfriend, Annie? well then, I'll get *you* two seats: one for *you* and one for him

b) *vous etc.*

vous, vos etc. correspond to the **vous** form of the verb (second person plural) and are used:

i) when speaking to more than one person:

> **dépêchez-***vous***, les gars!** *vous* **allez manquer le train**
> hurry up, guys! *you*'ll miss the train

ii) when speaking to one person you do not know well or to someone older. They represent the formal or polite form of address:

> **je regrette, Monsieur, mais** *vous* **ne pouvez pas garder**
> *votre* **chien avec** *vous* **dans ce restaurant**
> I'm sorry, sir, but *you* can't keep *your* dog with *you* in this restaurant

c) when speaking or writing to one person, you must not mix words from both sets, but have to decide whether you are being formal or familiar, and use the same form of address throughout:

> **Cher Michel,**
> **Merci de** *ta* **lettre. Comment vas-***tu?* . . .
> Dear Michel,
> Thanks for *your* letter. How are *you*? . . .

> **Monsieur,**
> **Pourriez-***vous* **me réserver une chambre dans** *votre*
> **hôtel pour le huit juin?**
> Dear Sir,
> Could *you* book a room for me in *your* hotel for the eighth of June?

vous etc. and **tu** etc. can only be used together when **vous** is plural (i.e. when it refers to more than one person):

> *tu* **sais, Jean,** *toi* **et** *ta* **sœur,** *vous vous* **ressemblez**
> *you* know, Jean, *you* and *your* sister look like *each other*

7. Noun phrases

A noun phrase is a combination of two nouns used together to name things or people. In English, the first of these nouns is used to describe the second one, e.g. 'a love story'. In French, however, the position of the two nouns is reversed, so that the describing noun comes second and is linked to the first one by the preposition **de** (or **d'**):

une histoire d'amour a love story	**un acteur de cinéma** a movie actor
un magasin de disques a record store	**un film d'aventure** an adventure film
un arrêt d'autobus a bus stop	**une boule de neige** a snowball
un coup de soleil sunstroke	**un match de football** a soccer game
un roman de science-fiction a science fiction novel	**un conte de fées** a fairy tale
le Pont de Brooklyn Brooklyn Bridge	**un employé de bureau** an office worker
un joueur de baseball a baseball player	

Note: when the describing noun refers to a material, the preposition **en** is often used instead of **de**:

un pull en laine a wool sweater	**un pantalon en cuir** leather pants
une bague en or a gold ring	**un sac en plastique** a plastic bag

8. Possession

In English, possession is often expressed by using a noun phrase and tagging **'s** onto the end of the first word, e.g.

my friend's cat

This is translated in French by: object + **de** + possessor:

le chat de mon ami

Note the use of the article **le/la/l'/les**.

le fiancé de ma sœur my sister's fiancé	**les amis de Chantal** Chantal's friends
les événements de la semaine dernière last week's events	

When **'s** is used in the sense of 'someone's house' or 'place' etc, it is translated by the preposition **chez**:

je téléphone de chez Paul I'm phoning from Paul's	**chez le dentiste** at/to the dentist's

Index
to
Grammar

Part II
Exercises

Questions

1. ARTICLES

A. THE DEFINITE ARTICLE

a) Insert *le*, *la*, *l'*, or *les*, as appropriate, in front of the following:

café	chauffeur	Italie
région	tennis	docteur
plage	secrétaire	usine
été	chambre	odeur
fin	avion	Afrique
radio	maths	hall
page	cuisine	hôtel
uniforme	magasin	automne
interview	Canada	Europe
géographie	Etats-Unis	histoire
Montagnes Rocheuses	homme	hôtesse
fromage	peau	nuit
musée	lumière	pluie
terre	verre	côté
leçon	ange	cœur

Score: ... × 2

b) Complete the following sentences using *au, à la, à l', aux.*

(1) Au printemps, je dois aller ..... Canada en voyage d'affaires.
(2) Il travaille depuis trois ans ..... usine de voitures.
(3) L'été, nous préférons aller en vacances ..... mer.
(4) Le directeur a emmené les clients. ..... restaurant, et ensuite ils iront ..... Opéra.
(5) Quand je vais à Paris, je descends toujours ..... hôtel Bristol.
(6) La société où je travaille se trouve ..... Champs-Elysées.
(7) Je n'ai pas parlé. ..... directeur, j'ai parlé ..... secrétaire.
(8) Autrefois, les touristes allaient manger une soupe ..... oignon aux Halles; maintenant, ils vont voir des expositions ..... Centre Pompidou.
(9) J'ai donné votre adresse ..... homme qui a téléphoné hier matin.
(10) Il doit venir nous chercher ..... aéroport ..... heure convenue.

(11) Il a un poste important: c'est le représentant de la France . . . . . Nations Unies.
(12) Une jeune fille a donné un bouquet . . . . . héros de la course.
(13) Leurs enfants ont appris l'anglais . . . . . école bilingue de Genève.
(14) Mon frère travaille depuis cinq ans . . . . . étranger.
(15) Elle est restée . . . . . maison du matin . . . . . soir.

Score: . . . × 5

c) Complete the following sentences with a word from the list.

du de la de l' des

(1) Paris est la capitale . . . . . France.
(2) La secrétaire est dans le bureau du directeur, avec le représentant . . . . . établissements Boussac.
(3) Cette usine est l'une . . . . . plus importantes . . . . . région.
(4) L'industrie automobile japonaise est sans doute la plus solide . . . . . monde.
(5) Le nombre . . . . . chômeurs a beaucoup augmenté ces dernières années.
(6) L'unité . . . . . Europe doit se faire rapidement.
(7) Le sommet . . . . . états européens doit avoir lieu au début . . . . . hiver.
(8) Le Président a encore souligné l'importance . . . . . l'équilibre européen.
(9) On espère une baisse . . . . . inflation et une augmentation . . . . . pouvoir d'achat pour la rentrée.
(10) Le personnel . . . . . aéroports est en grève illimitée.
(11) A la demande . . . . . habitants . . . . . île, le stationnement des voitures a été limité à partir de 6 heures . . . . . soir.
(12) La connissance . . . . . anglais est essentielle de nos jours, dans tous les pays . . . . . monde, particulièrement dans le domaine du marketing, ... affaires, et . . . . . finance.

Score: . . . × 5

d) Practice using the definite article by translating the following sentences into French.

(1) English grammar is easier than French grammar.
(2) I don't like jazz. I prefer classical music.
(3) In France, banks are open until 4:30 p.m.
(4) I hate skiing: last year at Aspen I broke my leg on the first day of the vacation!
(5) France and the United States don't always agree on Africa.

(6) I love French food and French wine, but French people drink a lot of coffee, and coffee gives me a headache.

(7) You will recognize him easily: he has white hair, blue eyes, and he will have a hat on his head and a newspaper in his hand.

(8) Poor Jean-Pierre! He always works on Saturdays.

(9) Nowadays, pupils study politics at school.

(10) President Chirac and Vice President Gore will go to Holland next month.

(11) They will talk about European unity.

(12) Queen Elizabeth II lives in Buckingham Palace. President Clinton lives in the White House.

Score: . . . × 5

B. THE INDEFINITE ARTICLE

a) **Practice using the indefinite article by translating the following into French.**

(1) He is a very good doctor

(2) Her father is a teacher, her mother is an architect.

(3) Gérard Depardieu, a great French actor, was on television yesterday.

(4) He received the news with great courage.

(5) She said surprising things.

(6) What a disaster! There are hundreds of people without a home.

(7) What a mess! There are papers and empty glasses everywhere!

(8) These are remarkable men and women.

(9) I'd like answers to my questions

(10) She would like children, but he prefers dogs.

Score: . . . × 10

C. THE PARTITIVE ARTICLE

a) **Fill in the blanks, choosing between *le, la, l', les*, and *du, de la, de l', des*.**

(1) C'est le week-end: je dois aller chercher . . . . . argent . . . . . banque.

(2) Dans notre groupe, il y avait . . . . . Français, ... Allemands, plusieurs Italiens, et surtout . . . . . Japonais.

(3) . . . . . eau minérale coûte presque aussi cher que . . . . . vin.

213

(4) . . . . . Français accordent beaucoup d'importance à . . . . . bonne cuisine.

(5) . . . . . bière belge est une des meilleures du monde.

(6) Les Allemands boivent surtout. . . . . bière blonde.

(7) . . . . . argent ne fait pas le bonheur.

(8) Dans certains pays, il vaut mieux ne boire que . . . . . eau minérale.

(9) . . . . . café m'empêche de dormir, alors en général je bois . . . . . thé.

(10) J'ai besoin . . . . . renseignements sur la Côte d'Azur.

(11) Je n'ai pas assez . . . . . temps pour écrire . . . . . lettres. J'ai trop . . . . . travail.

(12) Je préfère donner . . . . . coups de téléphone.

Score: . . . × 5 ◯

b) Put the following sentences into the negative.

(1) Elle a de la chance: elle a eu une augmentation de salaire.

(2) Il a des problèmes dans son travail.

(3) L'école organise des séjours linguistiques.

(4) Elle a toujours du retard.

(5) Nous avons une réservation.

(6) Il y a un avion pour Madrid ce matin.

(7) Les pays européens ont une politique économique commune.

(8) Paris a des espaces verts.

(9) J'ai encore de l'argent: je peux prendre un taxi.

(10) Le gouvernement a trouvé une solution au problème de la pollution industrielle.

Score: . . . × 10 ◯

2. NOUNS

A. GENDER

a) Give the gender of the following nouns.

boulanger	personne	santé
bonheur	lion	voix
Seine	école	communisme
faim	musée	écrivain
bonté	rêve	dimanche
charme	grève	pommier
puissance	boisson	professeur
uniforme	gloire	auteur
théorème	lycée	mer
soif		

b)

nation	victime	cuiller
soirée	lumière	cour
terre	monde	eau
tonnerre	loi	médecin
danse	mois	prison
peur	zèle	phénomène
verre	dent	portefeuille
feuille		

Score: ... × 2 ◯

215

B. THE FORMATION OF THE FEMININE

a) Give the feminine form of these masculine nouns.

un Français   un chirurgien   un médecin
un cousin   un danseur   un comte
un étudiant   un roi   un vieux
un cuisinier   un Allemand   un dieu
un Italien   un tourtereau   un voisin
un chanteur   un fermier   un pharmacien
un fils   un frère   un acteur
un fou   un cheval   un chien
un héros   un homme   un neveu
un maître   un prisonnier   un directeur
un boulanger   un chat   un duc
un vendeur   un instituteur   un prince
un ami   un jumeau   un coq
un beau-père

Score: . . . × 2

C. THE FORMATION OF THE PLURAL

a) Give the plural of these singular nouns.

l'Anglais   Mademoiselle   le travail
l'époux   le chou-fleur   la fille
le choix   le luxe   le cadeau
le gouvernement   le thé   le cheval
le professeur   Madame   l'oiseau
le jeu   l'hôtel   l'œuf
le fils   le prix   le pneu
l'eau   le bijou   le cheveu
le journal   le drame   le trou
Monsieur   le festival   le genou
l'homme   l'apéritif   le radis
le cri   le pays   le fou
l'œil   l'os   la clef
la fois

Score: . . . × 2

D. COLLECTIVE NOUNS/NOUNS WHICH ARE PLURAL IN FRENCH AND SINGULAR IN ENGLISH AND VICE VERSA

a) **Translate the following sentences into French.**

   (1) The police are looking for a man seen near the scene of the crime.
   (2) The family have refused to answer the journalists' questions.
   (3) The cattle had to be put to death because of the disease.
   (4) The news is very disturbing at the moment.
   (5) These pants don't fit me.
   (6) His pajamas are too small for him.
   (7) The furniture is too big for the room.
   (8) All the baggage was inspected at the airport.
   (9) Grapes are very expensive in this country.
   (10) We always have a terrific vacation when we go to France.
   (11) Chess is a very difficult game.

Score: . . . × 5

3. ADJECTIVES

A. AGREEMENT OF ADJECTIVES

a) Make the adjectives in parentheses agree with the nouns to which they refer.

une plaisanterie (amusant)
de (beau) sculptures
mes (nouveau) amies
les voitures (neuf)
des conversations (secret)
de (mauvais) nouvelles
des chaussures (neuf)
une (cruel) maladie
la (dernier) fois
des femmes (heureux)
une voix (doux)
une jeune fille (roux)
mon émission (favori)
de (vieux) maisons
l'histoire (ancien)
de l'eau (frais)
une fille (gentil)
une (long) attente

des apparences (trompeur)
une robe (blanc)
une vie très (actif)
une (meilleur) santé
une attitude (positif)
des accidents (fatal)
des enfants (normal)
une (petit) fille
des hommes (brutal)
une chance (fou)
un (beau) été
un (nouveau) élève
un (vieux) hôtel
une écharpe et un manteau
(vert)
une paix et un bonheur
(complet)
une voiture et un appartement (neuf)
un père et une mère (inquiet)

Score: . . . × 2

B. POSITION OF ADJECTIVES

a) Translate the following into French—the French adjective is given in parentheses, in the masculine.

(1) I have bought a beautiful painting. (beau)
(2) I met my former boss yesterday. (ancien)
(3) I went to see a very good film last week. (bon, dernier)
(4) He is a great actor. (grand)
(5) I must write to my dear mother. (cher)
(6) Poor woman! She is very sick. (pauvre)
(7) It is the last day of the vacation. (dernier)
(8) She is the only woman in the group. (seul)

(9) They live in a very expensive house. (cher)
(10) She is a tall and beautiful woman. (grand, beau)
(11) I love old furniture. (ancien)
(12) She has a definite taste for expensive jewelry. (certain, cher)
(13) She is a very lonely woman. (seul)
(14) There are too many poor countries in the world. (pauvre)
(15) Did you see the beautiful old houses in the old neighborhood? (beau, ancien, vieux)
(16) He has a very tiring job. (fatigant)

Score: . . . × 5

C. COMPARATIVE OF ADJECTIVES

a) Make up sentences to compare data, as in the model sentences provided below.

La France/grand/l'Angleterre. (plus)
La France est plus grande que l'Angleterre

L'Airbus/rapide/le Concorde (moins)
L'Airbus est moins rapide que le Concorde

(1) L'Amérique/peuplée/la France (plus)
(2) Le Mont Blanc/haut/l'Everest (moins)
(3) New-York/grand/Paris (plus)
(4) Le T.G.V. français/rapide/les trains américains (plus)
(5) Le métro newyorkais/cher/le métro parisien (plus)
(6) Les trains américains/confortables/les trains français (moins)
(7) Les restaurants français/chers/les restaurants américains (moins)
(8) La cuisine française/variée/la cuisine américaine (plus)
(9) Le taux de chômage en France/élevé/le taux de chômage aux Etats-Unis (plus)
(10) La France/étendue/les Etats-Unis (moins)
(11) Paris/pollué/New-York (aussi)
(12) L'histoire américaine/n'est pas intéressante/l'histoire de France (aussi)

Score: . . . × 5

D. SUPERLATIVE OF ADJECTIVES

a) Translate the following into French.

(1) The southwest is the hottest region in France.
(2) Baseball is the most popular sport in the United States.
(3) Dolphins are the most intelligent animals in the world.
(4) He is the most famous actor in France.

(5) French highways are the most expensive in Europe.
(6) German cars are the most solid and the fastest.
(7) Unemployment is the most serious problem at the moment.
(8) Traffic and strikes are the worst problems for Parisians.
(9) German grammar is perhaps the most difficult of all.
(10) Chartres cathedral is probably the most beautiful in France.
(11) Some people don't have the slightest desire to learn foreign languages.
(12) The most important thing is to be in good health.

Score:... × 5

4. ADVERBS

a) Make the corresponding adverb from these adjectives.

gentil	lent	violent
absolu	bon	récent
simple	meilleur	bruyant
vrai	bref	savant
pauvre	mauvais	suffisant
sale	gai	aimable
final	nouveau	souple
énorme	précis	libre
prudent	fou	heureux
évident	franc	léger
aveugle	commun	dernier
brillant	doux	cruel

Score: . . . × 5

b) Translate the following sentences into French.

(1) There is too much sun: I can't see clearly.
(2) The boss refused point blank to talk to the employees.
(3) Venice smells bad in summer.
(4) France isn't near the United States, and it costs a lot to fly to Paris.
(5) You must work very hard if you want to speak French fluently.
(6) They were talking, but they stopped short when I came in.
(7) The children don't like him, because he speaks gruffly to them.
(8) She didn't seem sick: she spoke very cheerfully on the phone.
(9) She always speaks happily of the past.
(10) I paid a lot for this radio, and it doesn't seem to work!
(11) She wanted to be an opera singer, but unfortunately she sings off key.
(12) The teacher spoke sternly to the children and they listened attentively.

Score: . . . × 5

c) Position of adverbs: put the adverbs given in parentheses into their correct position in the sentence.

(1) Je n'aime pas les gens qui parlent d'argent. (toujours)
(2) Les Français conduisent en ville. (dangereusement)
(3) Elle parle anglais et italien. (couramment)
(4) Vous êtes allée en France? (déjà)
(5) J'ai voyagé, mais je préfère rester chez moi. (beaucoup, maintenant)
(6) J'ai besoin de prendre des vacances. (vraiment)
(7) Je l'ai rencontrée mais je ne lui ai pas parlé. (souvent, encore)
(8) Elle est là?—Non, elle est partie! (encore, enfin)
(9) Les Français parlent de politique. (toujours, beaucoup)
(10) Nous avons attendu sa lettre. Il nous a écrit. (longtemps, enfin)

Score: . . . × 10

d) Comparative and superlative of adverbs: in each case, make the two sentences given into a single sentence, as in the model and using the word in parentheses.

J'y vais une fois par an. Avant, j'y allais quatre fois par an. (souvent)
J'y vais moins souvent qu'avant.

(1) Autrefois on pouvait rouler à 100 km/heure sur cette route. Maintenant, on ne peut rouler qu'à 80 km/heure. (vite)
(2) Il y a quelques années, nous voyions nos amis français tous les ans. Maintenant, nous les voyons tous les deux ou trois ans seulement. (rarement)
(3) Elle habite à un quart d'heure du centre-ville. Nous, nous habitons à une demi-heure du centre-ville. (loin)
(4) Elle parle anglais couramment. Il parle anglais sans faire de fautes. (bien)
(5) Elle écrit à ses parents tous les jours. Son frère leur écrit une fois par semaine. (souvent)
(6) La librairie ferme à sept heures et demie. La pharmacie ferme à huit heures. (tard)
(7) Quinze jours à St Tropez coûtent vingt mille francs. Un mois en Bretagne coûte vingt mille francs. (cher)
(8) Nous sommes montés à 1200 mètres. Nos amis sont montés jusqu'à 1600 mètres. (haut)
(9) Il a réussi son examen sans réviser beaucoup. J'ai réussi mon examen mais j'ai révisé pendant des mois. (facilement)
(10) Quand elles sont rentrées hier soir, j'ai entendu Marie, mais je n'ai pas entendu Claire. (doucement)

Score: . . . × 10

e) **Comparative and superlative of adverbs: translate the following sentences into French, using the comparative or superlative given in parentheses.**

  (1) I like math better than French. (mieux)
  (2) Japanese cars cost less than German cars. (moins)
  (3) I speak French better than German. (mieux)
  (4) I like Italian food less than French food. (moins)
  (5) Nowadays children watch television more than before. (plus)
  (6) Summer is the season I like the most. (le plus)
  (7) Provence is the region of France I know best. (le mieux)
  (8) Last year, the state of the economy was bad, but this year it's going from bad to worse. (de mal en pis)
  (9) I know Paris and Rome well: Madrid is the capital I know the least. (le moins).
  (10) Before, people used to go to the theater a lot, but now they go out less and they watch television more. (beaucoup, moins, plus)
  (11) She's the one who suffered the most when her father left home. (le plus)
  (12) I enjoyed myself most when we went to Spain on vacation. (le plus)
  (13) The suspect must be found as soon as possible. (aussi . . . que possible)
  (14) Paris is a very tiring city: I go there as rarely as possible. (aussi . . . que possible)
  (15) Drivers should drink as little as possible and drive as carefully as possible. (aussi . . . que possible)

Score: . . . × 2

5. PRONOUNS AND CORRESPONDING ADJECTIVES

A. DEMONSTRATIVES

a) **Complete the following sentences with** *ce*, *cet*, *cette*, **or** *ces*.

(1) ..... ordinateur est plus moderne, mais ..... machine à traitement de texte est moins chère.

(2) ..... livre vaut vraiment la peine d'être lu.

(3) ..... été, je vais faire un stage dans une société américaine.

(4) ..... enfants apprennent le français depuis l'école primaire.

(5) Je n'aime pas beaucoup ..... homme-là; ..... genre de gens ne m'intéresse pas.

(6) Nous avons choisi ..... hôtel, en fin de compte, car il est beaucoup moins cher que ..... pension de famille.

(7) Rouen, Auxerre, Quimper, Dijon: toutes ..... villes de province ont des zones piétonnes.

(8) ..... haricots verts sont vraiment délicieux!—Oui, je les ai cueillis ..... après-midi dans le jardin.

(9) ..... gens ne parlent pas un mot de français: c'est pour ça qu'ils ne comprennent pas ..... pancarte.

(10) ..... aéroport n'est plus assez grand pour un si grand nombre de voyageurs.

(11) ..... hommes d'affaires prennent ..... avion toutes les semaines.

(12) Je n'ai pas vu ..... ami depuis longtemps—heureusement, il doit venir nous voir ..... hiver.

(13) ..... animaux ont l'air malheureux. C'est sans doute parce que leur cage n'est pas assez grande.

Score: ... × 5 ◯

b) **Fill in the blanks using** *celui, celle, ceux,* **or** *celles,* **as in the example provided.**

Je préfère mon ordinateur à . . . . . de Jean-Claude.

Je préfère mon ordinateur à celui de Jean-Claude.

    (1) Maintenant, c'est le métro parisien qui est plus moderne que . . . . . de New-York.

    (2) Nous avons déjà choisi l'école de notre fils, mais pas . . . . . de notre fille.

    (3) Dans les pays pauvres, les problèmes des enfants sont encore plus urgents que . . . . . des adultes.

    (4) Notre maison vaut moins cher que . . . . . de nos voisins.

    (5) Les résultats du brevet sont excellents cette année, tandis que . . . . . du baccalauréat sont très décevants.

    (6) Le climat du Nord de la France ressemble beaucoup à . . . . . de la Nouvelle Angleterre.

    (7) D'après les statistiques, l'espérance de vie des hommes est plus courte que . . . . des femmes.

    (8) Les parcs newyorkais sont moins nombreux et moins grands que . . . . . de la capitale française.

    (9) Je n'ai jamais perdu les clefs de mon appartement, mais je perds souvent . . . . . de ma voiture.

    (10) Vous avez vu des expositions pendant votre séjour à Paris?— Oui, j'ai vu . . . . . du Musée d'Orsay, qui était excellente.

Score: . . . × 10   ◯

c) *Ce, il, elle,* **or** *ça*? **Translate the following sentences into French, taking care to avoid a literal translation.**

    (1) He is a very good doctor, very gentle and calm.

    (2) Do you like Polish jokes?—No, I must confess don't find them very funny.

    (3) Some friends have invited me to go to Norway with them, but it doesn't tempt me.

    (4) At his age, it is preferable to wait a little before getting married!

    (5) You enjoy skiing I bet?—Yes, I love it.

    (6) His life? It's like a novel!

    (7) It is very hard to find somewhere to live in Paris nowadays.

    (8) Do you like the car I just bought?—Yes, it's really beautiful!

    (9) Eat, it will give you strength!

    (10) Do you know the Florets?—Yes, they are friends of mine.

    (11) Do you speak German?—Oh no, it's too difficult for me!

    (12) Do you mind if I open the window?

    (13) It's better to avoid the Côte d'Azur in August: it's too crowded.

    (14) She is a very conscientious teacher, but she has a few discipline problems.

(15) This letter must be answered as soon as possible: it is very important.
(16) I don't like their house: it's too small.
(17) He has a good job: he's an engineer in a big multinational company.
(18) It is late: let's go or we'll miss the train.
(19) He's an excellent sales manager: profits have gone up since his arrival.
(20) They are good administrators, but they aren't very good businessmen.

Score: . . . × 10

B. INDEFINITE ADJECTIVES AND PRONOUNS

a) Translate the following sentences into French.

(1) Each passenger is checked at customs.
(2) He has made several mistakes in the exercise.
(3) He phoned me a few days ago.
(4) He met with such problems that he didn't go on.
(5) Do you know the people who are here today?—Some, not all of them.
(6) I see my parents every month.
(7) We need someone very competent.
(8) What did he tell you?—Nothing very interesting.
(9) There are thirty pupils in the class, but several of them are sick.
(10) I saw the principal and no one else.
(11) If you can't help me, I'll ask someone else.
(12) Do you have many American friends?—I have a few.
(13) I liked this novel but I have read others that weren't as good.
(14) I love these apples!—Have a few!
(15) No one knows where she is.
(16) I was there. I heard everything.
(17) I waited, but I didn't see anyone.
(18) I'm not hungry, I don't want to eat anything.
(19) She reads all the Sunday papers every week.
(20) I haven't seen any of his films.—I have seen some of them, but not many.

Score: . . . × 10

b) **Translate the following sentences into French, using the indefinite pronoun *on*.**

 (1) In France, people drink wine and eat snails.
 (2) At the beginning she's a little strange, but after a while you get used to her.
 (3) Someone knocked on the door but I didn't answer.
 (4) I was told to wait.
 (5) They were asked to come back later.
 (6) Shall we go to the movies or shall we stay home?
 (7) If you go to that clinic, you'll be very well taken care of.
 (8) You should never despair.
 (9) English spoken here.
 (10) You never know, we might be asked to testify.

Score: . . . × 10

C. INTERROGATIVE AND EXCLAMATORY PRONOUNS

a) **Here are the answers, but what are the corresponding questions?** (For many answers you can invent a number of questions.)

Example:

  A. J'ai le lundi et le mardi libres.
  Q. Quels jours as-tu de libres?

 (1) Je préfère les rouges.
 (2) J'ai acheté la Volvo.
 (3) Je suis né en janvier.
 (4) J'y vais le samedi et le dimanche.
 (5) Je suis ingénieur électronicien.
 (6) Quinze ans.
 (7) Paris, Lyon, et Marseille.
 (8) A l'hôtel de la Plage.
 (9) Je préfère le tennis et la natation.
 (10) C'est Paris.

Score: . . . × 10

b) Complete the following sentences with one of the words below:

quel(le)(s), ce qui, ce que, qu'est-ce que, qu'est-ce qui

(1) . . . . . accidents terribles! Il faut limiter la vitesse sur les routes!

(2) . . . . . vous préférez lire? Des romans ou des biographies?

(3) . . . . . ne va pas? Vous êtes malade?

(4) . . . . . est important, c'est de ne pas perdre espoir.

(5) J'ai cherché à savoir . . . . . s'était passé, mais il est difficile d'obtenir des informations.

(6) . . . . . tout le monde espère, c'est que la situation économique va s'améliorer.

(7) . . . . . vous plaît le plus? La France ou l'Italie?

(8) Il ne sait jamais . . . . . il veut. Il est incapable de prendre une décision.

(9) . . . . . bonnes nouvelles! Je suis ravi que tu aies réussi ton examen et ton permis de conduire!

(10) J'aime beaucoup le Japon . . . . . . pays raffiné!

Score: . . . × 10 ◯

c) Fill in the blanks in these sentences, using the appropriate form of *lequel* or *qui*.

(1) C'est la voisine, à . . . . . j'ai parlé hier, qui m'a renseigné.

(2) . . . . . de ces bicyclettes convient le mieux à un enfant de cet âge?

(3) Nous avons décidé d'acheter un ordinateur, mais nous ne savons pas . . . . . choisir.

(4) . . . . . trouvez-vous les plus jolis? Les villages français ou les petites villes américaines?

(5) Plusieurs villes ont été touchées par les bombardements, mais on ne sait pas encore . . . . .

(6) Dans . . . . . de ces maisons habite la famille Destouches?

(7) . . . . . de ces personnes avez-vous parlé l'autre jour?

(8) . . . . . de ces hommes vous êtes-vous adressé?

(9) Je n'ai pas très bien compris à . . . . . il faisait allusion.

(10) L'ami à . . . . . j'ai prêté notre appartement en Bretagne doit revenir demain.

Score: . . . × 10 ◯

d) **Translate the following sentences into French, using** *qui*, *que*, *quoi*, *ce qui*, *ce que*, **as appropriate.**

(1) Nobody knows the man who was elected president.
(2) I'm the man whom the workers chose to represent them.
(3) I don't know who he is. I've never seen him.
(4) I can't remember all the countries which I visited, but I've often been to France.
(5) There are lots of people who go abroad on vacation nowadays.
(6) That's the picture which I showed you in the local paper a few days ago.
(7) What did you put the passports in?
(8) Do you like the people you work for?
(9) The book which he wrote has not been published yet.
(10) Who are you going for vacation with this year?
(11) What do you think about during those long trips on the highway?
(12) What did you pay with when you bought the theater tickets?
(13) Tell me what you need and I'll go get it.
(14) I spent a year in France, which helped me a lot in my studies.
(15) He told me he was going to go live in Paris, which I already knew.
(16) The government has adopted some measures which are very unpopular.
(17) I don't know what happened. She left without saying a word.
(18) Nobody understands what she says. She speaks with a very strong accent.
(19) What is important is to be well informed about the situation.
(20) He talks about cars and sports all the time, which bores me terribly.

Score: . . . × 25 ◯

D. PERSONAL PRONOUNS

a) Replace the noun in italics with the appropriate object pronoun, as in the examples.

Q. J'aime voir jouer *les gamins*.
A. J'aime les voir jouer.
Q. J'ai parlé à *Marc*.
A. Je lui ai parlé.

(1) Je ne trouve pas *mon dossier*.
(2) J'admire beaucoup *la culture française*.
(3) J'ai donné mon adresse à *mes amis de Chicago*.
(4) Les enfants ont toujours beaucoup de questions à poser à *leurs parents*.
(5) Hier, j'ai cherché *mes lunettes* partout.
(6) Tu devrais téléphoner à *ton père* un peu plus souvent.

(7) Vous parlez à *vos enfants* en quelle langue, anglais ou français?

(8) J'espère voir *mes collègues* américains lors de leur passage à Paris.

(9) Le ministre des finances a expliqué les nouvelles mesures économiques au *grand public*.

(10) Tu ne devrais jamais prêter ta voiture à *tes amis*. C'est trop dangereux.

Score: . . . × 10

b) Translate the following sentences into French, paying particular attention to the order of the pronouns.

(1) She gives it to them. (l'argent)

(2) He explains them to us.

(3) I'm going to show it to you. (la bague)

(4) They will ask you for it. (la facture)

(5) Take it to her! (la lettre)

(6) Send them to us!

(7) He doesn't want to sell it to us. (la table)

(8) Lend it to her! (le vélo)

(9) She buys them for us.

(10) I'll give it back to you next week. (la cassette)

Score: . . . × 10

c) Complete the following sentences using *en* or *y*.

(1) Si vous voulez des précisions, je peux vous. . . . . donner.

(2) J'adore la France, j' . . . . . vais plusieurs fois par an.

(3) Je suis très attachée à mon enfance: je n' . . . . . parle pas beaucoup, mais j' . . . . . pense souvent.

(4) Laissons la voiture ici: nous n' . . . . . avons pas besoin, le théâtre est tout près.

(5) Je pense sérieusement aller m'installer aux Etats-Unis: j' . . . . . ai envie depuis longtemps.

(6) C'est ma mère qui ma donné ce vase: fais- . . . . . attention, j' . . . . . tiens beaucoup.

(7) Tu as réussi à trouver un appartement, finalement? -Oui, j' . . . . . suis finalement arrivé, mais ça n'a pas été simple!

(8) Tu veux que je te prête mes livres de français? Je ne m' . . . . . suis jamais servi.

(9) Tu te rappelles le week-end que nous avons passé à Boston?—Oui, je m' . . . . . souviens très bien.

(10) Ne t'inquiète pas pour les billets: je m' . . . . . occupe!

Score: . . . × 10

6. VERBS

A. REGULAR CONJUGATIONS

a) Complete the following sentences by putting the verbs in parentheses into the present tense.

(1) Ils (décider) toujours de leurs vacances au dernier moment.
(2) En été nous (jouer) au tennis le plus souvent possible.
(3) Comment (oser)-vous dire une chose pareille?
(4) Elle (grossir) chaque fois qu'elle a des ennuis.
(5) Je te (rendre) ta machine à écrire: je n'en ai plus besoin.
(6) Chaque année au printemps, nous (choisir) d'aller nous reposer dans un endroit calme.
(7) De nos jours, la plupart des gens se (nourrir) très mal.
(8) Parlez plus fort: il n' (entendre) pas très bien.
(9) On dit souvent que la musique (adoucir) les mœurs.
(10) Trop souvent nous (démolir) de vieilles maisons pour ensuite le regretter.

Score: . . . × 10 ⃝

b) Put the following verbs into the imperfect, future, and conditional, in the *je*, *nous*, and *ils* forms, as in the example given.

téléphoner

IMPERFECT	*FUTURE*	*CONDITIONAL*
je téléphonais	je téléphonerai	je téléphonerais
nous téléphonions	nous téléphonerons	nous téléphonerions
ils téléphonaient	ils téléphoneront	ils téléphoneraient

(1) entrer
(2) entendre
(3) descendre
(4) saisir
(5) réfléchir

(6) rendre
(7) tomber
(8) attendre
(9) rougir

Score: . . . × 10 ⃝

231

c) Put the verbs in parentheses into the present subjunctive.

(1) Il faut absolument que je (finir) mon travail avant de sortir ce soir.

(2) Je préférerais que vous (choisir) la date et l'heure vous-même.

(3) Elle veut que nous (vendre) la voiture pour en acheter une autre, plus grande.

(4) Il se peut qu'elles (arriver) en retard demain, à cause de la circulation.

(5) Le spectacle a beaucoup de succès. Il n'est pas rare que la salle (se remplir) en cinq minutes.

(6) Il est possible que nous (rentrer) de vacances un peu plus tôt, afin d'éviter les embouteillages sur les routes.

(7) J'ai mis la radio un peu plus fort, pour que vous (entendre) mieux.

(8) J'aimerais vous voir un peu plus longtemps, pour que vous me (fournir) tous les détails concernant votre plan.

(9) Je suis tout prêt à donner mon accord, pourvu que vous ne (dépasser) pas le budget fixe.

(10) Mon père aimerait mieux que nous lui (demander) son avis avant de prendre une décision.

Score: . . . × 10

B. STANDARD SPELLING IRREGULARITIES

a) Conjugate the following verbs in the present indicative, future, and conditional.

(1) avancer
(2) bouger
(3) épeler
(4) projeter
(5) grommeler
(6) nettoyer
(7) achever
(8) emmener
(9) élever
(10) ennuyer

Score: . . . × 10

b) Give the first person singular, and the first and third person plural, of the present indicative, future, and conditional of the following verbs.

- **(1)** célébrer
- **(2)** compléter
- **(3)** protéger
- **(4)** libérer
- **(5)** régler
- **(6)** préférer
- **(7)** récupérer
- **(8)** répéter
- **(9)** suggérer
- **(10)** tolérer

Score: . . . × 10

c) Put the verbs in parentheses into the correct form of the present subjunctive in the following sentences.

- **(1)** Il faut que vous (appeler) votre mère immédiatement: c'est urgent.
- **(2)** Même dans le Midi, il arrive de temps en temps que les routes (geler) l'hiver.
- **(3)** Il est essentiel que les entreprises (employer) le plus de jeunes possible.
- **(4)** Tous les hommes politiques présents ont formulé le désir que nos deux pays (jeter) ensemble les bases d'une coopération future.
- **(5)** Il se pourrait qu'il (racheter) la société Balland, qui est en faillite.
- **(6)** Je crains que le spectacle ne vous (ennuyer) si vous ne comprenez pas tout.
- **(7)** Cela m'étonnerait beaucoup que les autorités (tolérer) cette situation.
- **(8)** Il est souhaitable que vous (régler) ces problèmes au plus tôt.
- **(9)** Il est absolument indispensable qu'à l'avenir, il (gérer) ses finances d'une manière plus rigoureuse.
- **(10)** J'aimerais que quelqu'un me (suggérer) une solution: j'ai tout essayé, sans résultat.

Score: . . . × 10

d) Give the first and third person singular, and the first and third person plural, of the imperfect indicative for the following verbs.

- **(1)** avancer
- **(2)** arranger
- **(3)** menacer
- **(4)** nager
- **(5)** lancer

233

C. AUXILIARIES AND THE FORMATION OF COMPOUND TENSES

a) Give the first person singular and plural of the *passé composé, plus-que-parfait,* and past conditional for the following verbs, paying attention to the ending of the past participle for the verbs conjugated with *être.*

(1) jouer
(2) mentir
(3) défendre
(4) affaiblir
(5) attendre

(6) arriver
(7) descendre
(8) applaudir
(9) rester
(10) monter

Score: . . . × 10

b) Translate the following sentences into French. Take special care with the choice of the auxiliary verb.

(1) She didn't go back to America after her divorce. She stayed in France with her children.
(2) The President and his wife came back very tired from their trip and have gone on vacation to the mountains.
(3) Did you get the baggage out of the trunk?—Yes, and I took it up to the attic.
(4) In France, many young people have left the villages, and some have become deserted.
(5) I'm sorry: my secretary didn't inform me that you had arrived.
(6) Unfortunately, the French skiing champion came down the slope too fast and fell.
(7) Like every fall, the shepherds have come down from the mountains and the farmers have brought the cattle in.
(8) Parisian designers have brought out their spring collections: hems have gone up again this year!
(9) The country hasn't come out of the recession yet, and the government hasn't managed to convince the voters.
(10) As usual this season, film directors from every country have come to the Cannes Film Festival to show their films, and they have answered questions from journalists and critics.

Score: . . . × 5

D. REFLEXIVE VERBS

a) **In the following sentences, put the verbs given in parentheses into the appropriate form of the present indicative. Remember that the reflexive pronoun will also have to be changed.**

(1) Les événements récents (se passer) de tout commentaire.
(2) Nous (se moquer) trop facilement de ce qui est différent de nous.
(3) Vous (s'appeler) comment?
(4) Je (se promener) souvent seul: cela m'aide à réfléchir.
(5) De nos jours, les pères (s'occuper) de plus en plus de leurs enfants.
(6) Le travail, c'est sa drogue: il ne (s'arrêter) jamais!
(7) Tous les grands hôtels de toutes les grandes villes (se ressembler).
(8) Nous (s'attendre) rarement aux malheurs qui nous arrivent.
(9) Pourquoi est-ce que vous (s'inquiéter) toujours pour des choses qui n'en valent pas la peine?
(10) Après plusieurs séjours à Paris, je sais où (se trouver) les meilleurs restaurants.

Score: . . . × 10

b) **Translate the following sentences into French.**

(1) Don't stop!
(2) Apologize immediately!
(3) Enjoy yourselves!
(4) Don't laugh at people's accents!
(5) Let's not get angry! It's not worth it!
(6) Inquire at the tourist bureau.
(7) Don't get mixed up in all that: it's too complicated!
(8) Expect an increase in the interest rate this year.
(9) Never get rid of old things: maybe they will become fashionable again some day!
(10) Let's hurry up, or we'll miss the train!

Score: . . . × 10

c) Put the following sentences into the *passé composé*. Verbs that are not underlined should remain in the present tense.

(1) Pourquoi est-ce que tu *t'endors* pendant ce film? Il est très intéressant!

(2) Dans son troisième roman, il *s'éloigne* de son style habituel.

(3) Les hommes politiques *setrompent* trop souvent en ce qui concerne l'économie.

(4) Les deux hommes d'état ne *se rencontrent* jamais mais ils se parlent très souvent au téléphone.

(5) Nous nous *reposons* bien quand nous allons en Auvergne: c'est une région où il n'y a pas beaucoup de touristes.

(6) Beaucoup d'événements importants et graves *se passent* pendant ce vingtième siècle.

(7) Un très grand nombre de femmes *s'arrêtent* de fumer avant la naissance de leur premier enfant.

(8) En raison des conditions de sécurité insuffisantes, beaucoup d'ouvriers *se blessent* au travail, particulièrement sur les chantiers de construction.

(9) Les autorités concernées ne *s'excusent* même pas auprès des familles des victimes.

(10) Des centaines de lettres *se perdent* pendant la grève des postiers.

Score: . . . × 10 ◯

E. IMPERSONAL VERBS

a) In the following sentences, fill in the blanks with a suitable impersonal verb chosen from the list below.

il fait beau   il y a des nuages   il neige   il y a du verglas
il est six heures   il pleut   il fait nuit   il est inutile   il est difficile
il gèle

(1) (——): les récoltes risquent d'être gravement endommagées.

(2) On voit que l'été s'achéve: (——) de plus en plus tôt!

(3) On va pouvoir faire du ski: (——) dans le Vermont.

(4) Les fermiers craignaient la sécheresse: heureusement, aujourd'hui (——) dans toute la région.

(5) (——): à mon avis, il va sûrement pleuvoir. Prends ton imperméable!

(6) (——): les routes vont être très dangereuses!

(7) S' (——) demain, tu peux faire un pique-nique?

(8) (——): la conférence de presse du Président doit commencer d'une minute à l'autre.

(9) (——) de retrouver du travail lorsqu'on est au chômage depuis plusieurs mois.

(10) (——) d'essayer d'acheter une maison en ce moment: rien ne se vend!

Score: . . . × 10 ⭕

b) Translate the following sentences into English.

(1) It is clear that she doesn't want to talk to me.

(2) They will probably leave right after the lecture.

(3) It seems he's decided to go live in France.

(4) It is possible that the situation might improve, but nobody knows when that will happen.

(5) It is doubtful that he will find another job at his age.

(6) I thought I had the complete collection but I am three copies short.

(7) What happened? I heard a noise but I didn't see the accident.

(8) I still have my memories, and that's all.

(9) It seems to me that nowadays people are more pessimistic than before.

(10) Mrs. Dubois?—Yes, what's it about?

Score: . . . × 10 ⭕

c) Fill in each blank with one of the verbs given (one or two verbs may have to be used more than once).

il faut   il vaut mieux   il suffit   il est difficile   il est vrai
il est facile   il existe   il est impossible

(1) (——) absolument aller voir ce film: c'est génial!

(2) (——) de me demander à la réception, et je viendrai vous chercher.

(3) (——) que l'économie s'est un peu améliorée, mais la situation est encore difficile pour beaucoup de gens.

(4) Vous pouvez essayer d'aller au théâtre sans réserver, mais à mon avis (——) louer vos places à l'avance: c'est une pièce qui a beaucoup de succès.

(5) (——) d'être critique, mais il est beaucoup plus difficile d'être artiste ou créateur.

237

(6) Beaucoup de gens prennent les transports en commun, car (——) de se garer dans le centre de Paris.

(7) (——) d'arrêter de fumer, mais avec de la volonté on y arrive quand même.

(8) Ce n'est vraiment pas compliqué: (——) que le gouvernement accepte de baisser les impôts, et des centaines d'emplois seront sauvés.

(9) (——) encore trop d'inégalités entre pays riches et pays pauvres.

(10) S'(——) interdire de fumer dans tous les établissements publics, nous sommes prêts à le faire, pour le bien de tous.

Score: . . . × 10

F. TENSES

a) Translate the following sentences into French.

(1) What is he doing?—He's coming; he's parking the car.

(2) Many countries are going through a difficult time right now.

(3) Call me tomorrow when you arrive at the office.

(4) The French drink less wine than twenty or thirty years ago.

(5) When I go see her, she always talks about the past.

(6) The manager is busy at the moment: he is talking to his partner on the phone.

(7) Children do not read much these days, because they watch too much television.

(8) I think he is writing his autobiography.

(9) I'll tell him next time I see him.

(10) Every time I'm watching something good on television he wants to watch something else.

Score: . . . × 10

b) Put the verbs in parentheses into the appropriate past tense, *passé composé* or imperfect.

Example: Comme il (faire) froid hier, je ne (sortir) pas.
Comme il faisait froid hier, je ne suis pas sorti(e).

(1) J'(aller) souvent au théâtre quand j' (habiter) près de New-York.

(2) Il y a quelques années, les femmes (occuper) peu de postes de responsabilité et (rester) souvent au foyer.

(3) Quand j' (être) étudiant, je (lire) quelquefois toute la nuit.

(4) Comme il (pleuvoir) très fort, les responsables (annuler) le match.

(5) Quand il me (téléphoner), je (penser) tout de suite à un accident.
(6) Il (réfléchir) à ses problèmes et il ne pas (voir) la voiture arriver.
(7) C'est un homme qui (gagner) beaucoup d'argent, et qui (faire) beaucoup de bien dans sa vie.
(8) Le ministre des transports (prendre) des mesures draconiennes, mais malgré cela le nombre des accidents de la route ne pas (diminuer).
(9) Les gens (parler) tellement fort que je ne pas (entendre) l'annonce faite dans le haut-parleur.
(10) La foule (commencer) à crier dès qu'elle (apercevoir) le cortège.

Score: . . . × 10 ◯

c) Translate the following sentences into French.

(1) When he arrived, I had already gone out.
(2) The postal workers had been on strike for two weeks when they accepted the raise.
(3) I had told her to be careful but she didn't listen to me.
(4) As soon as I get to Paris, I am going to look for work.
(5) He will phone us when he's bought the tickets.
(6) I will get back to work when I have fully recovered.
(7) He has been working in Paris for twenty years.
(8) I lived in an apartment for six years, and then I bought this house.
(9) There have been fewer problems since they built this highway.
(10) He has been teaching at this university since 1991.

Score: . . . × 10 ◯

d) Complete the following sentences by choosing the correct verb form from the ones given in parentheses.

(1) Je (viens/venais/suis venu) de m'endormir lorsqu'un bruit bizarre m'a réveillé.
(2) J'ai l'intention de partir pour les Etats-Unis quand je (passe/passerai/aurai passé) mes examens.
(3) Je viendrai chercher ma robe quand elle (sera/est/était) prête.
(4) Les pourparlers (ont duré/durent/duraient) depuis plus de quinze jours lorsque les participants sont enfin arrivés à un accord.
(5) Je (n'ai/n'avais/n'aurai) pas eu de ses nouvelles depuis plusieurs années lorsque je l'ai rencontré à la gare.

(6) Les choses commenceront à changer lorsque les hommes politiques (comprennent/auront compris/ont compris) que les gens en ont assez.

(7) Ils ont promis qu'ils m'écriraient dès qu'ils (prenaient/avaient pris/auraient pris) une décision.

(8) Il y a plusieurs mois que nous les (avons connus/connaissions/connaissons) mais nous ne savons toujours pas où ils habitent.

(9) J'étais fatiguée parce que je (suis allée/j'étais allée/j'allais) me coucher tard.

(10) Téléphone-moi dès que tu (connais/auras connu/connaîtras) l'heure d'arrivée de ton train.

Score: . . . × 10

G. THE SUBJUNCTIVE

a) **Turn each set of two sentences into one by using *que* + the appropriate form of the subjunctive, as in the examples below.**

Examples: Je suis triste. Elle est partie. Je suis triste qu'elle soit partie.

Tenez-moi au courant régulièrement. Je le souhaite. Je souhaite que vous me teniez au courant régulièrement.

(1) Mes parents sont très contents. J'ai réussi à mes examens.
(2) Elle était désolée. Je donne ma démission.
(3) Je suis très heureux. Vous avez pris cette décision.
(4) J'étais surprise. Ils ne m'ont pas écrit.
(5) Il roule trop vite, et j'ai peur. Il aura un accident.
(6) Je regrette beaucoup. Tu ne peux pas m'accompagner à Paris.
(7) Ils sont étonnés. Tu ne viens pas.
(8) Je vais revenir plus tard. Tu veux?
(9) Ce ne sera pas possible de vous donner une réponse avant la fin du mois. Je le crains.
(10) Dis-moi la vérité. Je préfère ça.

Score: . . . × 10

b) **Using the impersonal verb in parentheses, and the given verb in the appropriate tense and form, complete the statements on the left.**

Examples: Ils sont en retard! (Il faut/se dépêcher!) Ils sont en retard! Il faut qu'ils se dépêchent!

Elles auraient pu régler le problème par téléphone. (Il n'était pas nécessaire / se déranger)

Elles auraient pu régler le problème par téléphone. Il n'était pas nécessaire qu'elles se dérangent.

    (1) Quand es-tu libre? (il est important / se voir au plus vite).

    (2) Mon mari doit aller aux Etats-Unis pour affaires en juin. (il est possible / m' emmener avec lui).

    (3) Je ne l'ai pas vue depuis une semaine. (Il se peut / être partie en vacances).

    (4) La police devrait interroger le concierge. (il est impossible / ne rien voir).

    (5) Ils devaient arriver avant huit heures. (Il est douteux / venir maintenant).

    (6) Tu sais bien que cette idée ne lui plaît pas. (Il est peu probable / réussir à le convaincre).

    (7) Elle a l'air très heureuse à l'université. (Il semble / s'être bien habituée à sa vie d'étudiante).

    (8) C'est un long voyage, et elle est malade. (Il serait préférable / rester chez elle).

    (9) Il ne connaît rien aux voitures. (Il vaudrait mieux/ ne pas acheter une voiture d'occasion).

    (10) J'aurais bien aimé vous voir quand vous étiez en France le mois dernier. (C'est dommage / ne pas me téléphoner).

Score: . . . × 10

c) **Answer the following questions, starting, as in the examples, with the expressions given in parentheses.**

Examples: Ils arrivent demain? (Il n'est pas certain) Il n'est pas certain qu'ils arrivent demain.

Ils ont réussi à avoir des places? (Je doute que) Je doute qu'ils aient réussi à avoir des places.

    (1) A ton avis, ça vaut la peine d'aller voir cette pièce? (ne pas croire que).

    (2) Tu crois qu'elle guérira bientôt? (ne pas penser que).

    (3) Les travaux seront finis avant l'été. (douter que).

    (4) Vous allez en France cette année, vous et votre famille? (ne pas être sûr que)

(5) L'inauguration aura lieu à la date prévue? (il n'est pas certain que)
(6) Selon toi, il sera élu? (il n'est pas évident que).
(7) Vous croyez que le niveau de vie a augmenté depuis une dizaine d'années? (il n'est pas vrai que).
(8) Le ministre a décidé de changer les programmes scolaires? (il semble que).
(9) D'après toi, les Républicains gagneront les élections cette fois-ci? (il n'est pas sûr que).
(10) Il y aura bientôt des élections? (il se pourrait que).

Score: . . . × 10

d) Fill in the blanks in these sentences by choosing the appropriate expression from the list below.

pourvu que   de peur que   sans que   à moins que   bien que   avant que   en attendant que   jusqu'à ce que   à condition que   pour que

(1) Il n'a pas gagné de médaille olympique, (——) il soit le meilleur skieur du monde.
(2) Les blessés sont morts de froid dans la neige, (——) il soit possible de les secourir.
(3) Il aurait fallu un plus grand théâtre, (——) plus de gens puissent voir le spectacle.
(4) Je laisse mes enfants sortir le soir, (——) ils ne rentrent pas trop tard.
(5) Beaucoup de jeunes sont obligés d'habiter chez leurs parents, (——) ils trouvent une maison ou un appartement à louer ou à acheter.
(6) J'ai l'intention de faire le voyage en voiture, (——) il ne fasse trop mauvais temps sur les routes.
(7) On a limité le nombre des spectateurs, (——) des incidents n'éclatent dans le stade.
(8) Je veux bien essayer de faire ce travail, (——) on m'aide un peu.
(9) Il faut absolument que j'arrive en ville (——) les banques ne ferment.
(10) (——) ma voiture soit réparée, je me sers de mon vélo pour aller travailler.

Score: . . . × 10

e) Translate the following sentences into French.

(1) She doesn't think she'll be able to come.
(2) I think I recognize her.
(3) She left without saying goodbye.
(4) She's working on Saturdays to earn some pocket money.
(5) It's better to rest before you go out.
(6) You can still see the play, provided you reserve seats now.
(7) I'd love to go to France but I am afraid I won't understand anything.
(8) He'll have to work very hard if he wants to pass this exam.
(9) I'll put the alarm on so that I won't forget to wake up.
(10) I am sorry I never met him.

Score: . . . × 10

f) In the following sentences, put the verbs in parentheses into the appropriate tense or form.

Examples: Si les amendes étaient plus élevées, il y (avoir) sans doute moins d'accidents. Si les amendes étaient plus élevées, il y aurait sans doute moins d'accidents.

Si tu m'avais prévenu, je (venir) te chercher. Si tu m'avais prévenu, je serais venu te chercher.

(1) S'il y avait moins de chômage, il y (avoir) sans doute moins de problèmes sociaux.
(2) Si j'avais beaucoup d'argent, je (faire) un voyage en Chine.
(3) Si j'avais su, je ne (pas venir).
(4) Si les prix étaient plus raisonnables, nous (aller) plus souvent au restaurant.
(5) S'il ne me (pas aider), je n'aurais jamais réussi à faire ça tout seul.
(6) Si je (pouvoir), je prendrais un mois de vacances par an.
(7) S'il y avait eu moins de circulation, nous ne (pas rater) notre avion.
(8) S'il n'y avait pas eu la grève des chemins de fer, nous (prendre) le train.
(9) Si le conducteur (rouler) moins vite, l'accident ne (pas arriver).
(10) Elle venait de téléphoner pour dire qu'elle (être) sans doute en retard.

Score: . . . × 10

g) **Rewrite the following sentences by putting the main verb into the imperative, as in the examples:**

Nous devons partir maintenant! Partons maintenant!

Tu dois te reposer maintenant! Repose-toi maintenant!

(1) Tu dois leur téléphoner!
(2) Vous devez faire attention!
(3) Nous ne devons pas oublier de prendre les imperméables!
(4) Tu dois nous accompagner!
(5) Vous devez nous prévenir à temps!
(6) Tu dois t'arrêter de fumer au plus vite!
(7) Nous devons nous préparer à sortir!
(8) Tu dois te souvenir de nos dernières vacances!
(9) Vous devez vous adresser aux responsables!
(10) Tu dois nous écrire à ton arrivée!

Score: . . . × 10

H. THE INFINITIVE

a) **Complete the following sentences by choosing the appropriate verb in the infinitive from the list below, and adding *à* or *de* in front of it when necessary.**

Examples: fermer battre le record du monde

Je n'arrive pas——la porte à clef. Je n'arrive pas à fermer la porte à clef.

La semaine prochaine à Tokyo, il va tenter——. La semaine prochaine à Tokyo, il va tenter de battre le record du monde.

sortir conduire habiter voler dire intervenir faire attendre mourir vendre

(1) Après des mois, ils se sont finalement décidés——leur maison.
(2) Le mois dernier, elle a failli——dans un accident de voiture.
(3) Si je voulais, je pourrais prendre des vacances maintenant, mais je préfère——jusqu'à l'été.
(4) Je n'ai jamais eu l'occasion de——en Concorde. Il paraît que c'est très confortable.
(5) Trop souvent, les parents modernes laissent leurs enfants——tout ce qu'ils veulent.
(6) J'ai trop de travail en ce moment: je n'ai pas le temps——.
(7) Les journalistes ont essayé de l'interviewer, mais il n'avait rien——.
(8) Elle s'ennuie: elle n'a pas l'habitude——à la campagne.
(9) La police a décidé——afin d'éviter des violences.
(10) Apprendre——n'est pas une chose facile.

Score: . . . × 10

b) **This time, complete the sentences below by choosing the main verb from the list below, and also the correct preposition, à or *de*, that should follow.**

Example: essaient acceptera

Depuis des années, les pays européens——régler ce problème.

Depuis des années, les pays européens essaient de régler ce problème.

Elle n'——jamais le laisser partir si loin.

Elle n'acceptera jamais de le laisser partir si loin.

chercher a invité a conseillé ai craint s'efforce empêchaient commencent sommes arrivés ont obligé viens

(1) Le docteur lui——aller à la montagne pour sa santé.
(2) Nous lui avons parlé pendant toute une heure, et finalement nous——la convaincre.
(3) Je ne lui ai pas tout dit: j'——l'ennuyer.
(4) Elle——attirer l'attention sur elle en s'habillant d'une manière très excentrique.
(5) Malheureusement, d'après les statistiques, les jeunes——fumer de plus en plus tôt.
(6) Il y avait de nombreux policiers sur les lieux de l'accident: ils——les gens——approcher.
(7) Après la projection du film, le metteur en scène——les spectateurs——lui poser des questions.
(8) Les autorités——tous les automobilistes——porter la ceinture de sécurité.
(9) Je ne peux pas rentrer chez moi: je——me rendre compte que j'avais oublié mes clefs au bureau.
(10) Le gouvernement——aider les jeunes sans emploi.

Score: . . . × 10

c) **Translate the following sentences into French, being careful to avoid literal translations.**

(1) I know how to drive, but I prefer to travel by train.
(2) She spends her time phoning her friends instead of studying for her exams.
(3) He was very sick during the night, so I sent for the doctor.
(4) I would like to help you, but I am busy just now.
(5) He has just finished a film and he is going to start another one.
(6) They didn't understand this exercise: I made them do it again.
(7) I hope to come and see you before leaving for France.
(8) You must have your hair cut; it's too long!—But I don't feel like going to the barber's!

(9) They kept us waiting at the airport for hours without giving any explanations.
(10) I've never eaten at the French restaurant that just opened near here, but I've heard that it is very good.

Score: . . . × 10 ◯

d) Rewrite the following sentences so as to say the same thing, but using the words given in parentheses and a verb in the infinitive, as in the examples.

Examples: Il ne peut pas vivre seul. (incapable) Il est incapable de vivre seul.

C'est un examen très difficile à réussir. (Il est) Il est très difficile de réussir cet examen.

(1) Ce problème est facile à résoudre. (Il est)
(2) Il a travaillé très dur. Il voulait obtenir la meilleure note. (pour)
(3) Il a donné un coup de téléphone important. Ensuite, il est sorti. (avant)
(4) Il est parti. Il n'a pas dit au revoir. (sans)
(5) Apprendre une langue étrangère est très difficile. (Il est)
(6) Ils n'ont pas pris l'autoroute. Ils ont emprunté les petites routes. (au lieu de)
(7) Il joue avec son ordinateur toute la journée. (passer son temps à)
(8) On règle le volume avec cette touche. (servir à)
(9) Elle ne prend pas souvent l'avion. (avoir l'habitude de)
(10) On ne peut pas visiter Paris et ne pas l'aimer (Il est impossible de . . . / . . . sans . . .)

Score: . . . × 10 ◯

e) In each case, transform the two sentences given into a single sentence, as in the examples below. This will involve using a verb in the past infinitive form.

Examples: Il a rencontré le Président. Ensuite, il a fait une déclaration. Après avoir rencontré le Président, il a fait une déclaration.

Elle s'est levée de bonne heure. Ensuite, elle a pris son petit déjeuner. Après s'être levée de bonne heure, elle a pris son petit déjeuner.

Je n'ai pas connu mes grands-parents. Je le regrette beaucoup. Je regrette beaucoup de n'avoir pas connu mes grands-parents.

Elle n'a pas pu venir au mariage de votre fille. Elle s'en excuse. Elle s'excuse de n'avoir pas pu venir au mariage de votre fille.

(1) Il a joué son dernier match. Puis, il a décidé d'abandonner le hockey.
(2) Vous m'avez écoutée très patiemment: je vous en remercie.
(3) Ils ont beaucoup réfléchi. Finalement, ils ont choisi de ne pas porter plainte.
(4) Elle est vraiment désolée: elle n'a pas pu nous aider.
(5) Nous avons beaucoup voyagé il y a quelques années. Ensuite, nous avons préféré nous fixer en France.
(6) Je l'ai rencontré à un dîner l'année dernière. Je m'en souviens.
(7) Elle s'est bien amusée dans sa jeunesse. Après cela, elle a fini par trouver du travail et mener une vie plus calme.
(8) Je n'ai pas pu vous recevoir hier: je m'en excuse.
(9) Les athlètes se sont reposés quelques jours, Après cela, ils ont recommencé leurs séances d'entraînement
(10) Je n'ai jamais étudié la musique. Je le regrette vraiment.

Score: . . . × 10

I. PARTICIPLES

a) First, give the present participle of each of the following verbs. Then, use the adjectives obtained in this way to fill in the blanks in the sentences below, remembering to make them agree, if necessary, with the nouns to which they refer.

amuser décevoir intéresser tenter étonner passionner vivre (se) méfier hésiter

amusant décevant intéressant tentant étonnant passionnant vivant méfiant hésitant

(1) Durant la discussion, plusieurs délégués ont fait des suggestions très——.
(2) Ces gâteaux au chocolat ont l'air très——. J'ai bien envie d'en acheter.
(3) Il me fait rire: ses plaisanteries sont très——.
(4) Ce livre raconte l'aventure——de la conquête de l'Espace.
(5) Je suis allé à hier: c'était une journée agréable, San Francisco et très——.
(6) Sur les marchés français on peut acheter des crevettes——.
(7) Il n'avait pas l'air très sûr de ce qu'il disait: il a répondu d'une voix——.
(8) Elle est devenue très——: elle n'ouvre pas sa porte aux inconnus.

247

   (9) Depuis qu'il a commencé à apprendre le français l'année
         dernière, il a fait des progrès——.
   (10) J'espérais obtenir de meilleurs résultats à mes examens: en
         fait, j'ai obtenu des notes très——.

Score: . . . × 10

**b) Translate the following sentences into French. In each, you
will need to use a present participle.**

   (1) She smiled when she saw herself in the mirror.
   (2) The children were laughing while opening their presents.
   (3) He made a lot of money in the eighties selling houses.
   (4) He succeeded by working very hard and knowing when to
       take risks.
   (5) I often listen to classical music while reading.
   (6) She left the hospital crying.
   (7) She pays for her studies by working part-time as a karate
       instructor.
   (8) Nowadays, many women choose to continue to work while
       bringing up their children.
   (9) He managed to get inside the house by breaking the bath-
       room window.
   (10) You won't get anywhere by losing your temper.

Score: . . . × 10

**c) Fill in the blanks in the sentences below with the
participles/adjectives taken from the list below. Then,
translate the completed sentences into English.**

allongés penchées étendus connue suspendus appréciée assises
couchée accoudée agenouillées

   (1) Les blessés étaient——sur des civières.
   (2) Plusieurs femmes priaient,——dans l'église.
   (3) Des centaines de touristes étaient——sur le sable, en plein
       soleil.
   (4) A la suite d'une forte grippe, elle est restée——quinze jours.
   (5) ——sur leur livre, elles ne l'avaient pas entendu entrer.
   (6) Les alpinistes ont dû rester——dans le vide en attendant du
       secours.

(7) ——à la fenêtre, la jeune femme posait pour le photographe.
(8) Aux heures d'affluence, il n'y a jamais assez de places——
dans les trains.
(9) ——de tous, elle était aussi particulièrement——des enfants.

Score: . . . × 10 ◯

d) Fill in the blank in each sentence with the most suitable verb from the selection given below. Since the missing verbs are given in the infinitive, you will have to put them into the past participle form, which must then agree with the preceding direct object.

Examples: porter rencontrer

C'est la robe que j'ai——au mariage de ma sœur.
C'est la robe que j'ai portée au mariage de ma sœur.

Nous nous sommes——chez un ami commun.
Nous nous sommes rencontrés chez un ami commun.

casser téléphoner voir visiter lire
parler amuser marier déguster faire

(1) Ma femme et moi avons vu un film comique hier soir; nous nous sommes beaucoup——.
(2) Elle s'est——la jambe en faisant du ski: elle a dû rester trois mois dans le plâtre.
(3) Pendant leur séparation, ils se sont——tous les jours.
(4) Anne et sa sœur ne se sont pas——depuis au moins trois ans.
(5) Les deux chefs de gouvernement se sont——longuement hier, pour la première fois depuis la fin de la guerre.
(6) Marie s'était souvent——pourquoi sa sœur ne s'était jamais mariée.
(7) Quels livres avez-vous——dans cette collection?
(8) Combien de voyages d'affaires avez-vous——cette année?
(9) Quels vins avez-vous——pendant votre voyage en Bourgogne?
(10) Parmi les capitales que j'ai——, je crois que Paris est celle que je préfère.

Score: . . . × 10 ◯

J. THE PASSIVE

a) Translate the following sentences into French.

(1) I was bought this dress for my birthday, and I was very pleased with my present.

(2) She gets some pocket money every week.

(3) They were taught French at a very early age.

(4) She was laughed at because of her strange name.

(5) When I was very young, children didn't use to speak unless they were spoken to.

(6) They were left a fortune when their parents died.

(7) I was assured that my passport would be ready the same day. I was told to wait here.

(8) She's very tired and she's been told to rest as much as possible.

(9) He's said to like France a lot and to speak very good French.

(10) English spoken (here).

Score: . . . × 10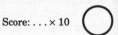

b) Translate the following sentences into English.

(1) On les a vus ensemble au théâtre la semaine dernière.

(2) Je ne sais pas comment elle s'appelle.

(3) Ce vin se boit très froid.

(4) On dit que c'est une très bonne joueuse de tennis.

(5) On parle de lui comme du prochain président.

(6) En France, la viande se mange moins cuite qu'aux Etats-Unis.

(7) On a dû faire venir le docteur en pleine nuit.

(8) On m'a envoyé une lettre de rappel au sujet de mon livre de bibliothèque.

(9) On l'a surpris en train de voler de l'argent à sa société.

(10) On l'a appelée la femme la plus célèbre du monde.

Score: . . . × 10

K. MODAL VERBS: VOULOIR, POUVOIR, DEVOIR, SAVOIR, FALLOIR

a) Choose the appropriate verb in the following sentences.

(1) Le médecin m'a dit que je (voulais / pouvais / devais) absolument prendre trois comprimés par jour.

(2) Elle (veut / doit / peut) être très contente d'avoir réussi (à) tous ses examens.

(3) L'avion (voudrait / devrait / pourrait) arriver à onze heures, mais il aura probablement du retard à cause du brouillard.

(4) C'est quelque chose qui (peut / sait / doit) arriver, mais c'est très rare.

(5) Je me réveille tous les matins avec une migraine épouvantable: je (dois / veux / peux) prendre rendezvous chez le médecin.

(6) Je préfère ne pas sortir: mon mari (peut / doit / veut) m'appeler des Etats-Unis vers sept heures.

(7) Ce n'est pas la peine que j'achète une voiture: je ne (sais / dois / peux) pas encore conduire.

(8) Je n'aime pas beaucoup aller en vacances à la mer, car je ne (sais / veux / peux) pas nager.

(9) J'ai essayé de téléphoner, mais pas de réponse: elle (a su / a dû / a pu) sortir.

(10) Ils auraient pu venir avec nous, (s'ils avaient dû / s'ils avaient pu / s'ils avaient voulu).

Score: . . . × 10 ◯

b) In the text below, fill in each blank with the appropriate verb in the correct tense and form.

vouloir   falloir   pouvoir   savoir   devoir

Some verbs will have to be used more than once.

Anne attend un coup de téléphone de son amie, avec qui elle—— partir en vacances. Elle——appeler vers sept ou huit heures. Elles ne——pas encore où elles——aller, mais il se——qu'elles choisissent l'Espagne. Anne——conduire, et une fois arrivées les deux jeunes filles——louer une voiture pour visiter la région. Elles—— déjà partir ensemble l'année dernière, mais elles n'——pas——, car Anne——acheter une nouvelle voiture.

Score: . . . × 10 ◯

c) **Match the following sentences with those below, paying attention to verb tenses.**

   (1) Elle aurait dû partir plus tôt/
   (2) Si tu ne veux pas finir à l'hôpital/
   (3) J'aurais bien voulu être médecin/
   (4) Elle voudrait bien lui dire la vérité/
   (5) Elle a beaucoup vieilli maintenant/
   (6) Tu pourrais au moins lui téléphoner pour la remercier/
   (7) On aurait pu éviter les grèves/
   (8) S'ils ne m'avaient pas aidé financièrement/
   (9) Vous devriez prendre des vacances plus souvent/
  (10) Finalement ils ont dû vendre leur maison/

si le gouvernement avait cédé aux revendications des ouvriers.
ce serait plus poli!
je n'aurais jamais pu surmonter mes difficultés.
vous avez l'air fatigué.
elle était devenue trop grande pour eux.
elle n'aurait pas raté son train.
tu devrais (t') arrêter de fumer.
mais je n'aurais jamais pu supporter la vue du sang.
mais elle a dû être très belle quand elle était jeune.
mais elle ne sait vraiment pas comment s'y prendre.

Score: . . . × 10

L. CONJUGATION PRACTICE

a) **Conjugate the following verbs in the present indicative.**

(1) manger	(6) vendre
(2) acheter	(7) mettre
(3) appeler	(8) finir
(4) jeter	(9) aller
(5) commencer	(10) faire

Score: . . . × 10

b) **Conjugate the following verbs in the imperfect tense: first and second person singular, and first person plural.**

(1) être	(4) faire
(2) avoir	(5) dire
(3) croire	

Score: . . . × 10

c) **Give the first person singular and plural of the future tense of each of the following verbs.**

(1) travailler	(6) pouvoir
(2) voir	(7) vouloir
(3) aller	(8) savoir
(4) faire	(9) tenir
(5) écrire	(10) venir

Score: . . . × 10 ◯

d) **Give the past participle of the following verbs.**

arriver	dormir
descendre	comprendre
partir	boire
rester	écrire
sortir	recevoir
entrer	devoir
venir	connaître
aller	lire
monter	vivre
revenir	rire

Score: . . . × 5 ◯

e) **Now, conjugate the above verbs in the passé composé.**

Score: . . . × 5 ◯

f) **Put the following verbs into the first person singular and plural of the present and passé composé.**

(1) se lever	(6) se demander
(2) s'amuser	(7) se dépêcher
(3) s'asseoir	(8) se réveiller
(4) se promener	(9) se tromper
(5) s'excuser	(10) s'endormir

Score: . . . × 10 ◯

g) **Conjugate the following verbs in the conditional, present and past.**

falloir (il faut)	devoir
être	préférer
avoir	dire
être aimé	savoir
faire	se souvenir

Score: . . . × 10 ◯

h) **Give the first person singular and plural of the plus-que-parfait of each of the following verbs.**

tomber	naître
partir	trouver
se coucher	revenir
se taire	espérer
sortir	courir

Score: . . . × 10 ◯

i) **Translate these verb forms into French.**

(1) they were playing
(2) I went
(3) they were eating
(4) you would like
(5) we should write
(6) they would have arrived
(7) they should have spoken
(8) I came back
(9) you used to laugh
(10) we are enjoying ourselves
(11) he will be coming
(12) they waited
(13) she is watching
(14) we should work
(15) they will be arriving
(16) they would prefer
(17) we had sat down
(18) they would have finished
(19) you should start
(20) it would have been necessary

Score: . . . × 5 ◯

j) **Give the present subjunctive (first person singular and plural) of the following verbs.**

(1) finir
(2) appeler
(3) croire
(4) commencer
(5) venir

(6) faire
(7) être
(8) avoir
(9) aller
(10) savoir

Score: . . . × 10

k) **Same exercise as above, for the past subjunctive of the following verbs.**

(1) essayer
(2) s'amuser
(3) se laver
(4) ouvrir
(5) mourir

(6) rentrer
(7) avoir
(8) devoir
(9) monter
(10) entendre

Score: . . . × 10

l) **Give the three forms of the imperative for each of these verbs.**

mettre
prendre
boire
manger
appeler

se réveiller
s'habiller
se lever
s'arrêter
se dépêcher

Score: . . . × 10

255

M. VERB CONSTRUCTIONS

a) Translate the following sentences into French.

(1) I waited for him but he didn't come.
(2) I was hoping for a letter but she didn't write.
(3) I paid for my vacation and now I don't have any money left.
(4) I didn't look at your book.
(5) He listens to lots of classical music.
(6) The professor never answers our questions clearly.
(7) She looks a lot like her father.
(8) He plays tennis and his sister plays the piano.
(9) Nowadays, few children obey their parents the way they used to.
(10) I will never forgive him.
(11) She didn't notice my presence.
(12) I wouldn't like to change places with him.
(13) You can use my pen if you want.
(14) I don't remember her at all.
(15) I'm sorry I'm late: I took the wrong bus!
(16) I suspected something but I didn't say anything.
(17) When the man came near the children, they ran away.
(18) I don't trust people who smile too much.
(19) It's not easy to give up tobacco and alcohol.
(20) His sense of humor doesn't appeal to everyone.

Score: . . . × 5

b) Fill in the blanks in the following sentences with the verbs from the list. Put the verbs into the right tense and add the correct preposition.

Examples: voler rêver

Il paraît qu'il——ce stylo en or——son camarade.
Il paraît qu'il a volé ce stylo en or à son camarade.

Elle——sa vie en Amérique, où elle a l'intention d'émigrer.
Elle rêve à sa vie en Amérique, où elle a l'intention d'émigrer.

traiter servir vivre remercier croire s'intéresser féliciter songer parler
dépendre

(1) Ça ne——rien de lui parler: elle n'écoute personne.
(2) Avez-vous déjà——changer de métier?
(3) Il n'a pas besoin de travailler. Il——ses rentes.
(4) J'aimerais beaucoup aller aux Etats-Unis cet été, mais ça——mes parents.
(5) C'est un livre très important, qui——conséquences de la deuxième guerre mondiale.

(6) Beaucoup de gens——fantômes, mais je dois avouer que ce n'est pas mon cas.

(7) N'oublie pas de téléphoner à Pierre et Françoise pour les——leur mariage.

(8) J'ai essayé de l'emmener avec moi au cinéma et au théâtre, et je lui ai prêté des livres, mais en fait elle ne——rien.

(9) Elle m'a téléphoné hier pour me——l'avoir aidée.

(10) Elle me——son mari très souvent mais je ne l'ai jamais vu.

Score: . . . × 10 ◯

c) Reorder correctly the mixed-up sentences below.

(1) Elle / a / avocat / sa sœur / voir / à / aller / conseillé / un / d'.

(2) Je / proposé / lui / de / ai / week-end / passer / un / nous / avec.

(3) Elle / me / toujours / moins / de / dit / vite / conduire.

(4) Il / préféré / maladie / sa famille / cacher / sa / a / à.

(5) Cette / moyens / ne / partir / pas / ont / permis / année / vacances / de / nos / nous / en.

(6) Le / m' / boire / vin / du / a / docteur / et / rouge / de / viande / le / défendu / de / de la / manger.

(7) A / parents / le / emprunté / ai / j' / mes / voiture / leur / week-end / pour.

(8) Aux / reprendre / travail / le / a / grévistes / gouvernement / de / ordonné / le.

(9) Fille / à / j' / promis / l' / ai / ma / emmener / cirque / de / au.

(10) Dit / plusieurs / qu' / on / il / l'argent / son / employeur / de / à / pris / années / pendant / a.

Score: . . . × 10 ◯

7. PREPOSITIONS

a) **Complete the following sentences, using the prepositions listed below. Some prepositions might have to be used more than once.**

dans   au   en   à   à la   chez   jusqu'à   à l'

(1) Je te retrouverai——arrêt d'autobus à huit heures.
(2) Il paraît qu'elle retourne——France trois fois par an.
(3) Elle a passé un an——Paris—— une famille française.
(4) Je préfère voyager——avion: c'est plus rapide!
(5) ——les cinémas américains il est interdit de fumer.
(6) Nous faisons du camping plutôt que de descendre——hôtel: c'est moin cher.
(7) ——France, il n'est pas nécessaire de se déplacer pour aller ——le docteur: le docteur vient vous voir——vous.
(8) Si ça vous arrange, je vous prête ma voiture——la semaine prochaine.
(9) En principe, il devrait arriver——deux heures.
(10) Il fait régulièrement du deux cent——heure avec sa voiture de sport, et un jour il a fait Paris-Lyon——moins de trois heures.
(11) Ils ont déménagé: maintenant, ils habitent——campagne—— quelques kilomètres de Caen,——Normandie.
(12) ——quelle année est-ce que vous êtes allé——vacances avec les Legrand——France?

Score: . . . × 5 ◯

b) **Translate the following sentences into French. Beware of literal translations!**

(1) She has lived in France for five years.
(2) They stayed with us for six weeks.
(3) She's coming to America for three months this summer.
(4) He is very pleased with his new car.
(5) Their living room is very big: it's about 10 yards long and 5 yards wide.
(6) Add a spoonful of milk.
(7) I saw a girl with blue eyes and glasses go in.
(8) There were a lot of people on the bus this morning.
(9) There is nothing interesting in the papers today.
(10) I can't find the teaspoons.

(11) He is the most famous man in France at the moment.
(12) I thought it was already 10 o'clock: my watch is ten minutes fast.
(13) I have never seen it in the movies but I saw it on television the other day.
(14) I haven't seen her since last week.
(15) They say that one child out of five cannot read.
(16) Don't stay out in the sun too long!
(17) I'm always very glad to see her; that's why I have invited her for Christmas.
(18) I speak as a father.
(19) I have lived in the same house for twenty years.
(20) In my opinion, she should take a vacation.

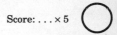

Score: . . . × 5

c) **Fill in the blanks in the following sentences with the appropriate preposition.**

(1) Elle habite——troisième étage.
(2) J'ai acheté une voiture d'occasion——mon frère, pour l'aider dans ses affaires.
(3) ——le mauvais temps, la foule est venue accueillir la vedette à l'aéroport.
(4) Elle a peur de conduire——son accident.
(5) ——exploits des champions d'autrefois, ce record n'a vraiment rien d'extraordinaire.
(6) Elle a eu une réaction difficile——expliquer.
(7) C'est un homme passionnant, et je suis vraiment content——l'avoir rencontré.
(8) Je ne me couche jamais——minuit; je n'arrive pas à m'endormir tôt.
(9) Il est plus prudent de vérifier les pneus——prendre la route.
(10) ——avoir vu la pièce, j'ai eu envie de visiter la France.
(11) Elle a pris un carnet——sa poche et elle a noté le numéro de téléphone.
(12) Le vin est meilleur si on le boit——les verres qui conviennent.
(13) Au cinéma, j'étais assise——quelqu'un——très grand et je n'ai rien vu.
(14) Je conduis——quinze ans, et——ici je n'ai jamais eu d'accident.
(15) —— son père, elle est beaucoup trop jeune——sortir le soir.
(16) Je suis très fâché——elle, car elle m'a parlé——un ton très désagréable.
(17) Les impôts sur le revenu ont baissé——le gouvernement républicain.

(18) L'accident a eu lieu——mes yeux, et malheureusement je n'ai rien pu faire.

(19) Il a——soixante-dix ans, mais il continue——faire beaucoup de sport et——courir le marathon.

(20) J'ai un comprimé à prendre quatre fois——jour.

Score: . . . × 5

d) Translate the above sentences into English.

Score: . . . × 5

8. CONJUNCTIONS

a) Complete the following sentences, using the most suitable conjunction from the list below.

ni ... ni pourtant or car mais
aussi ou ... ou alors toutefois soit ... soit

(1) Elle ne parle pas beaucoup,——elle est très timide.
(2) Elle a la grippe,——elle va travailler quand meâme.
(3) Les Legrand ont été cambriolés dans la nuit.——, on a vu un individu suspect près de la maison hier soir.
(4) Je ne la connais pas très bien.——, j'ai l'impression qu'elle est très intelligente.
(5) Elle n'avait pas l'air très enthousiaste,——n'ai-je pas insisté.
(6) ——ses parents——ses amis n'ont réussi à la convaincre.
(7) Vous pouvez payer——par chèque,——avec votre carte de crédit.
(8) Elle se reposait,——je n'ai pas voulu la déranger.
(9) Il ne peut y avoir que deux raisons à son silence:——elle est malade,——elle ne souhaite pas nous revoir.
(10) Elle s'est perdue en route.——, je lui avais donné des indications très précises.

Score: ... × 10

b) Rewrite the following sentences, using the conjunctions in parentheses, as shown in the examples.

Examples: Elle n'avait pas fini son travail. Elle n'est pas sortie. (comme)
Comme elle n'avait pas fini son travail, elle n'est pas sortie.
Je viendrai te chercher vers 8 heures. Je ne suis pas retenu au bureau. (à moins que)
Je viendrai te chercher vers 8 heures, à moins que je ne sois retenu au bureau.

(1) Ce programme a commencé il y a trois semaines. Depuis, les indices d'écoute n'ont cessé d'augmenter. (depuis que)
(2) Ils vont attendre; quand il aura passé tous ses examens, ils se marieront. (jusqu'à ce que)
(3) Quand tu auras de ses nouvelles, téléphone-moi tout de suite. (aussitôt)
(4) Il n'arrive pas à trouver du travail. Pourtant, il a beaucoup de diplômes. (bien que)
(5) Le gouvernement va adopter de nouvelles mesures. Grâce à celles-ci, le chômage va diminuer. (pour que)

   (6) Demain, nous allons passer la journée à la campagne, s'il ne
       pleut pas. (pourvu que)
   (7) Je préfère ne pas l'inviter. Elle refuserait sûrement, je le
       crains. (de peur que)
   (8) Il va faire son possible pour nous aider. Il me l'a dit. (que)
   (9) Elle est intelligente, mais son frère l'est encore plus. (que)
(10) N'arrivez pas trop tard. Ainsi, nous aurons tout notre temps
       pour visiter l'exposition. (de sorte que)

Score: . . . × 10

9. NUMBERS AND QUANTITY

a) Write the following numbers in full.

4   14   15   40   50   17   19   71   73   79   80   95   99   101
120   123   500   1,312   100,000   789,500

Score: . . . × 5 ◯

b) Complete the following sentences, writing the correct ordinal number in full, as shown in the examples.

Examples: C'est le (1) jour des vacances et il pleut!
C'est le premier jour des vacances et il pleut!

Il y a une place (de) libre au (8) rang, sur la droite.
Il y a une place (de) libre au huitième rang, sur la droite.

- **(1)** C'est la (1) fois que je le vois.
- **(2)** Nous allons partir en France le (5) jour des vacances.
- **(3)** Nous avons organisé une petite fête: c'est son (60) anniversaire.
- **(4)** C'est le printemps! Les (1) fleurs sont apparues dans le jardin.
- **(5)** Ils se sont mariés en 1968: c'est leur (29) anniversaire de mariage.
- **(6)** L'année dernière, on a fêté la (1,000) représentation de la pièce.
- **(7)** Le supermarché a offert des vacances gratuites à sa (100) cliente.
- **(8)** C'est sa (2) crise cardiaque: il devrait faire attention!
- **(9)** C'est à Cannes, dans le Midi de la France, que se sont tenues les (41) Rencontres Cinématographiques.
- **(10)** Il s'est marié tard: il était dans sa (39) année.

Score: . . . × 10 ◯

c) Write the following fractions and arithmetical expressions in full. (Note that French uses a comma instead of a decimal point.)

- **(1)** 2/3
- **(2)** 3/10

- **(6)** 10.4
- **(7)** 13 + 7

(3) 1/20
(4) 1/2
(5) 3.5

(8) 9×4
(9) $48 \div 8$
(10) 9/8

Score: . . . × 10 ◯

d) Translate the following sentences into French.

(1) In the middle, the lake is nearly/almost 4 meters deep.
(2) The living room is 3 meters high and 20 meters long.
(3) This plank is 3 centimeters thick.
(4) It's not very far to my school. We don't have to take the car.
(5) Our house is 2.5 kilometers from downtown.
(6) Her present cost me 200 francs.
(7) How much did you pay for these shoes?
(8) I have seen some strawberries in the market, but they cost 13 francs a kilo. The melons cost 4F50 each.
(9) How much do all these things come to?
(10) In America good wine costs at least $5 a bottle.

Score: . . . × 10 ◯

e) In each case, choose the appropriate expression of quantity and rewrite the entire sentence.

(1) J'habite cette région depuis 10 ans, mais je n'ai jamais vu (trop de / un peu de / autant de) neige!
(2) Depuis quelques mois, je n'ai plus le temps de sortir ou de voir mes amis: j'ai (assez de / trop de / moins de) travail.
(3) (La plupart des / Plus d' / Peu d') enfants aiment le chocolat et les bonbons.
(4) Si vous voulez vivre longtemps, il vaut mieux manger (assez de / plus de / peu de) beurre ou de crème, et ne pas boire (plus de / tellement de / trop de) vin.
(5) (La plupart du / Beaucoup de / Trop de) temps, je prends ma voiture pour aller travailler.
(6) J'ai acheté une paire (de / des) chaussures hier mais malheureusement elles sont trop petites.
(7) Voulez-vous une tasse (de / du) café avant de partir?
(8) J'aime le vin, mais je (le / en) bois peu.
(9) Combien de chocolats est-ce qu'elle a mangés? (Elle a / Elle les a / Elle en a) mangé une douzaine.
(10) J'ai gagné beaucoup d'argent dans ma vie, mais (je l'ai / j'en ai) aussi beaucoup dépensé.

Score: . . . × 10 ◯

10. EXPRESSIONS OF TIME

a) **Write out the following times in full, using the 12-hour clock.**

Examples:
It's 9 a.m. Il est neuf heures du matin.
It's 10 p.m. Il est dix heures du soir.

    (1) It's 1 a.m.   **(6)** It's 11:45 p.m.
    (2) It's 2:15 a.m.   **(7)** It's 12:25 a.m.
    (3) It's 11:50 a.m.   **(8)** It's 4:30 a.m.
    (4) It's 3:37 p.m.   **(9)** It's 8:25 p.m.
    (5) It's 12:06 p.m.   **(10)** It's 9:40 p.m.

Score: . . . × 10

b) **Write out the following times in full, using the 24-hour clock, common in France.**

Examples:
It's 11:12 a.m. Il est onze heures douze.
It's 13:12 p.m. Il est treize heures douze.

    (1) It's 20:13   **(6)** It's 22:19
    (2) It's 14:30   **(7)** It's 6:25
    (3) It's 23:02   **(8)** It's 15:40
    (4) It's 17:15   **(9)** It's 21:58
    (5) It's 18:18   **(10)** It's 13:05

Score: . . . × 10

c) Write the dates mentioned in the following sentences in French, and in full. (Note that, in French, the numerals represent the day first and the month second.)

Examples:

Ils se sont mariés le 1/1/78.
Ils se sont mariés le premier janvier mil neuf cent soixante-dix-huit.

Ils sont revenus de vacances le 19/8.
Ils sont revenus de vacances le dix-neuf août.

   (1) Son anniversaire est le 16/3.
   (2) Il est né le 23/4/1948.
   (3) Je suis arrivée en France le 2/10/1972.
   (4) L'année scolaire commence le 15/9.
   (5) Le traité a été signé le 1/2/1698.
   (6) Le 31/12, en France, on célèbre le Réveillon du Jour de l'An.
   (7) Il a eu cinquante ans le 26/6.
   (8) L'Armistice a été déclarée le 11/11/1918.
   (9) Le 25/12, toute la famille vient déjeuner à la maison.
   (10) Le 14/7, c'est la Fête Nationale en France.

Score: . . . × 10

d) Fill in the blanks in the following sentences, using the appropriate word or phrase from the list below.

les années soixante   au plus tard   en retard   la journée
le lendemain   il y a   une heure passée   la matinée
passer   son temps à   soirée

   (1) J'ai passé———à écrire des lettres.
   (2) Nous avons passé une excellente———au théâtre hier soir.
   (3) Je passerai te voir dans———, je ne sais pas à quelle heure exactement.
   (4) Je suis arrivé———, et j'ai manqué le début du concert.
   (5) Lundi soir, je me suis couché très tard.———je ne me suis pas réveillé pour aller travailler.
   (6) Il faudra arriver à la gare à cinq heures et quart———, si nous ne voulons pas rater le train.
   (7) ———quinze jours, je suis tombée dans l'escalier. Depuis, j'ai mal à la cheville quand je marche.
   (8) Il est———et il n'est toujours pas là. Je me demande ce qui lui est arrivé.
   (9) Elle———lire des magazines au lieu de faire ses devoirs.
   (10) Dans———, j'étais étudiante à Paris. Tout cela semble très loin maintenant!

Score: . . . × 10

11. THE SENTENCE

a) **Make up sentences with the words given below. In each case, as in the examples given, you will have to: put the words in the right order, add some extra words, and put the verbs into the right tense and person.**

Examples:

Nous / manger / restaurant / très bien / hier / italien.
Hier, nous avons très bien mangé dans un restaurant italien.

Demain / robe / acheter / pour / soie / ma sœur / le mariage / aller / blanche / je.
Demain, je vais acheter une robe en soie blanche pour le mariage de ma sœur.

   (1) Maison / je / dont / décider / parler / te / nous / d'acheter.
   (2) Téléphone / mon sac / sonner / poser / à peine / que.
   (3) Pas du tout / il / français / aussi / parler / content / être / notre aide / de.
   (4) Déménager / cet été / aller / nous / peut-être.
   (5) Pays / le passé / dont / être / très riche / c'est.
   (6) Je / avoir / dont / les parents / une amie / maison / le mois dernier / dans le sud de la France / acheter.
   (7) Nombre / affirmer / Le Ministre des Transports / diminuer / d'accidents de la route.
   (8) Cuir / année / acheter / dernière / Espagne / vacances / être / quand / très / sac / beau.
   (9) Je / le bracelet / donner / perdre / mon mari / mon anniversaire / argent.
   (10) Vieux / avoir / disques / je / mais / leur / quand / déménager / vendre / je / les / de jazz.

Score: . . . × 10 ◯

b) **Fill in the blanks in the following sentences with the appropriate words / phrases from the list below.**

ne . . . jaemais   ne . . . rien   ne . . . guère   ni . . . ni   ne . . . aucun(e)
ne . . . pas   ne . . . que   ne . . . personne   ne . . . nulle part   ne . . . plus

   (1) Elle a changé de quartier: elle——habite——près de l'Opéra depuis septembre dernier.
   (2) J'essaie de la contacter depuis quinze jours mais elle—— répond——au téléphone.
   (3) Pas étonnant qu'elle soit si maigre: elle——mange——, ou presque.

(4) Avant son accident, elle voyageait beaucoup, mais maintenant elle——va——.
(5) Pour le moment, nous venons d'arriver dans la région et nous——connaissons——.
(6) Je l'ai rencontrée une ou deux fois et je——la trouve——sympathique.
(7) Elle——a——seize ans mais elle est déjà excellente musicienne.
(8) Mon mari voudrait aller travailler à l'étranger mais je n'ai vraiment——envie de quitter la France.
(9) Je——ai——le temps——l'argent nécessaire pour apprendre à jouer au golf.
(10) ——me demande——de te prêter de l'argent: je n'en ai pas!

Score: . . . × 10 ◯

c) **Put the negations in parentheses correctly into the following sentences, so that the new sentences make sense. In some cases, the negative word will replace a word in the original sentence.**

Examples:

J'aime beaucoup le Bordeaux. (ne . . . pas)
Je n'aime pas beaucoup le Bordeaux.

Elle sort le soir: c'est très dangereux maintenant. (ne . . . plus)
Elle ne sort plus le soir: c'est très dangereux maintenant.

Il y avait du monde dans les grands magasins. (ne . . . personne)
Il n'y avait personne dans les grands magasins.

(1) Moi, j'ai visité Paris. (ne . . . jamais)
(2) Ils sont rentrés aux Etats-Unis. (ne . . . pas encore)
(3) Quelqu'un a téléphoné aujourd'hui. (personne)
(4) J'ai eu un ou deux problèmes. (aucun)
(5) J'aimerais mieux le savoir. (ne . . . pas)
(6) Finalement, j'ai décidé de retourner là-bas. (ne . . . jamais plus)
(7) Je la lui ai donnée. (ne . . . pas)
(8) Il y a quelqu'un chez eux à cette heure-ci. (ne . . . personne)
(9) Elle en a acheté une. (aucune).
(10) Je vois des gens. (ne . . . plus personne)

Score: . . . × 10 ◯

d) Translate the following sentences into French.

    (1) Did you like the movie?——Not much.
    (2) She's going, but I'm not.
    (3) He never talks to anyone.
    (4) We've never gone back there.
    (5) I never saw him or his sister again.
    (6) I never drink wine with lunch.
    (7) Many children never eat anything but burgers and fries.
    (8) The four-day work week? Not a very original idea!
    (9) I didn't understand what he said, did you?—No, neither did I.
    (10) He's happy living in the country, but I'm not.

Score: . . . × 10 ◯

e) Ask the appropriate questions that would elicit the answers below, as in the two examples given. Most of these sentences are very open-ended, so you can ask any questions you like, provided they fit the given answer. Whenever possible, give all three different ways of asking the same question.

Examples:

Answer: J'ai mangé des céréales avec du lait.
Question: Qu'est-ce que tu as mangé au petit déjeuner ce matin?

Answer: Elle est à 300 mètres.
Question: Où se trouve la poste? /
Où est-ce que la poste se trouve? /
Où la poste se trouve-t-elle?

    (1) Il arrive à quinze heures quinze.
    (2) J'ai mal à la tête.
    (3) Oui, très bien, merci. C'était un excellent repas.
    (4) Non, elle est sortie, mais elle va revenir bientôt.
    (5) Non, j'étais trop fatiguée. Je suis restée à la maison.
    (6) Non, une fois tous les deux ans seulement. Le voyage est/coûte trop cher.
    (7) En taxi avec une amie.
    (8) La semaine dernière.
    (9) Non, pas encore. Je vais le lire en vacances.
    (10) Non, mais j'espère faire sa connaissance bientôt.

Score: . . . × 10 ◯

f) Turn the direct questions below into indirect questions, as in the examples given.

Examples:

Ça s'est passé comment? Je ne comprends pas!
Je ne comprends pas comment ça s'est passé!

Il va venir? Demande-lui.
Demande-lui s'il va venir.

   (1) Pourquoi est-ce qu'il n'est jamais revenu? Je ne sais pas!
   (2) Ils doivent se dépêcher. Dis-leur!
   (3) Pourquoi est-ce que les trains ont autant de retard? Je me le demande!
   (4) Où est-ce que l'autobus s'arrête? Montre-lui!
   (5) Comment est-ce qu'on téléphone à l'étranger? Explique-moi!
   (6) Où avez-vous rangé mes livres? Dites-le-moi!
   (7) Comment a-t-il fait pour se casser une jambe? Je ne comprends vraiment pas!
   (8) Quand est-ce que vous avez acheté la maison? Rappelez-moi.
   (9) A quelle heure part le bateau? Je ne sais pas.
 (10) Pourquoi est-ce que vous avez changé d'avis si brusquement? Expliquez-moi.

Score: . . . × 10

g) Translate the following sentences into idiomatic English.

   (1) Tu étais très fatiguée, hein?
   (2) C'est délicieux, non?
   (3) Tu téléphoneras, hein?
   (4) Elle voulait rentrer chez elle, n'est-ce pas?
   (5) Vous avez un frère?—Oui.
   (6) Vous avez entendu parler de Gérard Depardieu?—Oui, bien sûr.
   (7) Vous vous êtes bien amusés?—Non, pas du tout.
   (8) Vous allez venir nous voir l'été prochain?—J'espère.
   (9) Il parle français?—Je ne crois pas.
 (10) Il est professeur.—Elle aussi.

Score: . . . × 10

12. TRANSLATION PROBLEMS

a) Translate the following sentences into French.

(1) American society must cope with today's problems.
(2) I like vacations abroad better.
(3) Prices go up every year.
(4) Children don't respect teachers as much as they used to.
(5) At school, I prefer history and math.
(6) Do they have beautiful children?
(7) Do you drink wine?—No, I hate wine.
(8) I would love to drink some champagne, but champagne is very expensive.
(9) Queen Cleopatra was very beautiful.
(10) Alcohol and disease are responsible for many deaths in that part of the world.

Score: . . . × 10 ◯

b) Fill in the blanks in the following sentences.

(1) De nos jours, les enfants obéissent rarement———leurs parents.
(2) Je lui écris, mais il ne répond jamais———mes lettres.
(3) J'ai vu les Legrand hier: le fils ressemble beaucoup———son père.
(4) Elle joue———tennis régulièrement: c'est pour ça qu'elle est si mince.
(5) Il joue———violon depuis l'âge de 5 ans.
(6) Il est dangereux de se fier———apparences. Elles sont souvent trompeuses.
(7) Je préfère téléphoner———ma famille et mes amis: je n'ai pas le temps d'écrire des lettres.
(8) Le docteur m'a prévenu: si je ne renonce pas———fumer, je ne vivrai pas longtemps.
(9) Il est très difficile pour les enfants de résister———la publicité, surtout à la télévision.
(10) Il te———a dit?
(11) Oui, je———sais depuis longtemps.
(12) Quand j'ai besoin———argent, j'en emprunte———ma sœur. Elle est très généreuse!

(13) Je ne peux rien cacher———mes parents: ils devinent tout!
(14) Demandez des renseignements———cet agent de police.
(15) Autrefois, les femmes se brossaient———cheveux cent fois, matin et soir.
(16) Cette lumière est trop forte: elle———fait mal———yeux.
(17) J'achète toujours des fleurs———ce fleuriste: ses roses sont magnifiques.
(18) Je ne peux plus faire de ski depuis que je———suis cassé———jambe il y a trois ans.
(19) J'ai vu un documentaire sur le transport des animaux, qui a ôté le goût de manger de la viande———beaucoup de spectateurs.
(20) C'est un plaisir de la rencontrer: elle a toujours le sourire———lèvres.

Score: . . . × 10 ◯

c) Translate into French.

(1) I think she'll come tomorrow.
(2) He's the man I saw yesterday at that dinner I told you about.
(3) Have you seen the dress I bought Saturday?
(4) I thought you wanted to stay home.
(5) I hope you're well.
(6) She said she would write.
(7) I'm sure you'll manage.
(8) The meal we had yesterday was delicious.
(9) I suppose you know she won't come back?
(10) That's the coat I want.

Score: . . . × 10 ◯

d) Translate the following sentences into French.

(1) It was a very tiring trip.
(2) I heard them laughing and having a good time.
(3) You should not judge without knowing the truth.
(4) Stop worrying.
(5) I don't like dancing very much.
(6) We enjoy going to the theater.
(7) I'm not used to swimming when it's so cold.
(8) I plan to keep working for as long as possible.
(9) Drinking and driving is not a good idea.
(10) I ended up walking there.
(11) She hasn't finished talking.
(12) He greeted his guests with a smile.
(13) I watched him backing the car up into the wall.
(14) I get used to traveling, although it is very tiring.

(15) Working while bringing up children requires a lot of energy and organization.
(16) Auto racing is a dangerous sport.
(17) It's no use complaining: you should have been more careful.
(18) Do you have an urge to eat out tonight?
(19) Check your tires before taking off in the car.
(20) I'm really not interested in working in a bank.

Score: . . . × 10

e) **Cherchez l'erreur: Find the mistake! There is at least one mistake per sentence below, and there are 15 mistakes in all for you to find. See if you can correct them all!**

(1) Je peux entendre les enfants jouant.
(2) Je préfère écouter à de la musique classique.
(3) Ils peuvent nager depuis trois ans: c'est leur père qui les a appris.
(4) J'ai beaucoup de mal à se réveiller dans le matin.
(5) Sur le samedi, en général, je vais danser.
(6) J'ai cherché partout pour mon stylo mais je ne peux pas le trouver.
(7) Je lui ai écrit plusieurs fois mais il ne répond jamais mes lettres.
(8) J'espère pour une augmentation le prochain mois.
(9) Les transports marchent très mal: en général j'attends pour l'autobus pendant au moins une demi-heure tous les soirs.
(10) J'ai de la chance: j'habite trois kilomètres seulement du bureau.

Score: . . . × 10

f) **In each of the following sentences, decide which is suitable: *il est, elle est,* or *c'est,* and fill in the blanks accordingly.**

Examples:

Tu as vu sa chambre?—Oui,———très petite.
Tu as vu sa chambre?—Oui, elle est trés petite.
———possible que je vienne.
Il est possible que je vienne.

(1) J'ai rencontré sa femme récemment.———très belle.
(2) Il a beaucoup de succès auprès des électeurs, et surtout des électrices.———un très bel homme.
(3) Il inspire confiance à ses malades.———un très bon médecin.
(4) J'adore me promener dans les villes la nuit:———beau!
(5) ———trop tard pour changer d'avis: il faut partir.

273

(6) Pierre nous a invités dans sa maison de campagne pour les vacances:———génial!

(7) En ce moment j'essaie de trouver du travail:———difficile!

(8) J'adore Paris:———une belle ville!

(9) ———facile de trouver un appartement à Paris si on a de l'argent.

(10) Le français,———une langue relativement facile à apprendre.

Score: ... × 10 ◯

g) **Complete the following sentences using the expressions given below and putting the verbs in these phrases into the appropriate tense or person.**

Examples: avoir faim   avoir soif

Arrêtons-nous dans un café: j'———.
Arrêtons-nous dans un café: j'ai soif.
Elle voudrait bien maigrir, mais c'est difficile: elle———toujours———.
Elle voudrait bien maigrir, mais c'est difficile: elle a toujours faim.
avoir peur faire beau avoir ... ans aller mieux avoir tort il y a du vent faire chaud avoir raison il y a des nuages avoir honte

(1) Je l'ai vue hier: elle———beaucoup———maintenant.

(2) Ouvre la fenêtre: il———trop———.

(3) Je ne crois pas que le beau temps va durer:———.

(4) Il veut absolument l'épouser, mais à mon avis il———.

(5) Elle m'assure qu'il n'y a aucun danger, mais j'———qu'elle ne se trompe.

(6) Elle a fait beaucoup de bêtises récemment, et maintenant elle en———.

(7) De nos jours, les jeunes veulent profiter de la vie au maximum, et je trouve qu'ils———bien———.

(8) Elle———presque———, mais elle n'en paraît que 25 ou 30.

(9) J'adorerais habiter dans le Midi de la France, car———y———toujours———.

(10) C'est le temps idéal pour faire de la voile: il fait du soleil et.———

Score: ... × 10 ◯

h) **Translate the following sentences into English.**

(1) J'habite aux Etats-Unis depuis douze mois.

(2) Elle traversait la rue quand l'accident est arrivé.

(3) Je ne me sentais pas très bien hier.

(4) En ce moment elle travaille dans une école.

(5) Je crois qu'il a du mal à trouver un nouveau travail.

(6) Je fais de gros efforts pour finir ce travail le plus vite possible.
(7) On lui demande de faire des sacrifices, et ça ne lui plaît pas.
(8) Vous me traitez de menteur?
(9) Où est-ce que vous passerez vos vacances cette année?
(10) Nous espérons aller en Espagne l'été prochain.

Score: . . . × 10 ◯

i) Translate the following sentences into French.

(1) I don't have any money.
(2) She doesn't want any salad.
(3) He doesn't like anybody.
(4) I don't want any.
(5) She doesn't have any left.
(6) Do you have any?
(7) Do you know any?
(8) Do you want any wine?
(9) Do you need any help?
(10) Have you had any soup?
(11) I'll take any one, I don't care.
(12) Buy any pair of shoes, they're all on sale.
(13) Any mother will understand what I mean.
(14) You can phone me any time, any day. I'll be there.
(15) You can't trust anybody.
(16) I'll go anywhere, it doesn't matter.
(17) Anyone can enter the competition.
(18) She never goes anywhere without her dog.
(19) I saw someone go in, but nobody came out.
(20) I'll do anything to help him.

Score: . . . × 10 ◯

j) Put the following sentences into the negative, as in the examples given.

Examples:

J'ai mangé du poisson. Je n'ai pas mangé de poisson.
Elle a vu quelqu'un. Elle n'a vu personne.

(1) Elle a acheté quelque chose.
(2) J'ai téléphoné à quelqu'un
(3) Elle a gagné de l'argent.
(4) Ils ont du temps libre.
(5) Quelqu'un m'a contacté hier à ce sujet.
(6) Il a tout fait pour réussir.

(7) Ils mangent toujours des bonbons.
(8) C'est simple: elle se plaît partout.
(9) Elle est très sociable: elle parle à tout le monde.
(10) Elle joue encore du violon.

Score: . . . × 10 ◯

k) **Complete the following sentences by translating into French the words given in parentheses, using either a personal pronoun, a possessive adjective (*ton, ta, tes, ses*, etc.) or a possessive pronoun (*le tien, la tienne, les miennes, les siens*, etc.).**

(1) Je ne trouve pas (my) stylo. Tu peux me prêter (yours)?
(2) J'aime beaucoup (your) photos de vacances. (Ours) ne sont pas aussi réussies.
(3) Si seulement (my) enfants travaillaient bien à l'école, comme (yours, familiar form).
(4) Nous avons acheté (our) voiture il y a cinq ans. Depuis combien de temps avez-vous (yours, polite form)?
(5) Il s'occupe de (her) enfants, à elle, comme si c'étaient (his).
(6) (My) robe vient d'un grand magasin. Anne a fait faire (hers).
(7) Monsieur, Je (you) remercie de (your) lettre du 2 avril.
(8) J'ai acheté deux gâteaux: un pour (you, familiar form) et un pour (me).
(9) Vous devriez (you) dépêcher! (Your) train part dans cinq minutes et il faut prendre (your) billets!
(10) Vous avez de la chance: vous (each other) entendez tellement bien, (you, familiar form) et (your, familiar form) frère!

Score: . . . × 10 ◯

l) **Translate the following sentences into French.**

(1) These lawn chairs are very comfortable.
(2) There's going to be a snowstorm.
(3) He likes war films the best.
(4) Have you visited the White House?
(5) I think it's the biggest toy shop in Los Angeles.
(6) My parents' friends are coming this weekend.
(7) I often listen to my brother's tapes when he's away.
(8) We're going to the Dubois's for dinner tonight.
(9) Where is yesterday's paper?
(10) I have to get to the drugstore by six.
(11) I often go to her house.
(12) I like staying home Sundays.
(13) I love reading the Sunday papers in bed.

(14) The mother of one of my mother's friends is going to sell me her car.

(15) If I had lots of money, I would buy a race horse.

(16) She's spending the night at her friend's.

(17) Close the garage door!

(18) I was at my grandmother's when he called.

(19) I found this newspaper article in John's desk.

(20) This year's fashions don't do anything for me.

Score: . . . × 5 ◯

m) Put the verbs in parentheses into the past infinitive, as in the example:

Example:

Nous sommes allés au restaurant après (voir) un film.
Nous sommes allés au restaurant après avoir vu un film.

(1) J'étais très fatiguée hier après (rentrer) du travail.

(2) Il était vraiment de bonne humeur après (recevoir) sa lettre.

(3) Je ne l'ai pas vue depuis au moins dix ans. Je regrette vraiment de la (manquer).

(4) Brigitte a téléphoné ce matin pour nous remercier de l'(inviter).

(5) Je ne me souviens pas du tout de la (rencontrer).

(6) Après (passer) son baccalauréat, elle a l'intention de voyager à l'étranger pendant quelques mois.

(7) Après (se casser) la jambe dans un accident de ski, elle a complètement arrêté de faire du sport.

(8) Après (se consulter), nous avons pris la décision de ne pas donner suite à sa demande.

(9) Après lui (parler) pendant plus d'une heure, j'espère bien la (convaincre) de prendre des vacances.

(10) Ils se sont excusés de nous (déranger) et ils sont partis tout de suite après.

Score: . . . × 10 ◯

n) Translate into English the sentences in the previous exercise.

Score: . . . × 10 ◯

ANSWERS

1. ARTICLES

A. THE DEFINITE ARTICLE

a)

le café	le chauffeur	l'Italie
la région	le tennis	le docteur
la plage	la secrétaire	l'usine
l'été	la chambre	l'odeur
la fin	l'avion	l'Afrique
la radio	les maths	le hall
la plage	la cuisine	l'hôtel
l'uniforme	le magasin	l'automne
l'interview	le Canada	l'Europe
la géographie	les Etats-Unis	l'histoire
les Montagnes Rocheuses	l'homme	l'hôtesse
le fromage	la peau	la nuit
le musée	la lumière	la pluie
la terre	le verre	le côté
la leçon	l'ange	le cœur

b) (1) Au printemps, je dois aller au Canada en voyage d'affaires.
-(2) Il travaille depuis trois ans à l'usine de voitures.-(3) L'été,
nous préférons aller en vacances à la mer.-(4) Le directeur a
emmené les clients au restaurant, et ensuite ils iront à l'Opéra.
-(5) Quand je vais à Paris, je descends toujours à l'hôtel Bristol.
-(6) La société où je travaille se trouve aux Champs-Elysées.
-(7) Je n'ai pas parlé au directeur, j'ai parlé à la secrétaire.
-(8) Autrefois, les touristes allaient manger une soupe à l'oignon
aux Halles; maintenant, ils vont voir des expositions au Centre
Pompidou. -(9) J'ai donné votre adresse à l'homme qui a téléphoné
hier matin.-(10) Il doit venir nous chercher à l'aéroport à l'heure
convenue.-(11) Il a un poste important: c'est le représentant de la
France aux Nations Unies.-(12) Une jeune fille a donné un bouquet au héros de la course.-(13) Leurs enfants ont appris l'anglais
à l'école bilingue de Genève.-(14) Mon frère travaille depuis cinq
ans à l'étranger-(15) Elle est restée à la maison du matin au soir.

c) **(1)** Paris est la capitale de la France.-**(2)** La secrétaire est dans le bureau du directeur, avec le représentant des établissements Boussac.-**(3)** Cette usine est l'une des plus importantes de la région-**(4)** L'industrie automobile japonaise est sans doute la plus solide du monde.-**(5)** Le nombre des chômeurs a beaucoup augmenté ces dernières années.-**(6)** L'unité de l'Europe doit se faire rapidement.-**(7)** Le sommet des états européens doit avoir lieu au début de l'hiver.-**(8)** Le Président a encore souligné l'importance de l'équilibre européen.-**(9)** On espère une baisse de l'inflation et une augmentation du pouvoir d'achat pour la rentrée.-**(10)** Le personnel des aéroports est en grève illimitée.-**(11)** A la demande des habitants de l'île, le stationnement des voitures a été limité à partir de 6 heures du soir.-**(12)** La connaissance de l'anglais est essentielle de nos jours, dans tous les pays du monde, particulièrement dans le domaine du marketing, des affaires, et de la finance.

d) **(1)** La grammaire anglaise est plus facile que la grammaire française.-**(2)** Je n'aime pas le jazz. Je préfère la musique classique.-**(3)** En France, les banques sont ouvertes jusqu'à quatre heures et demie.-**(4)** Je déteste le ski: l'année dernière à Aspen je me suis cassé la jambe le premier jour des vacances!-**(5)** La France et les Etats-Unis ne sont pas toujours d'accord sur l'Afrique. -**(6)** J'adore la cuisine française et le vin français, mais les Français boivent beaucoup de café, et le café me donne mal à la tête.-**(7)** Vous le reconnaîtrez facilement: il a les cheveux blancs, les yeux bleus, et il aura un chapeau sur la tête et un journal à la main.-**(8)** Pauvre Jean-Pierre! Il travaille toujours le samedi. -**(9)** De nos jours, les élèves étudient la politique à l'école. -**(10)** Le président Chirac et le vice-président Gore iront en Hollande le mois prochain.-**(11)** Ils parleront de l'unité européenne.-**(12)** La reine Elisabeth II habite à Buckingham Palace. Le président Clinton habite à la Maison Blanche.

B. THE INDEFINITE ARTICLE

a) **(1)** C'est un très bon docteur/médecin.-**(2)** Son père est professeur, sa mère est architecte.-**(3)** Gérard Depardieu, grand acteur français, était à la télévision hier.-**(4)** Il a accueilli la nouvelle avec un grand courage.-**(5)** Elle a dit des choses surprenantes. -**(6)** Quel désastre! Il y a des centaines de gens sans toit/maison/abri.-**(7)** Quel désordre! Il y a des papiers et des verres vides partout!-**(8)** Ce sont des hommes et des femmes remarquables.-**(9)** J'aimerais des réponses à mes questions.-**(10)** Elle voudrait des enfants, mais il préfère les chiens.

C. THE PARTITIVE ARTICLE

a) **(1)** C'est le week-end: je dois aller chercher de l'argent à la banque.-**(2)** Dans notre groupe, il y avait des Français, des Allemands, plusieurs Italiens, et surtout des Japonais.-**(3)** L'eau minérale coûte presque aussi cher que le vin.-**(4)** Les Français accordent beaucoup d'importance à la bonne cuisine.-**(5)** La bière belge est une des meilleures du monde.-**(6)** Les Allemands boivent surtout de la bière blonde.-**(7)** L'argent ne fait pas le bonheur. -**(8)** Dans certains pays, il vaut mieux ne boire que de l'eau minérale.-**(9)** Le café m'empêche de dormir, alors en général je bois du thé.-**(10)** J'ai besoin de renseignements sur la Côte d'Azur. -**(11)** Je n'ai pas assez de temps pour écrire des lettres. J'ai trop de travail.-**(12)** Je préfère donner des coups de téléphone.

b) **(1)** Elle n'a pas de chance: elle n'a pas eu d'augmentation de salaire.-**(2)** Il n'a pas de problèmes dans son travail.-**(3)** L'école n'organise pas de séjours linguistiques.-**(4)** Elle n'a jamais de retard.-**(5)** Nous n'avons pas de réservation.-**(6)** Il n'y a pas d'avion pour Madrid ce matin.-**(7)** Les pays européens n'ont pas de politique économique commune.-**(8)** Paris n'a pas d'espaces verts. -**(9)** Je n'ai plus d'argent: je ne peux pas prendre de taxi.-**(10)** Le gouvernement n'a pas trouvé de solution au problème de la pollution industrielle.

2. NOUNS

A. GENDER

a)
le boulanger
le bonheur
la Seine
la faim
la bonté
le charme
la puissance
l(e)' uniforme
le théorème
la soif

la personne
le lion
l(a)'école
le musée
le rêve
la grève
la boisson
la gloire
le lycée

la santé
la voix
le communisme
l(e)'écrivain
le dimanche
le pommier
le professeur
l(e)'auteur
la mer

b)
la nation
la soirée
la terre
le tonnerre
la danse
la peur
le verre
la feuille

la victime
la lumière
le monde
la loi
le mois
le zèle
la dent

la cuiller
la cour
l(a)'eau
le médecin
la prison
le phénomène
le portefeuille

B. THE FORMATION OF THE FEMININE

a) une Française

une cousine

un chirurgien (no feminine) or:
une femme chirurgien
un médecin (no feminine) or:
une femme médecin

une étudiante
une cuisinière
une Italienne
une chanteuse
une fille
une sœur
une folle
une héroïne
une maîtresse
une boulangère
une vendeuse
une amie
une belle-mère

une danseuse
une reine
une Allemande
une tourterelle
une fermière
une actrice
une jument
une femme
une prisonnière
une chatte
une institutrice
une jumelle

une comtesse
une vieille
une déesse
une voisine
une pharmacienne
une chienne
une nièce
une directrice
une duchesse
une princesse
une poule

284

C. THE FORMATION OF THE PLURAL

a) les Anglais
les époux
les choix
les gouvernements
les professeurs
les jeux
les fils
les eaux
les journaux
Messieurs
les hommes
les cris
les yeux
les fois

Mesdemoiselles
les choux-fleurs
les luxes
les thés
Mesdames
les hôtels
les prix
les bijoux
les drames
les festivals
les apéritifs
les pays
les os

les travaux
les filles
les cadeaux
les chevaux
les oiseaux
les œufs
les pneus
les chevaux
les trous
les genoux
les radis
les fous
les clefs

D. COLLECTIVE NOUNS/NOUNS THAT ARE PLURAL IN FRENCH AND SINGULAR IN ENGLISH AND VICE VERSA

a) **(1)** La police recherche un homme aperçu près du lieu du crime.
-**(2)** La famille a refusé de répondre aux questions des journalistes.-**(3)** Le bétail a dû être abattu en raison/à cause de la maladie. -**(4)** Les informations/nouvelles sont très inquiétantes en ce moment.-**(5)** Ce pantalon ne me va pas.-**(6)** Son pyjama est trop petit pour lui.-**(7)** Les meubles sont trop grands pour la pièce. -**(8)** Tous les bagages ont été vérifiés à l'aéroport.-**(9)** Le raisin est très cher dans ce pays.-**(10)** Nous passons toujours des vacances formidables quand nous allons en France.-**(11)** Les échecs sont un jeu très difficile.

3. ADJECTIVES

A. AGREEMENT OF ADJECTIVES

a) une plaisanterie amusante
de belles sculptures
mes nouvelles amies
les voitures neuves
des conversations secrètes
de mauvaises nouvelles
des chaussures neuves
une cruelle maladie
la dernière fois
des femmes heureuses
une voix douce
une jeune fille rousse
mon émission favorite
de vieilles maisons
l'histoire ancienne
de l'eau fraîche
une fille gentille
une longue attente

des apparences trompeuses
une robe blanche
une vie très active
une meilleure santé
une attitude positive
des accidents fatals
des enfants normaux
une petite fille
des hommes brutaux
une chance folle
un bel été
un nouvel élève
un vieil hôtel
une écharpe et un manteau verts
une paix et un bonheur complets
une voiture et un appartement
  neufs
un père et une mère inquiets

B. POSITION OF ADJECTIVES

a) **(1)** J'ai acheté un beau tableau.-**(2)** J'ai rencontré mon ancien patron hier.-**(3)** Je suis allé voir un très bon film la semaine dernière.- **(4)** C'est un grand acteur.-**(5)** Je dois écrire à ma chère mère.-**(6)** Pauvre femme! Elle est très malade.-**(7)** C'est le dernier jour des vacances.-**(8)** C'est la seule femme du groupe.-**(9)** Ils habitent dans une maison très chère.-**(10)** C'est une femme grande et belle.-**(11)** J'adore les meubles anciens-**(12)** Elle a un certain goût pour les bijoux chers.-**(13)** C'est une femme très seule. -**(14)** Il y a trop de pays pauvres dans le monde.-**(15)** Tu as vu les belles maisons anciennes dans le vieux quartier?-**(16)** Il a un métier très fatigant.

C. COMPARATIVE OF ADJECTIVES

a) **(1)** L'Amérique est plus peuplée que la France.-**(2)** Le Mont Blanc est moins haut que l'Everest.-**(3)** New-York est plus grand que Paris.-**(4)** Le T.G.V. français est plus rapide que les trains américains.-**(5)** Le métro newyorkais est plus cher que le métro parisien.-**(6)** Les trains américains sont moins confortables que les trains français.-**(7)** Les restaurants américains sont plus chers que les restaurants français.-**(8)** La cuisine française est plus variée que la cuisine américaine.-**(9)** Le taux de chômage en France est plus élevé que le taux de chômage aux Etats-Unis.-**(10)** La France est moins étendue que les Etats-Unis.-**(11)** Paris est aussi pollué que New-York.-**(12)** L'histoire américaine n'est pas aussi intéressante que l'histoire de France.

D. SUPERLATIVE OF ADJECTIVES

a) **(1)** Le sud-ouest est la région la plus chaude de France.
-**(2)** Le baseball est le sport le plus populaire des Etats-Unis.
-**(3)** Les dauphins sont les animaux les plus intelligents du monde.-**(4)** C'est l'acteur le plus célèbre de France.
-**(5)** Les autoroutes françaises sont les plus chères d'Europe.
-**(6)** Les voitures allemandes sont les plus solides et les plus rapides.-**(7)** Le chômage est le problème le plus grave en ce moment.-**(8)** La circulation et les grèves sont les pires problèmes pour les Parisiens.-**(9)** La grammaire allemande est peut-être la plus difficile de toutes.-**(10)** La cathédrale de Chartres est sans doute la plus belle de France.-**(11)** Il y a des gens qui n'ont pas la moindre envie d'apprendre des langues étrangères.-**(12)** La chose la plus importante est d'être en bonne santé.

4. ADVERBS

a)

gentiment	lentement	violemment
absolument	bien	récemment
simplement	mieux	bruyamment
vraiment	brièvement	savamment
pauvrement	mal	suffisamment
salement	gaiement	aimablement
finalement	nouvellement	souplement
énormément	précisément	librement
prudemment	follement	heureusement
évidemment	franchement	légèrement
aveuglément	communément	dernièrement
brillamment	doucement	cruellement

b) **(1)** Il y a trop de soleil: je ne vois pas clair.-**(2)** Le patron a refusé net de parler aux employés.-**(3)** Venise sent mauvais en été.-**(4)** La France n'est pas proche des Etats-Unis, et ça coûte cher d'aller à Paris en avion.-**(5)** Il faut travailler très dur si on veut parler français couramment.-**(6)** Ils étaient en train de parler, mais ils se sont arrêtés court quand je suis entré.-**(7)** Les enfants ne l'aiment pas, parce qu'il leur parle avec colère.-**(8)** Elle n'avait pas l'air malade: elle a parlé très joyeusement/d'une manière/voix très joyeuse au téléphone.-**(9)** Elle parle toujours avec bonheur du passé/du passé avec bonheur.-**(10)** J'ai payé cette radio cher, et elle n'a pas l'air de marcher!-**(11)** Elle voulait être chanteuse d'opéra, mais malheureusement elle chante faux.-**(12)** Le professeur a parlé sévèrement aux enfants et ils ont écouté attentivement.

c) **(1)** Je n'aime pas les gens qui parlent toujours d'argent.-**(2)** Les Français conduisent dangereusement en ville.-**(3)** Elle parle anglais et italien couramment/couramment (l')anglais et (l')italien. -**(4)** Vous êtes déjà allée en France?-**(5)** J'ai beaucoup voyagé, mais maintenant je préfère rester chez moi.-**(6)** J'ai vraiment besoin de prendre des vacances.-**(7)** Je l'ai souvent rencontrée mais je ne lui ai pas encore parlé.-**(8)** Elle est encore là?—Non, elle est enfin partie!-**(9)** Les Français parlent toujours beaucoup de politique.-**(10)** Nous avons attendu longtemps sa lettre/sa lettre longtemps. Il nous a enfin écrit.

d) **(1)** Maintenant, on roule moins vite qu'autrefois.-**(2)** Maintenant, nous les voyons plus rarement qu'il y a quelques années/qu'avant. -**(3)** Nous habitons plus loin qu'elle du centre-ville.-**(4)** Il parle anglais aussi bien qu'elle.-**(5)** Son frère leur écrit moins souvent qu'elle./Elle écrit à ses parents plus souvent que lui.-**(6)** La pharmacie ferme plus tard que la librairie.-**(7)** Quinze jours à St Tropez coûtent aussi cher qu'un mois en Bretagne.-**(8)** Nos amis sont montés plus haut que nous./Nous sommes montés moins haut que nos amis.-**(9)** Il a réussi son examen plus facilement que moi./J'ai réussi mon examen moins facilement que lui.-**(10)** Claire a parlé/parlait plus doucement que Marie./Marie a parlé/parlait moins doucement que Claire.

e) **(1)** J'aime mieux les maths que le français.-**(2)** Les voitures japonaises coûtent moins (cher) que les voitures allemandes.-**(3)** Je parle mieux le français que l'allemand.-**(4)** J'aime moins la cuisine italienne que la cuisine française./la cuisine italienne moins que la cuisine française.-**(5)** De nos jours les enfants regardent la télévision plus qu'avant.-**(6)** L'été est la saison que j'aime le plus.-**(7)** La Provence est la région de France que j'aime le mieux.-**(8)** L'année dernière, l'état de l'économie était mauvais, mais cette année ça va de mal en pis.-**(9)** Je connais bien Paris et Rome: Madrid est la capitale que je connais le moins.-**(10)** Avant, les gens allaient beaucoup au théâtre, mais maintenant ils sortent moins et ils regardent plus la télévision.-**(11)** C'est elle qui a le plus souffert quand son père a quitté la maison./le foyer.-**(12)** Je me suis le plus amusé lorsque nous sommes allés en vacances en Espagne./C'est quand nous sommes allés en vacances en Espagne que je me suis le plus amusé.-**(13)** Il faut trouver le suspect le plus vite possible. -**(14)** Paris est une ville très fatigante: j'y vais aussi rarement que possible.-**(15)** Les automobilistes devraient boire aussi peu que possible et conduire aussi prudemment que possible.

5. PRONOUNS AND CORRESPONDING ADJECTIVES

A. DEMONSTRATIVES

a) (1) Cet ordinateur est plus moderne, mais cette machine à traitement de texte est moins chère.-(2) Ce livre vaut vraiment la peine d'être lu.-(3) Cet été, je vais faire un stage dans une société américaine.-(4) Ces enfants apprennent le français depuis l'école primaire.—(5) Je n'aime pas beaucoup cet homme-là; ce genre de gens ne m'intéresse pas.-(6) Nous avons choisi cet hôtel, en fin de compte, car il est beaucoup moins cher que cette pension de famille.-(7) Rouen, Auxerre, Quimper, Dijon: toutes ces villes de province ont des zones piétonnes.-(8) Ces haricots verts sont vraiment délicieux!-Oui, je les ai cueillis cet après-midi dans le jardin.-(9) Ces gens ne parlent pas un mot de français: c'est pour ça qu'ils ne comprennent pas cette pancarte.-(10) Cet aéroport n'est plus assez grand pour un si grand nombre de voyageurs. -(11) Ces hommes d'affaires prennent cet avion toutes les semaines.-(12) Je n'ai pas vu cet ami depuis longtemps—heureusement, il doit venir nous voir cet hiver.-(13) Ces animaux ont l'air malheureux. C'est sans doute parce que leur cage n'est pas assez grande.

b) (1) Maintenant, c'est le métro parisien qui est plus moderne que celui de New-York.-(2) Nous avons déjà choisi l'école de notre fils, mais pas celle de notre fille.-(3) Dans les pays pauvres, les problèmes des enfants sont encore plus urgents que ceux des adultes.-(4) Notre maison vaut moins cher que celle de nos voisins.-(5) Les résultats du brevet sont excellents cette année, tandis que ceux du baccalauréat sont très décevants.-(6) Le climat du Nord de la France ressemble beaucoup à celui de la Nouvelle Angleterre.-(7) D'après les statistiques, l'espérance de vie des hommes est plus courte que celle des femmes.-(8) Les parcs newyorkais sont moins nombreux et moins grands que ceux de la capitale française.-(9) Je n'ai jamais perdu les clefs de mon appartement, mais je perds souvent celles de ma voiture. -(10) Vous avez vu des expositions pendant votre séjour à Paris?—Oui, j'ai vu celle du Musée d'Orsay, qui était excellente.

ANSWERS

c) **(1)** C'est un très bon docteur, très doux et calme.-**(2)** Vous aimez les blagues polonaises?—Non, je dois avouer que je ne trouve pas ça drôle.-**(3)** Des amis m'ont invitée à aller en Norvège avec eux, mais ça ne me / tente pas / dit rien.-**(4)** A son âge, il est préférable d'attendre un peu avant de se marier!-**(5)** Tu aimes le ski, je crois?—Oui, j'adore ça.-**(6)** Sa vie? C'est comme un roman! / Ça ressemble à un roman!-**(7)** Il est très difficile de trouver quelque part où se loger / à se loger à Paris, de nos jours.- **(8)** Tu aimes la voiture que je viens d'acheter?—Oui, elle est vraiment très belle! -**(9)** Mange, ça te donnera des forces!-**(10)** Tu connais les Floret?— Oui, ce sont des amis à moi.-**(11)** Vous parlez allemand?—Oh non, c'est trop difficile pour moi!-**(12)** Ça ne vous dérange pas que / si j'ouvre la fenêtre?-**(13)** Il vaut mieux éviter la Côte d'Azur en août: il y a trop de monde.-**(14)** C'est une enseignante très consciencieuse, mais elle a quelques problèmes de discipline.-**(15)** Il faut répondre au plus vite à cette lettre: c'est très important. -**(16)** Je n'aime pas leur maison: c'est trop petit. / elle est trop petite.-**(17)** Il a une bonne situation: il est ingénieur dans une grande multinationale.**(18)** Il est tard: partons ou nous allons rater le train.-**(19)** C'est un excellent directeur des ventes: les bénéfices ont augmenté depuis son arrivée.-**(20)** Ce sont de bons administrateurs, mais ce ne sont pas de très bons hommes d'affaires.

B. INDEFINITE ADJECTIVES AND PRONOUNS

a) **(1)** Chaque voyageur est contrôlé à la douane.-**(2)** Il a fait plusieurs fautes dans l'exercice.-**(3)** Il m'a téléphoné il y a quelques jours.-**(4)** Il a rencontré de tels problèmes qu'il n'a pas continué-**(5)** Vous connaissez les gens qui sont ici aujourd'hui?— Certains, pas tous.-**(6)** Je vois mes parents tous les mois.-**(7)** Nous avons besoin de quelqu'un de très compétent.-**(8)** Qu'est-ce qu'il t'a dit?—Rien de très intéressant.-**(9)** Il y a trente élèves dans la classe, mais il y en a plusieurs de malades.-**(10)** J'ai vu le directeur et personne d'autre.-**(11)** Si vous ne pouvez pas m'aider, je demanderai à quelqu'un d'autre.-**(12)** Tu as beaucoup d'amis américains?—J'en ai quelques-uns.-**(13)** Ce roman m'a bien plu, mais j'en ai lu d'autres qui n'étaient pas aussi bons.-**(14)** J'adore ces pommes!—Prends-en quelques-unes!-**(15)** Personne ne sait où elle est.-**(16)** J'étais là. J'ai tout entendu.-**(17)** J'ai attendu, mais je n'ai vu personne.-**(18)** Je n'ai pas faim, je ne veux rien manger. -**(19)** Elle lit tous les journaux du dimanche toutes les semaines. -**(20)** Je n'ai vu aucun de ses films.—(Moi), j'en ai vu certains, mais pas beaucoup.

b) **(1)** En France, on boit du vin et on mange des escargots.-**(2)** Au début elle est un peu bizarre, mais au bout d'un moment on s'habitue à elle.-**(3)** On a frappé à la porte mais je n'ai pas répondu.-**(4)** On m'a dit d'attendre.-**(5)** On leur a demandé de revenir plus tard.-**(6)** On va au cinéma ou on reste à la maison?-**(7)** Si tu vas dans cette clinique, on / s'occupera très bien de toi / te soignera très bien.-**(8)** On ne doit jamais désespérer.-**(9)** Ici on parle anglais.-**(10)** On ne sait jamais, on pourrait nous demander de témoigner.

C. INTERROGATIVE AND EXCLAMATORY PRONOUNS

a) **(1)** Quelles chaussures préférez-vous?-**(2)** Quelle voiture est-ce que tu as achetée.-**(3)** En quel mois est-ce que vous êtes né?-**(4)** Quels jours est-ce que vous allez au golf?-**(5)** Quel est votre métier? / Quelle est votre profession?-**(6)** Quel âge avez-vous? / a votre frère / sœur? etc.-**(7)** Quelles sont les trois villes françaises / les plus importantes? / principales?-**(8)** A / Dans quel hôtel est-ce que vous êtes descendu? / logez? / êtes?-**(9)** Quels sports est-ce vous préférez?-**(10)** Quelle est la capitale de la France?

b) **(1)** Quels accidents terribles! Il faut limiter la vitesse sur les routes!-**(2)** Qu'est-ce que vous préférez lire? Des romans ou des biographies?-**(3)** Qu'est-ce qui ne va pas? Vous êtes malade?-**(4)** Ce qui est important, c'est de ne pas perdre espoir.-**(5)** J'ai cherché à savoir ce qui s'était passé, mais il est difficile d'obtenir des informations.-**(6)** Ce que tout le monde espère, c'est que la situation économique va s'améliorer.-**(7)** Qu'est-ce qui vous plaît le plus? La France ou l'Italie?-**(8)** Il ne sait jamais ce qu'il veut. Il est incapable de prendre une décision.-**(9)** Quelles bonnes nouvelles! Je suis ravi que tu aies réussi ton examen et ton permis de conduire!-**(10)** J'aime beaucoup le Japon. Quel pays raffiné!

c) **(1)** C'est la voisine, à qui j'ai parlé hier, qui m'a renseigné.-**(2)** Laquelle de ces bicyclettes convient le mieux à un enfant de cet âge?-**(3)** Nous avons décidé d'acheter un ordinateur, mais nous ne savons pas lequel choisir.-**(4)** Lesquels trouvez-vous les plus jolis? Les villages français ou les petites villes américaines?-**(5)** Plusieurs villes ont été touchées par les bombardements, mais on ne sait pas encore lesquelles.-**(6)** Dans laquelle de ces maisons habite la famille Destouches?-**(7)** A laquelle de ces personnes avez-vous parlé l'autre jour?-**(8)** Auquel de ces hommes vous êtes-vous adressé?-**(9)** Je n'ai pas très bien compris à qui il faisait allusion.-**(10)** L'ami à qui j'ai prêté notre appartement en Bretagne doit revenir demain.

d) **(1)** Personne ne connaît l'homme qui a été élu président.-**(2)** Je suis l'homme que les travailleurs ont choisi pour les représenter.-

(3) Je ne sais pas qui c'est. Je ne l'ai jamais vu.-(4) Je ne me rappelle pas tous les pays que j'ai visités, mais je suis souvent allé en France.-(5) Il y a beaucoup de gens qui vont en vacances à l'étranger, de nos jours.-(6) C'est la photo que je t'ai montrée dans le journal local il y a quelques jours.-(7) Dans quoi est-ce que tu as mis les passeports?-(8) Tu aimes bien les gens pour qui tu travailles?-(9) Le livre qu'il a écrit n'a pas encore été publié. -(10) Avec qui est-ce que tu vas en vacances cette année?-(11) A quoi est-ce que vous pensez pendant ces longs trajets sur l'autoroute?-(12) Avec quoi est-ce que tu as payé quand tu as acheté les places de théâtre?-(13) Dis-moi de quoi tu as besoin et j'irai le chercher.-(14) J'ai passé une année en France, ce qui m'a beaucoup aidé dans mes études.-(15) Il m'a dit qu'il allait aller habiter à Paris, ce que je savais déjà.-(16) Le gouvernement a adopté des mesures qui sont très impopulaires.-(17) Je ne sais pas ce qui s'est passé. Elle est partie sans dire un mot.-(18) Personne ne comprend ce qu'elle dit. Elle parle avec un très fort accent.-(19) Ce qui est important, c'est d'être bien informó sur la situation.-(20) Il parle tout le temps de voitures et de sport, ce qui m'ennuie terriblement.

D. PERSONAL PRONOUNS

a) (1) Je ne le trouve pas.-(2) Je l'admire beaucoup.-(3) Je leur ai donné mon adresse.-(4) Les enfants ont toujours beaucoup de questions à leur poser.-(5) Hier, je les ai cherchées partout.-(6) Tu devrais lui téléphoner un peu plus souvent.-(7) Vous leur parlez en quelle langue, anglais ou français?-(8) J'espère les voir lors de leur passage à Paris.-(9) Le ministre des finances lui a expliqué les nouvelles mesures économiques.-(10) Tu ne devrais jamais leur prêter ta voiture. C'est trop dangereux.

b) (1) Elle le leur donne.
   (2) Il nous les explique.
   (3) Je vais vous/te la montrer.
   (4) Ils vous/te la demanderont.
   (5) Porte/Portez-la-lui!
   (6) Envoie/Envoyes-les-nous!
   (7) Il ne veut pas nous la vendre.
   (8) Prête/Prêtez-le-lui!
   (9) Elle nous les achète.
   (10) Je vous/te la rendrai la semaine prochaine.

c) (1) Si vous voulez des précisions, je peux vous en donner.
   -(2) J'adore la France, j'y vais plusieurs fois par an.-(3) Je suis très attachée à mon enfance: je n'en parle pas beaucoup, mais j'y pense souvent.-(4) Laissons la voiture ici: nous n'en avons pas besoin, le

théâtre est tout près.-**(5)** Je pense sérieusement aller m'installer aux Etats-Unis: j'en ai envie depuis longtemps.-**(6)** C'est ma mère qui m'a donné ce vase: fais-y attention, j'y tiens beaucoup!-**(7)** Tu as réussi à trouver un appartement, finalement?—Oui, j'y suis finalement arrivé, mais ça n'a pas été simple!-**(8)** Tu veux que je te prête mes livres de français? Je ne m'en suis jamais servi.-**(9)** Tu te rappelles le week-end que nous avons passé à Boston?—Oui, je m'en souviens très bien.-**(10)** Ne t'inquiète pas pour les billets: je m'en occupe!

6. VERBS

A. REGULAR CONJUGATIONS

a) **(1)** Ils décident toujours de leurs vacances au dernier moment. -**(2)** En été nous jouons au tennis le plus souvent possible. -**(3)** Comment osez-vous dire une chose pareille?-**(4)** Elle grossit chaque fois qu'elle a des ennuis.-**(5)** Je te rends ta machine à écrire: je n'en ai plus besoin.-**(6)** Chaque année au printemps, nous choisissons d'aller nous reposer dans un endroit calme.-**(7)** De nos jours, la plupart des gens se nourrissent très mal.-**(8)** Parlez plus fort: il n'entend pas très bien.-**(9)** On dit souvent que la musique adoucit les mœurs.-**(10)** Trop souvent nous démolissons de vieilles maisons pour ensuite le regretter.

	IMPERFECT	FUTURE	CONDITIONAL
b) (1)	j'entrais	j'entrerai	j'entrerais
	nous entrions	nous entrerons	nous entrerions
	ils entraient	ils entreront	ils entreraient
(2)	j'entendais	j'entendrai	j'entendrais
	nous entendions	nous entendrons	nous entendrions
	ils entendaient	ils entendront	ils entendraient
(3)	je descendais	je descendrai	je descendrais
	nous descendions	nous descendrons	nous descendrions
	ils descendaient	ils descendront	ils descendraient
(4)	je saisissais	je saisirai	je saisirais
	nous saisissions	nous saisirons	nous saisirions
	ils saisissaient	ils saisiront	ils saisiraient
(5)	je réfléchissais	je réfléchirai	je réfléchirais
	nous réfléchissions	nous réfléchirons	nous réfléchirions
	ils réfléchissaient	ils réfléchiront	ils réfléchiraient
(6)	je rendais	je rendrai	je rendrais
	nous rendions	nous rendrons	nous rendrions
	ils rendaient	ils rendront	ils rendraient
(7)	je tombais	je tomberai	je tomberais
	nous tombions	nous tomberons	nous tomberions
	ils tombaient	ils tomberont	ils tomberaient
(8)	j'attendais	j'attendrai	j'attendrais
	nous attendions	nous attendrons	nous attendrions
	ils attendaient	ils attendront	ils attendraient
(9)	je rougissais	je rougirai	je rougirais
	nous rougissions	nous rougirons	nous rougirions
	ils rougissaient	ils rougiront	ils rougiraient

c) **(1)** Il faut absolument que je finisse mon travail avant de sortir ce soir.-**(2)** Je préférerais que vous choisissiez la date et l'heure vous-même.-**(3)** Elle veut que nous vendions la voiture pour en acheter une autre, plus grande.-**(4)** Il se peut qu'elles arrivent en retard demain, à cause de la circulation.-**(5)** Le spectacle a beaucoup de succès. Il n'est pas rare que la salle se remplisse en cinq minutes. -**(6)** Il est possible que nous rentrions de vacances un peu plus tôt, afin d'éviter les embouteillages sur les routes.-**(7)** J'ai mis la radio un peu plus fort, pour que vous entendiez mieux.-**(8)** J'aimerais vous voir un peu plus longtemps, pour que vous me fournissiez tous les détails concernant votre plan.-**(9)** Je suis tout prêt à donner mon accord, pourvu que vous ne dépassiez pas le budget fixe. -**(10)** Mon père aimerait mieux que nous lui demandions son avis avant de prendre une décision.

B. STANDARD SPELLING IRREGULARITIES

a) **(1)** j'avance tu avances il/elle avance nous avançons vous avancez ils/elles avancent
j'avancerai tu avanceras il/elle avancera nous avancerons vous avancerez ils/elles avanceront
j'avancerais tu avancerais il/elle avancerait nous avancerions vouz avanceriez ils/elles avanceraient

(2) je bouge tu bouges il/elle bouge nous bougeons vous bougez ils/elles bougent
je bougerai tu bougeras il/elle bougera nous bougerons vous bougerez ils/elles bougeront
je bougerais tu bougerais il/elle bougerait nous bougerions vous bougeriez ils/elles bougeraient

(3) j'épelle tu épelles il/elle épelle nous épelons vous épelez ils/elles épellent
j'epellerai tu épelleras il/elle épellera nous épellerons vous épellerez ils/elles épelleront
j'épellerais tu épellerais il/elle épellerait nous épellerions vous épelleriez ils/elles épelleraient

(4) je projette tu projettes il/elle projette nous projetons vous projetez ils/elles projettent
je projetterai tu projetteras il/elle projettera nous projetterons vous projetterez ils/elles projetteront
je projetterais tu projetterais il/elle projetterait nous projetterions vous projetteriez ils/elles projetteraient

(5) je grommelle tu grommelles il/elle grommelle nous grommelons vous grommelez ils/elles grommellent
je grommellerai tu grommelleras il/elle grommellera nous grommellerons vous grommellerez

ils/elles grommelleront
je grommellerais tu grommellerais il/elle grommellerait
nous grommellerions ils/elles grommelleraient

(6) je nettoie tu nettoies il/elle nettoie nous nettoyons
vous nettoyez ils/elles nettoient
je nettoierai tu nettoieras il/elle nettoiera nous nettoierons
vous nettoierez ils/elles nettoieront
je nettoierais tu nettoierais il/elle nettoierait
nous nettoierions vous nettoieriez ils/elles nettoieraient

(7) j'achève tu achèves il/elle achève nous achevons
vous achevez ils/elles achèvent
j'achèverai tu achèveras il/elle achèvera nous achèverons
vous achèverez ils/elles achèveront
j'achèverais tu achèverais il/elle achèverait
nous achèverions vous achèveriez ils/elles achèveraient

(8) j'emmène tu emmènes il/elle emmène nous emmenons
vous emmenez ils/elles emmènent
j'emmènerai tu emmèneras il/elle emmènera
nous emmènerons vous emmènerez ils/elles emmèneront
j'emmènerais tu emmènerais il/elle emmènerait
nous emmènerions vous emmèneriez
ils/elles emmèneraient

(9) j'élève tu élèves il/elle élève nous élevons vous élevez
ils/elles élèvent
j'élèverai tu élèveras il/elle élèvera nous élèverons
vous élèverez ils/elles élèveront
j'élèverais tu élèverais il/elle élèverait nous élèverions
vous élèveriez ils/elles élèveraient

(10) j'ennuie tu ennuies il/elle ennuie nous ennuyons
vous ennuyez ils/elles ennuient
j'ennuierai tu ennuieras il/elle ennuiera nous ennuierons
vous ennuierez ils/elles ennuieront
j'ennuierais tu ennuierais il/elle ennuierait
nous ennuierions vous ennuieriez ils/elles ennuieraient

b) **(1)** je célèbre nous célébrons ils/elles célèbrent
je célébrerai nous célébrerons ils/elles célébreront
je célébrerais nous célébrerions ils/elles célébreraient

(2) je complète nous complétons ils/elles complètent
je compléterai nous compléterons ils/elles compléteront
je compléterais nous compléterions ils/elles compléteraient

(3) je protège nous protégeons ils/elles protègent
je protégerai nous protégerons ils/elles protégeront
je protégerais nous protégerions ils/elles protégeraient

(4) je libère nous libérons ils/elle libèrent
je libérerai nous libérerons ils/elles libéreront
je libérerais nous libérerions ils/elles libéreraient

(5) je règle nous réglons ils/elles règlent
je réglerai nous réglerons ils/elles régleront
je réglerais nous réglerions ils/elles régleraient

(6) je préfère nous préférons ils/elles préfèrent
je préférerai nous préférerons ils/elles préféreront
je préférerais nous préférerions ils/elles préféreraient

(7) je récupère nous récupérons ils/elles récupèrent
je récupérerai nous récupérerons ils/elles récupéreront
je récupérerais nous récupérerions ils/elles récupéreraient

(8) je répète nous répétons ils/elles répètent
je répéterai nous répéterons ils/elles répéteront
je répéterais nous répéterions ils/elles répéteraient

(9) je suggère nous suggérons ils/elles suggèrent
je suggérerai nous suggérerons ils/elles suggéreront
je suggérerais nous suggérerions ils/elles suggéreraient

(10) je tolère nous tolérons ils/elles tolèrent
je tolérerai nous tolérerons ils/elles toléreront
je tolérerais nous tolérerions ils/elles toléreraient

c) **(1)** appeliez-**(2)** gèlent-**(3)** emploient-**(4)** jettent-**(5)** rachète
-**(6)** ennuie-**(7)** tolèrent-**(8)** régliez-**(9)** gère-**(10)** suggère

d) **(1)** j'avançais il/elle avançait nous avancions
ils/elles avançaient

(2) j'arrangeais il/elle arrangeait nous arrangions
ils/elles arrangeaient

(3) je menaçais il/elle menaçait nous menacions
ils/elles menaçaient

(4) je nageais il/elle nageait nous nagions
ils/elles nageaient

(5) je lançais il/elle lançait nous lancions
ils/elles lançaient

C. AUXILIARIES AND THE FORMATION OF COMPOUND TENSES

a) **(1)** j'ai joué j'avais joué j'aurais joué
nous avons joué nous avions joué nous aurions joué

(2) j'ai menti j'avais menti j'aurais menti
nous avons menti nous avions menti
nous aurions menti

(3) j'ai défendu j'avais défendu j'aurais défendu
nous avons défendu nous avions défendu
nous aurions défendu

(4) j'ai affaibli j'avais affaibli j'aurais affaibli
nous avons affaibli nous avions affaibli
nous aurions affaibli

(5) j'ai attendu j'avais attendu j'aurais attendu
nous avons attendu nous avions attendu
nous aurions attendu

(6) je suis arrivé(e) j'étais arrivé(e) je serais arrivé(e)
nous sommes arrivé(e)s nous étions arrivé(e)s
nous serions arrivé(e)s

(7) j'ai descendu / je suis descendu(e) j'avais descendu/j'étais
descendu(e)
j'aurais descendu / je serais descendu(e)
nous avons descendu / nous sommes descendu(e)s
nous avions descendu / nous étions descendu(e)s
nous aurions descendu / nous serions descendu(e)s

(8) j'ai applaudi j'avais applaudi j'aurais applaudi
nous avons applaudi nous avions applaudi
nous aurions applaudi

(9) je suis resté(e) j'étais resté(e) je serais resté(e)
nous sommes resté(e)s nous étions resté(e)s
nous serions resté(e)s

(10) j'ai monté / je suis monté(e) j'avais monté / j'étais monté(e)
j'aurais monté / je serais monté(e)
nous avons monté / nous sommes monté(e)s
nous avions monté / nous étions monté(e)s
nous aurions monté / nous serions monté(e)s

b) (1) Elle n'est pas retournée en Amérique après son divorce. Elle
est restée en France avec ses enfants.-**(2)** Le président et sa
femme sont revenus très fatigués de leur voyage et sont partis
(allés) en vacances à la montagne.-**(3)** Vous avez sorti les bagages
du coffre?--Oui, et je les ai montés au grenier.-**(4)** En France, beaucoup de jeunes ont quitté les villages, et certains sont devenus
déserts.-**(5)** Je suis désolé: ma secrétaire ne m'a pas prévenu que
vous étiez arrivé(e/s).-**(6)** Malheureusement, le champion de ski
français a descendu la pente trop vite et il est tombé.-**(7)** Comme
chaque automne, les bergers sont descendus des montagnes et les
fermiers ont rentré le bétail.-**(8)** Les couturiers parisiens ont sorti
leurs collections de printemps: les ourlets sont remontés cette
année!-**(9)** Le pays n'est pas encore sorti de la récession, et le gouvernement n'est pas parvenu à convaincre les électeurs.
-**(10)** Comme d'habitude à cette saison, des metteurs en scène de
tous les pays sont venus au Festival de Cannes présenter leurs
films, et ils ont répondu aux questions des journalistes et des
critiques.

D. REFLEXIVE VERBS

a) **(1)** Les événements récents se passent de tout commentaire. -**(2)** Nous nous moquons trop facilement de ce qui est différent de nous.-**(3)** Vous vous appelez comment?-**(4)** Je me promène souvent seul: cela m'aide à réfléchir.-**(5)** De nos jours, les pères s'occupent de plus en plus souvent de leurs enfants.-**(6)** Le travail, c'est sa drogue: il ne s'arrête jamais!-**(7)** Tous les grands hôtels de toutes les grandes villes se ressemblent.-**(8)** Nous nous attendons rarement aux malheurs qui nous arrivent.-**(9)** Pourquoi est-ce que vous vous inquiétez toujours pour des choses qui n'en valent pas la peine?-**(10)** Après plusieurs séjours à Paris, je sais où se trouvent les meilleurs restaurants.

b) **(1)** Ne vous arrêtez pas! / Ne t'arrête pas!-**(2)** Excusez-vous / Excuse-toi immédiatement!-**(3)** Amusez-vous (bien).-**(4)** Ne vous moquez / Ne te moque pas de l'accent des gens!-**(5)** Ne nous mettons pas en colère! Ce n'est pas la peine! / Ça n'en vaut pas la peine!-**(6)** Renseignez-vous / Renseigne-toi au Syndicat d'Initiative / à l'Office du Tourisme.-**(7)** Ne vous mêlez / Ne te mêle pas de tout ça: c'est trop compliqué!-**(8)** Attendez-vous / Attends-toi à une augmentation du taux d'intérêt cette année.-**(9)** Ne vous débarrassez / Ne te débarrasse jamais de(s) vieilles choses: elles redeviendront peut-être à la mode un jour!-**(10)** Dépêchons-nous, ou nous manquerons le train!

c) **(1)** Pourquoi est-ce que tu t'es endormi(e) pendant ce film? Il est très intéressant!-**(2)** Dans son troisième roman, il s'est éloigné de son style habituel.-**(3)** Les hommes politiques se sont trompés trop souvent en ce qui concerne l'économie.-**(4)** Les deux hommes d'état ne se sont jamais rencontrés mais ils se sont parlé très souvent au téléphone.-**(5)** Nous nous sommes bien reposé(e)s quand nous sommes allé(e)s en Auvergne: c'est une région où il n'y a pas beaucoup de touristes.-**(6)** Beaucoup d'événements importants et graves se sont passés pendant ce vingtième siècle.-**(7)** Un très grand nombre de femmes se sont arrêtées de fumer avant la naissance de leur premier enfant.-**(8)** En raison des conditions de sécurité insuffisantes, beaucoup d'ouvriers se sont blessés au travail, particulièrement sur les chantiers de construction.-**(9)** Les autorités concernées ne se sont même pas excusées auprès des familles des victimes.-**(10)** Des centaines de lettres se sont perdues pendant la grève des postiers.

E. IMPERSONAL VERBS

a) (1) Il gèle-(2) Il fait nuit-(3) Il neige-(4) Il pleut-(5) Il y a des nuages-(6) Il y a du verglas-(7) Il fait beau-(8) Il est six heures -(9) Il est difficile-(10) Il est inutile

b) (1) Il est évident qu'elle ne veut pas me parler.-(2) Il est probable qu'ils partiront tout de suite après la conférence.-(3) Il paraît qu'il a décidé d'aller vivre en France.-(4) Il est possible que la situation s'améliore, mais personne ne sait quand cela arrivera.-(5) Il est douteux qu'il trouve un autre emploi à son âge.-(6) Je croyais que j'avais la collection complète mais il me manque trois exemplaires.-(7) Qu'est-ce qui s'est passé? J'ai entendu un bruit mais je n'ai pas vu l'accident.-(8) Il me reste mes souvenirs, et c'est tout. -(9) Il me semble que de nos jours les gens sont plus pessimistes qu'avant.-(10) Mme Dubois?--Oui, de quoi s'agit-il?

c) (1) Il faut-(2) Il suffit-(3) Il est vrai-(4) Il vaut mieux-(5) Il est facile-(6) Il est impossible-(7) Il est difficile-(8) Il suffit-(9) Il existe-(10) Il faut

F. TENSES

a) (1) Qu'est-ce qu'il fait? / est en train de faire?--Il arrive; il gare / est en train de garer la voiture.-(2) Beaucoup de pays traversent une période difficile en ce moment.-(3) Appelle-moi demain quand tu arriveras au bureau.-(4) Les Français boivent moins de vin qu'il y a vingt ou trente ans.-(5) Quand je vais la voir, elle parle toujours du passé.-(6) Le directeur est occupé en ce moment: il parle au téléphone à / avec son associé.-(7) Les enfants ne lisent pas beaucoup de nos jours, parce qu'ils regardent trop la / de télévision.-(8) Je crois qu'il est en train d'écrire son autobiographie. -(9) Je lui dirai la prochaine fois que je le verrai.-(10) Chaque fois / Toutes les fois que je suis en train de regarder quelque chose de bien à la télévision, il veut regarder autre chose.

b) (1) J'allais souvent au théâtre quand j'habitais près de New-York.-(9) Il y a quelques années, les femmes occupaient peu de postes de responsabilité et restaient souvent au foyer.-(3) Quand j'étais étudiant, je lisais quelquefois toute la nuit.-(4) Comme il pleuvait très fort, les responsables ont annulé le match.-(5) Quand il m'a téléphoné, j'ai pensé tout de suite à un accident.-(6) Il réfléchissait à ses problèmes et il n'a pas vu la voiture arriver.-(7) C'est un homme qui a gagné beaucoup d'argent, et qui a fait beaucoup de bien dans sa vie.-(8) Le ministre des transports a pris des mesures draconiennes, mais malgré cela le nombre des accidents de la route n'a pas diminué.-(9) Les gens parlaient tellement fort que je n'ai pas entendu l'annonce faite dans le haut-parleur.-(10) La foule a commencé à crier dès qu'elle a aperçu le cortège.

c) **(1)** Quand il est arrivé, j'étais déjà sorti.-**(2)** Les postiers étaient en grève depuis quinze jours quand ils ont accepté l'augmentation de salaire.-**(3)** Je lui avais dit de faire attention mais elle ne m'a pas écouté.-**(4)** Dès que j'arriverai à Paris je vais chercher du travail. -**(5)** Il nous téléphonera quand il aura acheté les billets.-**(6)** Je retournerai travailler quand je serai complètement guéri.-**(7)** Il travaille à Paris depuis vingt ans. / Il y vingt ans qu'il travaille à Paris. / Ça fait vingt ans qu'il travaille à Paris.-**(8)** J'ai habité dans un appartement pendant six ans, et puis j'ai acheté cette maison. -**(9)** Il y a moins de problèmes depuis qu'ils ont construit cette autoroute. -**(10)** Il enseigne dans cette université depuis 1991.

d) **(1)** Je venais de m'endormir lorsqu'un bruit bizarre m'a réveillé. -**(2)** J'ai l'intention de partir pour les Etats-Unis quand j'aurai passé mes examens.-**(3)** Je viendrai chercher ma robe quand elle sera prête.-**(4)** Les pourparlers duraient depuis plus de quinze jours lorsque les participants sont enfin arrivés à un accord.-**(5)** Je n'avais pas eu de ses nouvelles depuis plusieurs années lorsque je l'ai rencontré à la gare.-**(6)** Les choses commenceront à changer lorsque les hommes politiques auront compris que les gens en ont assez.-**(7)** Ils ont promis qu'ils m'écriraient dès qu'ils auraient pris une décision.-**(8)** Il y a plusieurs mois que nous les connaissons mais nous ne savons toujours pas où ils habitent.-**(9)** J'étais fatiguée parce que j'étais allée me coucher tard.-**(10)** Téléphone-moi dès que tu connaîtras l'heure d'arrivée de ton train.

G. THE SUBJUNCTIVE

a) **(1)** Mes parents sont très contents que j'aie réussi (à) mes examens. -**(2)** Elle était désolée que je donne ma démission.-**(3)** Je suis très heureux que vous ayez pris cette décision.-**(4)** J'étais surprise qu'ils ne m'aient pas écrit.-**(5)** Il roule trop vite, et j'ai peur qu'il n'ait un accident.-**(6)** Je regrette beaucoup que tu ne puisses pas m'accompagner à Paris.-**(7)** Ils sont étonnés que tu ne viennes pas.-**(8)** Tu veux que je revienne plus tard?-**(9)** Je crains que ce ne soit pas possible de vous donner une réponse avant la fin du mois. -**(10)** Je préfère que tu me dises la vérité.

b) **(1)** Quand es-tu libre? Il est important que nous nous voyions au plus vite.-**(2)** Mon mari doit aller aux Etats-Unis pour affaires en juin. Il est possible qu'il m'emmène avec lui.-**(3)** Je ne l'ai pas vue depuis une semaine. Il se peut qu'elle soit partie en vacances. -**(4)** La police devrait interroger le concierge. Il est impossible qu'il n'ait rien vu.-**(5)** Ils devaient arriver avant huit heures. Il est douteux qu'ils viennent maintenant.-**(6)** Tu sais bien que cette idée ne lui plaît pas. Il est peu probable que tu/vous/nous réussisses/réussissiez/réussissions à le convaincre.-**(7)** Elle a l'air très heureuse à l'université. Il semble qu'elle se soit bien habituée à sa vie d'étudiante.-**(8)** C'est un long voyage, et elle est malade. Il serait préférable qu'elle reste chez elle.-**(9)** Il ne connaît rien aux voitures. Il vaudrait mieux qu'il n'achète pas une voiture d'occasion.-**(10)** J'aurais bien aimé vous voir quand vous étiez en France le mois dernier. C'est dommage que vous ne m'ayez pas téléphoné.

c) **(1)** Je ne crois pas que ça vaille la peine d'aller voir cette pièce. -**(2)** Je ne pense pas qu'elle guérisse bientôt.-**(3)** Je doute que les travaux soient finis avant l'été.-**(4)** Je ne suis pas sûr que nous allions en France cette année.-**(5)** Il n'est pas certain que l'inauguration ait lieu à la date prévue.-**(6)** Il n'est pas évident qu'il soit élu.-**(7)** Il n'est pas vrai que le niveau de vie ait augmenté depuis une dizaine d'années.-**(8)** Il semble que le ministre ait décidé de changer les programmes scolaires.-**(9)** Il n'est pas sûr que les Républicains gagnent les élections cette fois-ci.-**(10)** Il se pourrait qu'il y ait bientôt des élections.

d) **(1)** Il n'a pas gagné de médaille olympique, bien qu'il soit le meilleur skieur du monde.-**(2)** Les blessés sont morts de froid dans la neige, sans qu'il soit possible de les secourir.-**(3)** Il aurait fallu un plus grand théâtre, pour que plus de gens puissent voir le spectacle.-**(4)** Je laisse mes enfants sortir le soir, pourvu qu'ils ne rentrent pas trop tard.-**(5)** Beaucoup de jeunes sont obligés d'habiter chez leurs parents, jusqu'à ce qu'ils trouvent une maison ou un appartement à louer ou à acheter.-**(6)** J'ai l'intention de faire le voyage en voiture, à moins qu'il ne fasse trop mauvais temps sur les routes.-**(7)** On a limité le nombre des spectateurs, de peur que des incidents n'éclatent dans le stade.-**(8)** Je veux bien essayer de faire ce travail, à condition qu'on m'aide un peu.-**(9)** Il faut absolument que j'arrive en ville avant que les banques ne ferment.-**(10)** En attendant que ma voiture soit réparée, je me sers de mon vélo pour aller travailler.

e) **(1)** Elle ne pense pas pouvoir venir.-**(2)** Je crois la connaître. -**(3)** Elle est partie sans dire au revoir.-**(4)** Elle travaille le samedi pour gagner de l'argent de poche.-**(5)** Il est préférable de vous reposer avant de sortir.-**(6)** Vous pouvez encore voir la pièce à condition de louer maintenant.-**(7)** J'aimerais aller en France, mais j'ai peur de ne rien comprendre.-**(8)** Il lui faudra travailler très dur s'il veut réussir (à) cet examen.-**(9)** Je mettrai le réveil de manière à ne pas oublier de me réveiller.-**(10)** Je regrette de ne l'avoir jamais rencontré.

f) **(1)** S'il y avait moins de chômage, il y aurait sans doute moins de problèmes sociaux.-**(2)** Si j'avais beaucoup d'argent, je ferais un voyage en Chine.-**(3)** Si j' avais su, je ne serais pas venu(e).-**(4)** Si les prix étaient plus raisonnables, nous irions plus souvent au restaurant.-**(5)** S'il ne m'avait pas aidé(e), je n'aurais jamais réussi à faire ça tout seul.-**(6)** Si je pouvais, je prendrais un mois de vacances par an.-**(7)** S'il y avait eu moins de circulation, nous n'aurions pas raté notre avion.-**(8)** S'il n'y avait pas eu la grève des chemins de fer, nous aurions pris le train.-**(9)** Si le conducteur avait roulé moins vite, l'accident ne serait pas arrivé.-**(10)** Elle venait de téléphoner pour dire qu'elle serait sans doute en retard.

g) (1) Téléphone-leur!-(2) Faites attention!-(3) N'oublions pas de prendre les imperméables!-(4) Accompagne-nous!-(5) Prévenez-nous à temps!-(6) Arrête-toi de fumer au plus vite! -(7) Préparons-nous à sortir!-(8) Souviens-toi de nos dernières vacances!-(9) Adressez-vous aux responsables!-(10) Ecris-nous à ton arrivée!

H. THE INFINITIVE

a) (1) Après des mois, ils se sont finalement décidés à vendre leur maison.-(2) Le mois dernier, elle a failli mourir dans un accident de voiture.-(3) Si je voulais, je pourrais prendre des vacances maintenant, mais je préfère attendre jusqu'à l'été.-(4) Je n' ai jamais eu l'occasion de voler en Concorde. Il paraît que c'est très confortable.-(5) Trop souvent, les parents modernes laissent leurs enfants faire tout ce qu'ils veulent.-(6) J'ai trop de travail en ce moment: je n'ai pas le temps de sortir.-(7) Les journalistes ont essayé de l'interviewer, mais il n'avait rien à dire.-(8) Elle s'ennuie: elle n'a pas l'habitude d'habiter à la campagne.-(9) La police a décidé d'intervenir afin d'éviter des violences.-(10) Apprendre à conduire n'est pas une chose facile.

b) (1) Le docteur lui a conseillé d'aller à la montagne pour sa santé.-(2) Nous lui avons parlé pendant toute une heure, et finalement nous sommes arrivés à la convaincre.-(3) Je ne lui ai pas tout dit: j'ai craint de l'ennuyer.-(4) Elle cherche à attirer l'attention sur elle en s'habillant d'une manière très excentrique. -(5) Malheureusement, d'après les statistiques, les jeunes commencent à fumer de plus en plus tôt.-(6) Il y avait de nombreux policiers sur les lieux de l'accident: ils empêchaient les gens d'approcher.-(7) Après la projection du film, le metteur en scène a invité les spectateurs à lui poser des questions.-(8) Les autorités ont obligé tous les automobilistes à porter la ceinture de sécurité.-(9) Je ne peux pas rentrer chez moi: je viens de me rendre compte que j'avais oublié mes clefs au bureau.-(10) Le gouvernement s'efforce d'aider les jeunes sans emploi.

c) (1) Je sais conduire, mais je préfère voyager par le train.-(2) Elle passe son temps à téléphoner à ses amis au lieu d'étudier pour ses examens.-(3) Il a été très malade pendant la nuit, alors j'ai envoyé chercher le docteur.-(4) J'aimerais t'aider, mais je suis occupé en ce moment.-(5) Il vient de terminer un film et il va en commencer un autre.-(6) Ils n'ont pas compris cet exercice: je le leur ai fait refaire.-(7) J'espère venir vous voir avant de partir pour la France.-(8) Il faut te faire couper les cheveux, ils sont trop longs! Mais je n'ai pas envie d'aller chez le coiffeur!-(9) Ils nous ont fait attendre des heures à l'aéroport sans donner d'explications.-(10) Je n'ai jamais dîné au restaurant français qui vient d'ouvrir près d'ici mais j'ai entendu dire que c'est très bien.

d) **(1)** Il est facile de résoudre ce problème.-**(2)** Il a travaillé très dur pour obtenir la meilleure note.-**(3)** Il a donné un coup de téléphone important avant de sortir.-**(4)** Il est parti sans dire au revoir. -**(5)** Il est très difficile d'apprendre une langue étrangère.-**(6)** Au lieu de prendre l'autoroute, ils ont emprunté les petites routes. -**(7)** Il passe son temps à jouer toute la journée avec son ordinateur.-**(8)** Cette touche sert à régler le volume.-**(9)** Elle n'a pas l'habitude de prendre l'avion.-**(10)** Il est impossible de visiter Paris sans l'aimer.

e) **(1)** Après avoir joué son dernier match, il a décidé d'abandonner le hockey.-**(2)** Je vous remercie de m'avoir écoutée très patiemment. -**(3)** Après avoir beaucoup réfléchi, ils ont choisi de ne pas porter plainte.-**(4)** Elle est vraiment désolée de ne pas avoir/n'avoir pas pu nous aider.-**(5)** Après avoir beaucoup voyagé il y a quelques années, nous avons préféré nous fixer en France.-**(6)** Je me souviens de l'avoir rencontré à un dîner l'année dernière.-**(7)** Après s'être bien amusée dans sa jeunesse, elle a fini par trouver du travail et menor uno vie plus calme.-**(8)** Je m'excuse de ne pas avoir/n'avoir pas pu vous recevoir hier.-**(9)** Après s'être reposés quelques jours, les athlètes ont recommencé leurs séances d'entraînement.-**(10)** Je regrette vraiment de n'avoir jamais étudié la musique.

I. PARTICIPLES

a) **(1)** Durant la discussion, plusieurs délégués ont fait des suggestions très intéressantes.-**(2)** Ces gâteaux au chocolat ont l'air très tentants. J'ai bien envie d'en acheter.-**(3)** Il me fait rire: ses plaisanteries sont très amusantes.-**(4)** Ce livre raconte l'aventure passionnante de la conquête de l'Espace.-**(5)** Je suis allé à San Francisco hier: c'était une journée agréable, et très intéressante. -**(6)** Sur les marchés français, on peut acheter des crevettes vivantes.-**(7)** Il n'avait pas l'air très sûr de ce qu'il disait: il a répondu d'une voix hésitante.-**(8)** Elle est devenu très méfiante: elle n'ouvre pas sa porte aux inconnus.-**(9)** Depuis qu'il a commencé à apprendre le français l'année dernière, il a fait des progrès étonnants.-**(10)** J'espérais obtenir de meilleurs résultats à mes examens: en fait, j'ai obtenu des notes très décevantes.

b) **(1)** Elle a souri en se voyant dans la glace.-**(2)** Les enfants riaient tout en ouvrant leurs cadeaux.-**(3)** Il a gagné beaucoup d'argent en vendant des maisons dans les années '80.-**(4)** Il a réussi en travaillant très dur et en sachant quand prendre des risques.-**(5)** J'écoute souvent de la musique classique tout en lisant.-**(6)** Elle a quitté l'hôpital en pleurant.-**(7)** Elle paie ses études en travaillant à mi-temps comme professeur de karaté.-**(8)** De nos jours, beaucoup de femmes choisissent de continuer à travailler tout en élevant leurs enfants.-**(9)** Il a réussi à pénétrer dans la maison en cassant la fenêtre de la salle de bains.-**(10)** Tu n'arriveras à rien en te fâchant.

c) **(1)** Les blessés étaient étendus sur des civières.-The wounded were lying on stretchers.-**(2)** Plusieurs femmes priaient, agenouillées dans l'église.-Several women were on their knees, praying in the church.-**(3)** Des centaines de touristes étaient allongés sur le sable, en plein soleil.-Hundreds of tourists were lying on the sand in the blazing sun.-**(4)** A la suite d'une forte grippe, elle est restée couchée quinze jours.-After a bad bout with the flu, she stayed in bed for two weeks.-**(5)** Penchées sur leur livre, elles ne l'avaient pas entendu entrer.-Bent over their books, they hadn't heard him come in.-**(6)** Les alpinistes ont dû rester suspendus dans le vide en attendant du secours.-The climbers had to remain dangling in space while they waited for help.-**(7)** Accoudée à la fenêtre, la jeune femme posait pour le photographe.-Leaning by the window, the young woman was posing for the photographer.-**(8)** Aux heures d'affluence, il n'y a jamais assez de places assises dans les trains.-There are never enough seats on the trains at rush hours.-**(9)** Connue de tous, elle était aussi particulièrement appréciée des enfants.-Known to one and all, she was also well liked especially by the children.

d) **(1)** Ma femme et moi avons vu un film comique hier soir; nous nous sommes beaucoup amusés.-**(2)** Elle s'est cassé la jambe en faisant du ski: elle a dû rester trois mois dans le plâtre. -**(3)** Pendant leur séparation, ils se sont téléphoné tous les jours. -**(4)** Anne et sa sœur ne se sont pas vues depuis au moins trois ans.-**(5)** Les deux chefs de gouvernement se sont parlé longuement hier, pour la première fois depuis la fin de la guerre.-**(6)** Marie s'é-tait souvent demandé pourquoi sa sœur ne s'était jamais mariée.-**(7)** Quels livres avez-vous lus dans cette collection? -**(8)** Combien de voyages d'affaires avez-vous faits cette année? -**(9)** Quels vins avez-vous dégustés pendant votre voyage en Bourgogne?-**(10)** Parmi les capitales que j'ai visitées, je crois que Paris est celle que je préfère.

J. THE PASSIVE

a) **(1)** On m'a acheté / offert cette robe pour mon anniversaire, et mon cadeau m'a fait grand plaisir.-**(2)** On lui donne de l'argent de poche toutes les semaines.-**(3)** On leur a appris le français très jeunes. / quand ils étaient très jeunes. / à un âge très tendre.-**(4)** On s'est moqué d'elle à cause de son drôle de nom.-**(5)** Quand j'étais très jeune, les enfants ne parlaient pas à moins qu'on ne leur parle.-**(6)** Ils ont hérité d'une fortune quand leurs parents sont morts.-**(7)** On m'a assuré que mon passeport serait prêt le même jour. On m'a dit d'attendre ici.-**(8)** Elle est très fatiguée et on lui a dit de se reposer le plus possible.-**(9)** On dit qu'il aime beaucoup la France et qu'il parle très bien (le) français.-**(10)** (Ici) on parle anglais.

b) **(1)** They were seen together at the theater last week.-**(2)** I don't know what her name is.-**(3)** This wine is drunk very cold.-**(4)** She is said to be a very good tennis player.-**(5)** He is being talked about as the next president.-**(6)** In France, meat is eaten less well done than in the United States.-**(7)** The doctor had to be sent for in the middle of the night.-**(8)** I was sent a reminder about my library book.-**(9)** He was caught stealing money from his company. -**(10)** She has been called the most famous woman in the world.

K. MODAL VERBS: *VOULOIR, POUVOIR, DEVOIR, SAVOIR, FALLOIR*

a) **(1)** Le médecin m'a dit que je devais absolument prendre trois comprimés par jour.-**(2)** Elle doit être très contente d'avoir réussi à tous ses examens.-**(3)** L'avion devrait arriver à onze heures, mais il aura probablement du retard à cause du brouillard.-**(4)** C'est quelque chose qui peut arriver, mais c'est très rare.-**(5)** Je me réveille tous les matins avec une migraine épouvantable: je dois prendre rendez-vouz chez le médecin.-**(6)** Je préfère ne pas sortir: mon mari doit m'appeler des Etats-Unis vers sept heures.-**(7)** Ce n'est pas la peine que j'achète une voiture: je ne sais pas encore conduire.-**(8)** Je n'aime pas beaucoup aller en vacances à la mer, car je ne sais pas nager.-**(9)** J'ai essayé de téléphoner, mais pas de réponse: elle a dû sortir.-**(10)** Ils auraient pu venir avec nous, s'ils avaient voulu.

b) Anne attend un coup de téléphone de son amie, avec qui elle doit partir en vacances. Elle doit appeler vers sept ou huit heures. Elles ne savent pas encore où elles veulent aller, mais il se peut qu'elles choisiront l'Espagne. Anne sait conduire, et une fois arrivées les jeunes filles voudraient louer une voiture pour visiter la région. Elles devaient déjà partir ensemble l'année dernière, mais elles n'ont pas pu, car Anne a dû acheter une nouvelle voiture.

c) **(1)** Elle aurait dû partir plus tôt, elle n'aurait pas raté son train. -**(2)** Si tu ne veux pas finir à l'hôpital, tu devrais (t')arrêter de fumer!-**(3)** J'aurais bien voulu être médecin, mais je n'aurais jamais pu supporter la vue du sang.-**(4)** Elle voudrait bien lui dire la vérité, mais elle ne sait vraiment pas comment s'y prendre. -**(5)** Elle a beaucoup vieilli maintenant, mais elle a dû être très belle quand elle était jeune.-**(6)** Tu pourrais au moins lui télépho-ner pour la remercier: ce serait plus poli!-**(7)** On aurait pu éviter les grèves si le gouvernement avait cédé aux revendications des ouvri-crs.-**(8)** S'ils ne m'avaient pas aidé financièrement, je n'aurais jamais pu surmonter mes difficultés.-**(9)** Vous devriez prendre des vacances plus souvent: vous avez l'air fatigué.-**(10)** Finalement ils ont dû vendre leur maison; elle était devenue trop grande pour eux.

L. CONJUGATION PRACTICE

a) **(1)** je mange   nous mangeons
tu manges   vous mangez
il }
elle } mange   ils }
on }   elles } mangent

(2) j'achète   nous achetons
tu achètes   vous achetez
il }
elle } achète   ils }
on }   elles } achètent

(3) j'appelle   nous appelons
tu appelles   vous appelez
il }
elle } appelle   ils }
on }   elles } appellent

(4) je jette   nous jetons
tu jettes   vous jetez
il }
elle } jette   ils }
on }   elles } jettent

(5) je commence   nous commençons
tu commences   vous commencez
il }
elle } commence   ils }
on }   elles } commencent

(6) je vends   nous vendons
tu vends   vous vendez
il }
elle } vend   ils }
on }   elles } vendent

(7) je mets   nous mettons
tu mets   vous mettez
il }
elle } met   ils }
on }   elles } mettent

(8) je finis   nous finissons
tu finis   vous finissez
il }
elle } finit   ils }
on }   elles } finissent

(9) je vais   nous allons
tu vas   vous allez
il }
elle } va   ils }
on }   elles } vont

(10) je fais   nous faisons
        tu fais   vous faites
        il }   ils }
        elle } fait   elles } font
        on }

b)
(1) j'étais	tu étais	nous étions
(2) j'avais	tu avais	nous avions
(3) je croyais	tu croyais	nous croyions
(4) je faisais	tu faisais	nous faisions
(5) je disais	tu disais	nous disions

c) (1) je travaillerai, nous travaillerons-**(2)** je verrai, nous verrons -**(3)** j'irai, nous irons-**(4)** je ferai, nous ferons-**(5)** j'écrirai, nous écrirons-**(6)** je pourrai, nous pourrons-**(7)** je voudrai, nous voudrons-**(8)** je saurai, nous saurons-**(9)** je tiendrai, nous tiendrons -**(10)** je viendrai, nous viendrons

d)
arrivé	dormi
descendu	compris
partı	bu
resté	écrit
sorti	reçu
entré	dû
venu	connu
allé	lu
monté	vécu
revenu	ri

e)
Je suis arrivé/e	Nous sommes arrivé/ées
Tu es arrivé/e	Vous êtes arrivés/ées
Il est arrivé	Ils sont arrivés
Elle est arrivée	Elles sont arrivées
On est arrivé	
Je suis descendu/e	Nous sommes descendus/es
Tu es descendu/e	Vous êtes descendus/es
Il est descendu	Ils sont descendus
Elle est descendue	Elles sont descendues
On est descendu	
Je suis parti/e	Nous sommes partis/es
Tu es partie/e	Vous êtes partis/es
Il est parti	Ils sont partis
Elle est partie	Elles sont parties
On est parti	
Je suis resté/e	Nous sommes restés/es
Tu es resté/e	Vous êtes restés/es
Il est resté	Ils sont restés
Elle est restée	Elles sont restées
On est resté	

Je suis sorti/e	Nous sommes sortis/es
Tu es sorti/e	Vous êtes sortis/es
Il est sorti	Ils sont sortis
Elle est sortie	Elles sont sorties
On est sorti	
Je suis entré/e	Nous sommes entrés/es
Tu es entré/e	Vous êtes entrés/es
Il est entré	Ils sont entrés
Elle est entrée	Elles sont entrées
On est entré	
Je suis venu/e	Nous sommes venus/es
Tu es venu/e	Vous êtes venus/es
Il est venu	Ils sont venus
Elle est venue	Elles sont venues
On est venu	
Je suis allé/e	Nous sommes allés/es
Tu es allé/e	Vous êtes allés/es
Il est allé	Ils sont allés
Elle est allée	Elles sont allées
On est allé	
Je suis monté/e	Nous sommes montés/es
Tu es monté/e	Vous êtes montés/es
Il est monté	Ils sont montés
Elle est montée	Elles sont montées
On est monté	
Je suis revenu/e	Nous sommes revenus/es
Tu es revenu/e	Vous êtes revenus/es
Il est revenu	Ils sont revenus
Elle est revenue	Elles sont revenues
On est revenu	
J'ai dormi	Nous avons dormi
Tu as dormi	Vous avez dormi
Il a dormi	Ils ont dormi
Elle a dormi	Elles ont dormi
On a dormi	
J'ai compris	Nous avons compris
Tu as compris	Vous avez compris
Il a compris	Ils ont compris
Elle a compris	Elles ont compris
On a compris	
J'ai bu	Nous avons bu
Tu as bu	Vous avez bu
Il a bu	Ils ont bu
Elle a bu	Elles ont bu
On a bu	

J'ai écrit	Nous avons écrit
Tu as écrit	Vous avez écrit
Il a écrit	Ils ont écrit
Elle a écrit	Elles ont écrit
On a écrit	
J'ai reçu	Nous avons reçu
Tu as reçu	Vous avez reçu
Il a reçu	Ils ont reçu
Elle a reçu	Elles ont reçu
On a reçu	
J'ai dû	Nous avons dû
Tu as dû	Vous avez dû
Il a dû	Ils ont dû
Elle a dû	Elles ont dû
On a dû	
J'ai connu	Nous avons connu
Tu as connu	Vous avez connu
Il a connu	Ils ont connu
Elle a connu	Elles ont connu
On a connu	
J'ai lu	Nous avons lu
Tu as lu	Vous avez lu
Il a lu	Ils ont lu
Elle a lu	Elles ont lu
On a lu	
J'ai vécu	Nous avons vécu
Tu as vécu	Vous avez vécu
Il a vécu	Ils ont vécu
Elle a vécu	Elles ont vécu
On a vécu	
J'ai ri	Nous avons ri
Tu as ri	Vous avez ri
Il a ri	Ils ont ri
Elle a ri	Elles ont ri
On a ri	

f) (1) Je me lève — Nous nous levons
Je me suis levé/e — Nous nous sommes levés/es

(2) Je m'amuse — Nous nous amusons
Je me suis amusé/e — Nous nous sommes amusés/es

(3) Je m'assieds — Nous nous asseyons
Je me suis assis/e — Nous nous sommes assis/es

(4) Je me promène — Nous nous promenons
Je me suis promené/e — Nous nous sommes promenés/es

(5) Je m'excuse — Nous nous excusons
Je me suis excusé/e — Nous nous sommes excusés/es

(6) Je me demande	Nous nous demandons
Je me suis demandé	Nous nous sommes demandé
(7) Je me dépêche	Nous nous dépêchons
Je me suis dépêché/e	Nous nous sommes dépêchés/es
(8) Je me réveille	Nous nous réveillons
Je me suis réveillé/e	Nous nous sommes réveillés/es
(9) Je me trompe	Nous nous trompons
Je me suis trompé/e	Nous nous sommes trompés/es
(10) Je m'endors	Nous nous endormons
Je me suis endormi/e	Nous nous sommes endormis/es
g) Il faudrait	Il aurait fallu

Je serais	Nous serions
Tu serais	Vous seriez
Il serait	Ils seraient
Elle serait	
On serait	

J'aurais été	Nous aurions été
Tu aurais été	Vous auriez été
Il aurait été	Ils auraient été
Elle aurait été	Elles auraient été
On aurait été	

J'aurais	Nous aurions
Tu aurais	Vous auriez
Il aurait	Ils auraient
Elle aurait	Elles auraient
On aurait	

J'aurais eu	Nous aurions eu
Tu aurais eu	Vous auriez eu
Il aurait eu	Ils auraient eu
Elle aurait eu	Elles auraient eu
On aurait eu	

Je serais aimé/e	Nous serions aimés/es
Tu serais aimé/e	Vous seriez aimés/es
Il serait aimé	Ils seraient aimés
Elle serait aimée	Elles seraient aimées
On serait aimé	

J'aurais été aimé/e	Nous aurions été aimés/es
Tu aurais été aimé/e	Vous auriez été aimés/es
Il aurait été aimé	Ils auraient été aimés
Elle aurait été aimée	Elles auraient été aimées
On aurait été aimé	

Je ferais	Nous ferions
Tu ferais	Vous feriez
Il ferait	Ils feraient
Elle ferait	Elles feraient
On ferait	

J'aurais fait	Nous aurions fait
Tu aurais fait	Vous auriez fait
Il aurait fait	Ils auraient fait
Elle aurait fait	Elles auraient fait
On aurait fait	
Je devrais	Nous devrions
Tu devrais	Vouz devriez
Il devrait	Ils devraient
Elle devrait	Elles devraient
On devrait	
J'aurais dû	Nous aurions dû
Tu aurais dû	Vous auriez dû
Il aurait dû	Ils auraient dû
Elle aurait dû	Elles auraient dû
On aurait dû	
Je préférerais	Nous préférerions
Tu préférerais	Vous préféreriez
Il préférerait	Ils préféreraient
Elle préférerait	Elles préféreraient
On préférerait	
J'aurais préféré	Nous aurions préféré
Tu aurais préféré	Vous auriez préféré
Il aurait préféré	Ils auraient préféré
Elle aurait préféré	Elles auraient préféré
On aurait préféré	
Je dirais	Nous dirions
Tu dirais	Vous diriez
Il dirait	Ils diraient
Elle dirait	Elles diraient
On dirait	
J'aurais dit	Nous aurions dit
Tu aurais dit	Vous auriez dit
Il aurait dit	Ils auraient dit
Elle aurait dit	Elles auraient dit
On aurait dit	
Je saurais	Nous saurions
Tu saurais	Vous sauriez
Il saurait	Ils sauraient
Elle saurait	Elles sauraient
On saurait	
J'aurais su	Nous aurions su
Tu aurais su	Vous auriez su
Il aurait su	Ils auraient su
Elle aurait su	Elles auraient su
On aurait su	

Je me souviendrais   Nous nous souviendrions
Tu te souviendrais   Vous vous souviendriez
Il se souviendrait   Ils se souviendraient
Elle se souviendrait   Elles se souviendraient
On se souviendrait

Je me serais souvenu/e   Nous nous serions
Tu te serais souvenu/e   souvenus/es
Il se serait souvenu   Vous vous seriez souvenus/es
Elle se serait souvenue Ils se seraient souvenus
On se serait souvenu   Elles se seraient souvenues

h) J'étais tombé/e   Nous étions tombés/es
J'étais parti/e   Nous étions partis/es
Je m'étais couché/e   Nous nous étions couchés/es
Je m'étais tu/e   Nous nous étions tus/es
J'étais sorti/e   Nous étions sortis/es
J'étais né/e   Nous étions nés/es
J'avais trouvé   Nous avions trouvé
J'étais revenu/e   Nous étions revenus/es
J'avais espéré   Nous avions espéré
J'avais couru   Nous avions couru

i) **(1)** ils/elles jouaient/étaient en train de jouer
   (2) je suis allé/e
   (3) ils/elles mangeaient/étaient en train de manger
   (4) tu aimerais/vous aimeriez
   (5) nous devrions écrire
   (6) ils/elles seraient arrivés/es
   (7) ils/elles auraient dû parler
   (8) je suis revenu/e
   (9) tu riais/vous riiez/tu avais/vous aviez l'habitude de rire
   (10) nous nous amusons/nous sommes en train de nous amuser
   (11) il viendra
   (12) ils/elles ont attendu
   (13) elle regarde/elle est en train de regarder
   (14) nous devrions travailler
   (15) ils/elles arriveront
   (16) ils/elles préféreraient
   (17) nous nous étions assis/es
   (18) ils/elles auraient fini
   (19) tu devrais/vous devriez commencer
   (20) il aurait fallu

j) **(1)** que je finisse   que nous finissions
   (2) que j'appelle   que nous appelions
   (3) que je croie   que nous croyions
   (4) que je commence   que nous commencions
   (5) que je vienne   que nous venions
   (6) que je fasse   que nous fassions
   (7) que je sois   que nous soyons

(8) que j'aie	que nous ayons	
(9) que j'aille	que nous allions	
(10) que je sache	que nous sachions	

k)

(1) que j'aie essayé	que nous ayons essayé
(2) que je me sois amusé/e	que nous nous soyons amusés/es
(3) que je me sois lavé/e	que nous nous soyons lavé/es
(4) que j'aie ouvert	que nous ayons ouvert
(5) que je sois mort/e	que nous soyons morts/es
(6) que je sois rentré/e	que nous soyons rentrés/es
(7) que j'aie eu	que nous ayons eu
(8) que j'aie dû	que nous ayons dû
(9) que je sois monté/e	que nous soyons montés/es
(10) que j'aie entendu	que nous ayons entendu

l)

mets,	mettons,	mettez
prends,	prenons,	prenez
bois,	buvons,	buvez
mange,	mangeons,	mangez
appelle,	appelons,	appelez
réveille-toi,	réveillons-nous,	réveillez-vous
habille-toi,	habillons-nous,	habillez-vous
lève-toi,	levons-nous,	levez-vous
arrête-toi,	arrêtons-nous,	arrêtez-vous
dépêche-toi,	dépêchons-nous,	dépêchez-vous

M. VERB CONSTRUCTIONS

a) (1) Je l'ai attendu mais il n'est pas venu.-**(2)** J'espérais une lettre mais elle n'a pas écrit.-**(3)** J'ai payé mes vacances et maintenant il ne me reste plus d'argent.-**(4)** Je n'ai pas regardé votre livre. -**(5)** Il écoute beaucoup de musique classique.-**(6)** Le professeur ne répond jamais clairement à nos questions.-**(7)** Elle ressemble beaucoup à son père.-**(8)** Il joue au tennis et sa sœur joue du piano.-**(9)** De nos jours peu d'enfants obéissent à leurs parents comme ils le faisaient autrefois.-**(10)** Je ne lui pardonnerai jamais.-**(11)** Elle ne s'est pas aperçue de ma présence.-**(12)** Je n'aimerais pas changer de place avec lui.-**(13)** Vous pouvez vous servir de mon stylo si vous voulez./Tu peux te servir de mon stylo si tu veux.-**(14)** Je ne me souviens pas du tout d'elle.-**(15)** Je suis désolé/e d'être en retard: je me suis trompé/e d'autobus.-**(16)** Je me doutais de quelque chose mais je n'ai rien dit.-**(17)** Lorsque l'homme s'est approché des enfants, ils se sont enfuis en courant. -**(18)** Je me méfie des gens qui sourient trop.-**(19)** Ce n'est pas facile de renoncer au tabac et à l'alcool.-**(20)** Son sens de l'humour ne convient pas à tout le monde.

b) **(1)** Ça ne sert à rien de lui parler: elle n'écoute personne.-**(2)** Avez-vous déjà songé à changer de métier?-**(3)** Il n'a pas besoin de travailler. Il vit de ses rentes.-**(4)** J'aimerais beaucoup aller aux Etats-Unis cet été, mais ça dépend de mes parents.-**(5)** C'est un livre très important, qui traite des conséquences de la deuxième guerre mondiale.-**(6)** Beaucoup de gens croient aux fantômes, mais je dois avouer que ce n'est pas mon cas.-**(7)** N'oublie pas de téléphoner à Pierre et Françoise pour les féliciter de leur mariage. -**(8)** J'ai essayé de l'emmener avec moi au cinéma et au théâtre, et je lui ai prêté des livres, mais en fait elle ne s'intéresse à rien. -**(9)** Elle m'a téléphoné hier pour me remercier de l'avoir aidée. -**(10)** Elle me parle de son mari très souvent mais je ne l'ai jamais vu.

c) **(1)** Elle a conseillé à sa sœur d'aller voir un avocat.-**(2)** Je lui ai proposé de passer un week-end avec nous.-**(3)** Elle me dit toujours de conduire moins vite.-**(4)** Il a préféré cacher sa maladie à sa famille.-**(5)** Cette année, nos moyens ne nous ont pas permis de partir en vacances.-**(6)** Le docteur m'a défendu de boire du vin et de manger de la viande rouge.-**(7)** J'ai emprunté leur voiture à mes parents pour le week-end.-**(8)** Le gouvernement a ordonné aux grévistes de reprendre le travail.-**(9)** J'ai promis à ma fille de l'emmener au cirque.-**(10)** On dit qu'il a pris de l'argent à son employeur pendant plusieurs années.

7. PREPOSITIONS

a) **(1)** Je te retrouverai à l'arrêt d'autobus à huit heures.-**(2)** Il paraît qu'elle retourne en France trois fois par an.-**(3)** Elle a passé un an à Paris dans une famille française.-**(4)** Je préfère voyager en avion: c'est plus rapide!-**(5)** Dans les cinémas américains il est interdit de fumer.-**(6)** Nous faisons du camping plutôt que de descendre à l'hôtel: c'est moins cher.-**(7)** En France, il n'est pas nécessaire de se déplacer pour aller chez le docteur: le docteur vient vous voir chez vous.-**(8)** Si ça vous arrange, je vous prête ma voiture jusqu'à la semaine prochaine.-**(9)** En principe, il devrait arriver dans deux heures.-**(10)** Il fait régulièrement du deux cent à l'heure avec sa voiture de sport, et un jour il a fait Paris-Lyon en moins de trois heures.-**(11)** Ils ont déménagé: maintenant, ils habitent à la campagne à quelques kilomètres de Caen, en Normandie.-**(12)** En quelle année est-ce que vous êtes allé en vacances avec les Legrand en France?

b) **(1)** Elle habite en France depuis cinq ans.-**(2)** Ils ont séjourné chez nous pendant six semaines.-**(3)** Elle vient en Amérique pour trois mois cet été.-**(4)** Il est très content de sa nouvelle voiture.-**(5)** Leur salle de séjour est très grande: elle est longue de dix mètres et large de cinq mètres.-**(6)** Ajoutez une cuillerée de lait.-**(7)** J'ai vu entrer une fille aux yeux bleus et à lunettes.-**(8)** Il y avait beaucoup de monde / gens dans l'autobus ce matin.-**(9)** Il n'y a rien d'intéressant dans les journaux aujourd'hui.-**(10)** Je ne trouve pas les cuillères/cuillers à thé.-**(11)** C'est l'homme le plus célèbre de France en ce moment.-**(12)** Je pensais qu'il était déjà dix heures: ma montre avance de dix minutes.-**(13)** Je ne l'ai jamais vu au cinéma mais je l'ai vu l'autre jour à la télévision.-**(14)** Je ne l'ai pas vue depuis la semaine dernière.-**(15)** On dit qu'un enfant sur cinq ne sait pas lire.-**(16)** Ne reste pas trop longtemps au soleil! -**(17)** Je suis toujours très contente de la voir; c'est pour ça que je l'ai invitée pour Noël.-**(18)** Je parle en tant que père.-**(19)** Je vis dans la même maison depuis vingt ans.-**(20)** A mon avis, elle devrait prendre des vacances.

c) **(1)** Elle habite au troisième étage.-**(2)** J'ai acheté une voiture d'occasion à mon frère, pour l'aider dans ses affaires.-**(3)** Malgré le mauvais temps, la foule est venue accueillir la vedette à l'aéroport.-**(4)** Elle a peur de conduire depuis/après son accident. -**(5)** Auprès des exploits des champions d'autrefois, ce record n'a vraiment rien d'extraordinaire.-**(6)** Elle a eu une réaction difficile à expliquer.-**(7)** C'est un homme passionnant, et je suis vraiment content de l'avoir rencontré.-**(8)** Je ne me couche jamais avant minuit: je n'arrive pas à m'endormir tôt.-**(9)** Il est plus prudent de vérifier les pneus avant de prendre la route.-**(10)** Après avoir vu la pièce, j'ai eu envie de visiter la France.-**(11)** Elle a pris un carnet dans sa poche et elle a noté le numéro de téléphone.-**(12)** Le vin est meilleur si on le boit dans les verres qui conviennent.-**(13)** Au cinéma, j'étais assise derrière quelqu'un de très grand et je n'ai rien vu.-**(14)** Je conduis depuis quinze ans, et jusqu'ici je n'ai jamais eu d'accident.-**(15)** Selon son père, elle est beaucoup trop jeune pour sortir le soir.-**(16)** Je suis très fâché contre elle, car elle m'a parlé sur un ton très désagréable.-**(17)** Les impôts sur le revenu ont baissé sous le gouvernement républicain. -**(18)** L'accident a eu lieu sous mes yeux, et malheureusement je n'ai rien pu faire.-**(19)** Il a environ soixante-dix ans, mais il continue à faire beaucoup de sport et à courir le marathon.-**(20)** J'ai un comprimé à prendre quatre fois par jour.

d) **(1)** She lives on the third floor.-**(2)** I bought a second-hand car from my brother, to help him with his business.-**(3)** In spite of the bad weather, the crowd came to greet the star at the airport. -**(4)** Since/After her accident, she has been afraid of driving. -**(5)** Next to the feats of champions in the past, this record really is nothing out of the ordinary.-**(6)** Her reaction was difficult to explain.-**(7)** He is a fascinating man, and I am really glad to have met him.-**(8)** I never go to bed until/before midnight: I can't fall asleep early.-**(9)** It is safer to check the tires before setting out on the road.-**(10)** After seeing the play, I felt like visiting France. -**(11)** She took a notebook out of her pocket and took down the phone number.-**(12)** Wine is better if it's drunk in the right glasses.-**(13)** At the movies I was sitting behind someone very tall and I didn't see a thing.-**(14)** I have been driving for fifteen years, and until now I have never had an accident.-**(15)** According to her father, she is much too young to go out at night.-**(16)** I'm very put out with her, because she spoke to me in a very nasty way. -**(17)** Income tax went down under the Republicans.-**(18)** The accident happened right before my eyes, and unfortunately I couldn't do anything.-**(19)** He is about seventy, but he keeps playing a lot of sports and running the marathon.-**(20)** I have to take a pill four times a day.

8. CONJUNCTIONS

a) (1) Elle ne parle pas beaucoup, car elle est très timide.-**(2)** Elle a la grippe, mais elle va travailler quand même.-**(3)** Les Legrand ont été cambriolés dans la nuit. Or, on a vu un individu suspect près de la maison hier soir.-**(4)** Je ne la connais pas très bien. Toutefois, j'ai l'impression qu'elle est très intelligente.-**(5)** Elle n'avait pas l'air très enthousiaste, aussi n'ai-je pas insisté.-**(6)** Ni ses parents ni ses amis n'ont réussi à la convaincre.-**(7)** Vous pouvez payer soit par chèque, soit avec votre carte de crédit.-**(8)** Elle se reposait, alors je n'ai pas voulu la déranger.-**(9)** Il ne peut y avoir que deux raisons à son silence: ou elle est malade, ou elle ne souhaite pas nous revoir.-**(10)** Elle s'est perdue en route. Pourtant, je lui avais donné des indications très précises.

b) (1) Depuis que ce programme a commencé il y a trois semaines, les indices d'écoute n'ont cessé d'augmenter.-**(2)** Ils vont attendre jusqu'à ce qu'il ait passé tous ses examens pour se marier. -**(3)** Téléphone-moi aussitôt que tu auras de ses nouvelles.-**(4)** Bien qu'il ait beaucoup de diplômes, il n'arrive pas à trouver du travail. -**(5)** Le gouvernement va adopter de nouvelles mesures pour que le chômage diminue-**(6)** Demain, nous allons passer la journée à la campagne, pourvu qu'il ne pleuve pas.-**(7)** Je préfère ne pas l'inviter de peur qu'elle ne refuse.-**(8)** Il m'a dit qu'il allait faire son possible pour nous aider.-**(9)** Son frère est encore plus intelligent qu'elle.-**(10)** N'arrivez pas trop tard, de sorte que nous ayons tout notre temps pour visiter l'exposition.

9. NUMBERS AND QUANTITY

a) quatre quatorze quinze quarante cinquante dix-sept dix-neuf soixante et onze soixante-treize soixante-dix-neuf quatre-vingts quatre-vingt-quinze quatre-vingt-dix-neuf cent un cent vingt cent vingt-trois cinq cents mille trois cent douze cent mille sept cent quatre-vingt-neuf mille cinq cents

b) **(1)** C'est la première fois que je le vois.-**(2)** Nous allons partir en France le cinquième jour des vacances.-**(3)** Nous avons organisé une petite fête: c'est son soixantième anniversaire.-**(4)** C'est le printemps! Les premières fleurs sont apparues dans le jardin. -**(5)** Ils se sont mariés en 1968: c'est leur vingt-neuvième anniversaire de mariage.-**(6)** L'année dernière, on a fêté la millième représentation de la pièce.-**(7)** Le supermarché a offert des vacances gratuites à sa centième cliente.-**(8)** C'est sa deuxième crise cardiaque: il devrait faire attention!-**(9)** C'est à Cannes, dans le Midi de la France, que se sont tenues les quarante et unièmes Rencontres Cinématographiques.-**(10)** Il s'est marié tard: il était dans sa trente-neuvième année.

c) **(1)** deux tiers-**(2)** trois dixièmes-**(3)** un vingtième-**(4)** un demi -**(5)** trois virgule cinq-**(6)** dix virgule quatre-**(7)** treize plus sept -**(8)** neuf multiplié par quatre-**(9)** quarante huit divisé par huit -**(10)** neuf huitièmes

d) **(1)** Au milieu, le lac a près de quatre mètres de profondeur.-**(2)** La salle de séjour fait trois mètres de haut et vingt mètres de long/est haute de trois mètres et longue de vingt mètres.-**(3)** Cette planche a trois centimètres d'épaisseur.-**(4)** Nous ne sommes pas très loin de mon école. Nous n'avons pas besoin de / Ce n'est pas la peine de prendre la voiture.-**(5)** Notre maison est à deux kilomètres et demi du centre-ville.-**(6)** Son cadeau m'a coûté deux cents francs. -**(7)** Combien as-tu payé ces chaussures?-**(8)** J'ai vu des fraises sur le marché, mais elles coûtent treize francs le kilo. Les melons coûtent quatre francs cinquante (la) pièce.-**(9)** A combien reviennent toutes ces choses? / Ça revient à combien, tout ça?-**(10)** En Amérique le bon vin coûte au moins cinq dollars la bouteille.

e) **(1)** J'habite cette région depuis 10 ans, mais je n'ai jamais vu autant de neige!-**(2)** Depuis quelques mois, je n'ai plus le temps de sortir ou de voir mes amis: j'ai trop de travail.-**(3)** La plupart des enfants aiment le chocolat et les bonbons.-**(4)** Si vous voulez vivre longtemps, il vaut mieux manger peu de beurre ou de crème, et ne pas boire trop de vin.-**(5)** La plupart du temps, je prends ma voiture pour aller travailler.-**(6)** J'ai acheté une paire de chaussures hier mais malheureusement elles sont trop petites. -**(7)** Voulez-vous une tasse de café avant de partir?-**(8)** J'aime le vin, mais j'en bois peu.-**(9)** Combien de chocolats est-ce qu'elle a mangés? Elle en a mangé une douzaine.-**(10)** J'ai gagné beaucoup d'argent dans ma vie, mais j'en ai aussi beaucoup dépensé.

10. EXPRESSIONS OF TIME

a) **(1)** Il est une heure du matin.-**(2)** Il est deux heures et quart du matin.-**(3)** Il est midi moins dix.-**(4)** Il est / trois heures trente-sept de l'après-midi. / quatre heures moins vingt-trois minutes de l'après-midi.-**(5)** Il est midi et six minutes.-**(6)** Il est minuit moins le quart.-**(7)** Il est minuit vingt-cinq.-**(8)** Il est quatre heures et demie du matin.-**(9)** Il est huit heures vingt-cinq du soir.-**(10)** Il est / neuf heures quarante du soir. / dix heures moins vingt du soir.

b) **(1)** Il est vingt heures treize.-**(2)** Il est quatorze heures trente.-**(3)** Il est vingt-trois heures deux.-**(4)** Il est dix-sept heures quinze.-**(5)** Il est dix-huit heures dix-huit.-**(6)** Il est vingt-deux heures dix-neuf. -**(7)** Il est six heures vingt-cinq.-**(8)** Il est quinze heures quarante. -**(9)** Il est vingt et une heures cinquante-huit.-**(10)** Il est treize heures cinq.

c) **(1)** Son anniversaire est le seize mars.-**(2)** Il est né le vingt-trois avril mil neuf cent quarante-huit.-**(3)** Je suis arrivée en France le deux octobre mil neuf cent soixante-douze.-**(4)** L'année scolaire commence le quinze septembre.-**(5)** Le traité a été signé le premier février mil neuf cent quatre-vingt-dix-huit.-**(6)** Le trente et un décembre, en France, on célèbre le Réveillon du Jour de l'An.-**(7)** Il a eu cinquante ans le vingt-six juin.-**(8)** L'Armistice a été déclaré le onze novembre mil neuf cent dix-huit.-**(9)** Le vingt-cinq décembre, toute la famille vient déjeuner à la maison.-**(10)** Le quatorze juillet, c'est la Fête Nationale en France.

d) **(1)** J'ai passé la journée à écrire des lettres.-**(2)** Nous avons passé une excellente soirée au théâtre hier soir.-**(3)** Je passerai te voir dans la matinée, je ne sais pas à quelle heure exactement.-**(4)** Je suis arrivé en retard, et j'ai manqué le début du concert.-**(5)** Lundi soir, je me suis couché très tard. Le lendemain, je ne me suis pas réveillé pour aller travailler.-**(6)** Il faudra arriver à la gare à cinq heures et quart au plus tard, si nous ne voulons pas rater le train.-**(7)** Il y a quinze jours, je suis tombée dans l'escalier. Depuis, j'ai mal à la cheville quand je marche.-**(8)** Il est une heure passée et il n'est toujours pas là. Je me demande ce qui lui est arrivé.-**(9)** Elle passe son temps à lire des magazines au lieu de faire ses devoirs. -**(10)** Dans les années soixante, j'étais étudiante à Paris. Tout cela semble très loin maintenant.

11. THE SENTENCE

a) **(1)** Nous avons décidé d'acheter la maison dont je t'ai / t'avais parlé.-**(2)** A peine avais-je posé mon sac que le téléphone a sonné. -**(3)** Il ne parle pas du tout français, aussi était-il / est-il très content de notre aide.-**(4)** Peut-être allons-nous déménager cet été.-**(5)** C'est un pays dont le passé est très riche.-**(6)** J'ai une amie dont les parents ont acheté une maison dans le sud de la France le mois dernier.-**(7)** Le nombre d'accidents de la route diminue / a diminué, affirme / a affirmé le Ministre des Transports.-**(8)** L'année dernière, quand j'étais en vacances en Espagne, j'ai acheté un très beau sac en cuir.-**(9)** J'ai perdu le bracelet en argent que mon mari m'a / m'avait donné pour mon anniversaire.-**(10)** J'avais des vieux disques de jazz mais je les leur ai vendus quand nous avons déménagé.

b) **(1)** Elle a changé de quartier: elle n'habite plus près de l'Opéra depuis septembre dernier.-**(2)** J'essaie de la contacter depuis quinze jours mais elle ne répond jamais au téléphone.-**(3)** Pas étonnant qu'elle soit si maigre: elle ne mange rien, ou presque. -**(4)** Avant son accident, elle voyageait beaucoup, mais maintenant elle ne va nulle part.-**(5)** Pour le moment, nous venons d'arriver dans la région et nous ne connaissons personne.-**(6)** Je l'ai rencontrée une ou deux fois et je ne la trouve guère sympathique. -**(7)** Elle n'a que seize ans mais elle est déjà excellente musicienne.-**(8)** Mon mari voudrait aller travailler à l'étranger mais je n'ai vraiment aucune envie de quitter la France.-**(9)** Je n'ai ni le temps ni l'argent nécessaire pour apprendre à jouer au golf. -**(10)** Ne me demande pas de te prêter de l'argent: je n'en ai pas!

c) **(1)** Moi, je n'ai jamais visité Paris.-**(2)** Ils ne sont pas encore rentrés aux Etats-Unis.-**(3)** Personne n'a téléphoné aujourd'hui.-**(4)** Je n'ai eu aucun problème.-**(5)** J'aimerais mieux ne pas le savoir. -**(6)** Finalement, j'ai décidé de ne jamais plus retourner là-bas. -**(7)** Je ne la lui ai pas donnée.-**(8)** Il n'y a personne chez eux à cette heure-ci.-**(9)** Elle n'en a acheté aucune.-**(10)** Je ne vois plus personne.

d) **(1)** Le film t'a plu? / Tu as aimé le film?—Pas beaucoup.-**(2)** Elle, elle y va, mais pas moi.-**(3)** Il ne parle jamais à personne.-**(4)** Nous n'y sommes jamais retournés.-**(5)** Je ne les ai plus jamais revus ni lui ni sa sœur. / Je ne l'ai plus jamais revu ni sa sœur non plus. -**(6)** Je ne bois jamais de vin au déjeuner. / à déjeuner. -**(7)** Beaucoup d'enfants ne mangent jamais que des hamburgers et des frites.-**(8)** La semaine de travail de quatre jours? Pas une idée très originale!-**(9)** Je n'ai pas compris ce qu'il a dit, et vous?— Non, moi non plus.-**(10)** Lui, il est heureux de vivre à la campagne, mais pas moi.

e) **(1)** L'avion arrive / atterrit à quelle heure? A quelle heure est-ce que l'avion atterrit? A quelle heure l'avion atterrit-il?-**(2)** Qu'est-ce que tu as? / vous avez? Qu'as-tu? / avez-vous?-**(3)** Vous avez bien mangé? Est-ce que vous avez bien mangé? Avez-vous bien mangé?-**(4)** Marie est là? Est-ce que Marie est là? Marie est-elle là?-**(5)** Tu es sortie hier soir? Est-ce que tu es sortie hier soir? Es-tu sortie hier soir? -**(6)** Vous allez / retournez souvent en France? Est-ce que vous allez / retournez souvent en France? Allez / Retournez-vous souvent en France?-**(7)** Tu es revenu comment hier soir? Comment est-ce que tu es revenu hier soir? Comment es-tu revenu hier soir?-**(8)** Vous êtes arrivé/e/s / vous êtes rentré/e/s quand? Quand est-ce que vous êtes arrivés / rentrés? Quand êtes-vous arrivés / rentrés?-**(9)** Tu as lu ce livre? Est-ce que tu as lu ce livre? As-tu lu ce livre?-**(10)** Vous connaissez Hélène? Est-ce que vous connaissez Hélène? Connaissez-vous Hélène?

f) **(1)** Je ne sais pas pourquoi il n'est jamais revenu!-**(2)** Dis-leur qu'ils doivent se dépêcher!-**(3)** Je me demande pourquoi les trains ont autant de retard!-**(4)** Montre-lui où l'autobus s'arrête! -**(5)** Explique-moi comment on téléphone à l'étranger!-**(6)** Dites-moi où vous avez rangé mes livres!-**(7)** Je ne comprends vraiment pas comment il a fait pour se casser une jambe!-**(8)** Rappelez-moi quand vous avez acheté la maison.-**(9)** Je ne sais pas à quelle heure part le bateau.-**(10)** Expliquez-moi pourquoi vous avez changé d'avis si brusquement.

g) **(1)** You were very tired, right?-**(2)** It's delicious, isn't it?-**(3)** You will phone, won't you?-**(4)** She wanted to come home, didn't she? -**(5)** Do you have a brother?—Yes, I do.-**(6)** Have you heard of Gérard Depardieu?—Of course I have.-**(7)** Did you enjoy yourselves?—No, not at all.-**(8)** Will you come see us next summer?—I hope so.-**(9)** Does he speak French?—I don't think so.-**(10)** He is a teacher.—So is she.

12. TRANSLATION PROBLEMS

a) **(1)** La société américaine doit faire face aux problèmes d'aujourd'hui.-**(2)** Je préfère les vacances à l'étranger.-**(3)** Les prix augmentent tous les ans.-**(4)** Les enfants ne respectent pas les professeurs autant qu'autrefois.-**(5)** A l'école, je préfère l'histoire et les maths.-**(6)** Est-ce qu'ils ont de beaux enfants?-**(7)** Vous buvez du vin?—Non, je déteste le vin.-**(8)** J'adorerais boire du Champagne, mais le Champagne est très cher.-**(9)** La reine Cléopâtre était très belle.-**(10)** L'alcool et la maladie sont les causes de nombreuses morts dans cette partie du monde.

b) **(1)** De nos jours, les enfants obéissent rarement à leurs parents. -**(2)** Je lui écris, mais il ne répond jamais à mes lettres.-**(3)** J'ai vu les Legrand hier: le fils ressemble beaucoup à son père.-**(4)** Elle joue au tennis régulièrement: c'est pour ça qu'elle est si mince.-**(5)** Il joue du violon depuis l'âge de 5 ans.-**(6)** Il est dangereux de se fier aux apparences. Elles sont souvent trompeuses.-**(7)** Je préfère téléphoner à ma famille et mes amis: je n'ai pas le temps d'écrire des lettres.-**(8)** Le docteur m'a prévenu: si je ne renonce pas à fumer, je ne vivrai pas longtemps.-**(9)** Il est très difficile pour les enfants de résister à la publicité, surtout à la télévision.-**(10)** Il te l'a dit? -**(11)** Oui, je le sais depuis longtemps.-**(12)** Quand j'ai besoin d'argent, j'en emprunte à ma sœur. Elle est très généreuse!-**(13)** Je ne peux rien cacher à mes parents: ils devinent tout!-**(14)** Demandez des renseignements à cet agent de police.-**(15)** Autrefois, les femmes se brossaient les cheveux cent fois, matin et soir.-**(16)** Cette lumière est trop forte: elle me fait mal aux yeux.-**(17)** J'achète toujours des fleurs à ce fleuriste: ses roses sont magnifiques.-**(18)** Je ne peux plus faire de ski depuis que je me suis cassé la jambe il y a trois ans. -**(19)** J'ai vu un documentaire sur le transport des animaux, qui a ôté le goût de manger de la viande à beaucoup de spectateurs. -**(20)** C'est un plaisir de la rencontrer: elle a toujours le sourire aux lèvres.

c) **(1)** Je crois qu'elle viendra demain.-**(2)** C'est l'homme que j'ai vu hier à ce dîner dont je t'ai parlé.-**(3)** Tu as vu la robe que j'ai achetée samedi?-**(4)** Je croyais que tu voulais rester à la maison.-**(5)** J'espère que tu te bien.-**(6)** Elle a dit qu'elle écrirait. -**(7)** Je suis sûr que tu te débrouilleras.-**(8)** Le repas que nous avons mangé hier était délicieux.-**(9)** Tu sais qu'elle ne reviendra pas, je suppose?-**(10)** C'est ce manteau-là que je veux.

d) (1) C'était un voyage très fatigant.-**(2)** Je les ai entendus rire et s'amuser.-**(3)** Vous ne devriez pas juger sans connaître la vérité. -**(4)** Arrêtez de vous inquiéter.-**(5)** Je n'aime pas beaucoup danser.-**(6)** Nous aimons aller au théâtre.-**(7)** Je n'ai pas l'habitude de nager quand il fait aussi froid.-**(8)** J'ai l'intention de continuer à travailler aussi longtemps que possible.-**(9)** Ce n'est pas une bonne idée que de boire quand on conduit. -**(10)** J'ai fini par y aller à pied.-**(11)** Elle n'a pas fini de parler. -**(12)** Il a salué ses invités en souriant.-**(13)** Je l'ai regardé / faire marche arrière et rentrer dans le mur. / rentrer dans le mur en marche arrière.-**(14)** Je m'habitue à voyager, bien que ce soit très fatigant.-**(15)** Travailler tout en élevant des enfants demande beaucoup d'énergie et d'organisation.-**(16)** La course de voitures est un sport dangereux.-**(17)** Ça ne sert à rien de vous plaindre: vous auriez dû / être plus prudent. / faire davantage attention.-**(18)** Ça te dit / Ça te plairait / de dîner au restaurant ce soir?-**(19)** Vérifiez vos pneus avant de partir en voiture. -**(20)** Ça ne m'intéresse vraiment pas de travailler dans une banque.

e) (1) J'entends les enfants jouer.-**(12)** Je préfère écouter de la musique classique.-**(3)** Ils savent nager depuis trois ans: c'est leur père qui leur a appris.-**(4)** J'ai beaucoup de mal à me réveiller le matin.-**(5)** Le samedi, en général, je vais danser.-**(6)** J'ai cherché partout mon stylo mais je ne le trouve pas.-**(7)** Je lui ai écrit plusieurs fois mais il ne répond jamais à mes lettres.-**(8)** J'espère une augmentation le mois prochain.-**(9)** Les transports marchent très mal: en général j'attends l'autobus pendant au moins une demi-heure tous les soirs.-**(10)** J'ai de la chance: j'habite à trois kilomètres seulement du bureau.

f) (1) J'ai rencontré sa femme récemment. Elle est très belle.-**(2)** Il a beaucoup de succès auprès des électeurs, et surtout des électrices. C'est un très bel homme.-**(3)** Il inspire confiance à ses malades. C'est un très bon médecin.-**(4)** J'adore me promener dans les villes la nuit: c'est beau!-**(5)** Il est trop tard pour changer d'avis: il faut partir.-**(6)** Pierre nous a invités dans sa maison de campagne pour les vacances: c'est génial!-**(7)** En ce moment j'essaie de trouver du travail: c'est difficile!-**(8)** J'adore Paris: c'est une belle ville!-**(9)** Il est facile de trouver un appartement à Paris si on a de l'argent.-**(10)** Le français, c'est une langue relativement facile à apprendre.

g) (1) Je l'ai vue hier: elle va beaucoup mieux maintenant.-**(2)** Ouvre la fenêtre: il fait trop chaud.-**(3)** Je ne crois pas que le beau temps va durer: il y a des nuages.-**(4)** Il veut absolument l'épouser, mais à mon avis il a tort.-**(5)** Elle m'assure qu'il n'y a aucun danger, mais j'ai peur qu'elle ne se trompe.-**(6)** Elle a fait beaucoup de bêtises récemment, et maintenant elle en a honte.-**(7)** De nos jours, les jeunes veulent profiter de la vie au maximum, et je trouve qu'ils ont bien raison.-**(8)** Elle a presque 40 ans, mais elle n'en paraît que 25 ou 30.-**(9)** J'adorerais habiter dans le Midi de la France, car il y fait toujours beau.-**(10)** C'est le temps idéal pour faire de la voile: il fait du soleil et il y a du vent.

h) **(1)** I have been living in the United States for 12 months.-**(2)** She was crossing the street when the accident happened.-**(3)** I wasn't feeling very well yesterday.-**(4)** At the moment she's working in a school.-**(5)** I think he is having trouble finding a new job.-**(6)** I'm trying very hard to finish this job as quickly as possible.-**(7)** She's being asked to make sacrifices, and she does-n't like it.-**(8)** Are you calling me a liar?-**(9)** Where will you be spending your vacation this year?-**(10)** We are hoping to go to Spain next summer.

i) **(1)** Je n'ai pas d'argent.-**(2)** Elle ne veut pas de salade.-**(3)** Il n'aime personne.-**(4)** Je n'en veux pas.-**(5)** Il ne lui en reste pas.-**(6)** Vous en avez?-**(7)** Vous en connaissez?-**(8)** Vous voulez du vin?-**(9)** Vous avez besoin d'aide?-**(10)** Vous avez pris de la soupe?-**(11)** Je prendrai n'importe lequel/laquelle, ça m'est égal.-**(12)** Achetez n'importe quelle paire de chaussures, elles sont toutes en solde.-**(13)** N'importe quelle mère comprendra ce que je veux dire.-**(14)** Vous pouvez me téléphoner n'importe quand, n'importe quel jour. Je serai là.-**(15)** On ne peut faire confiance à personne, de nos jours.-**(16)** J'irai n'importe où, ça m'est égal.-**(17)** N'importe qui peut faire le concours.-**(18)** Elle ne va jamais nulle part sans son chien.-**(19)** J'ai vu entrer quelqu'un, mais personne n'est sorti.-**(20)** Je ferai tout pour l'aider.

j) **(1)** Elle n'a rien acheté.-**(12)** Je n'ai téléphoné à personne.-**(3)** Elle n'a pas gagné d'argent.-**(4)** Ils n'ont pas de temps libre.-**(5)** Personne ne m'a contacté hier à ce sujet.-**(6)** Il n'a rien fait pour réussir.-**(7)** Ils ne mangent jamais de bonbons.-**(8)** Ce n'est pas simple: elle ne se plaît nulle part.-**(9)** Elle n'est pas très sociable: elle ne parle à personne.-**(10)** Elle ne joue plus du violon.

k) **(1)** Je ne trouve pas mon stylo. Tu peux me prêter le tien? -**(2)** J'aime beaucoup vos photos de vacances. Les nôtres ne sont pas aussi réussies.-**(3)** Si seulement mes enfants travaillaient bien à l'école, comme les tiens!-**(4)** Nous avons acheté notre voiture il y a cinq ans. Depuis combien de temps avez-vous la vôtre?-**(5)** Il s'occupe de ses enfants, à elle, comme si c'étaient les siens.-**(6)** Ma robe vient d'un grand magasin. Anne a fait faire la sienne.-**(7)** Monsieur, Je vous remercie de votre lettre du 2 avril. -**(8)** J'ai acheté deux gâteaux: un pour toi, et un pour moi.-**(9)** Vous devriez vous dépêcher! Votre train part dans cinq minutes et il faut prendre vos billets!-**(10)** Vous avez de la chance: vous vous entendez tellement bien, toi et ton frère.

l) **(1)** Ces chaises de jardin sont très confortables.-**(2)** Il va y avoir une tempête de neige.-**(3)** Ce sont les films de guerre qu'il aime le mieux.-**(4)** Vous avez visité la Maison Blanche?-**(5)** Je crois que c'est le plus grand magasin de jouets de Los Angeles.-**(6)** Les amis de mes parents viennent ce week-end.-**(7)** J'écoute souvent les cassettes de mon frère quand il n'est pas là.-**(8)** Nous allons dîner chez les Dubois ce soir.-**(9)** Où est le journal d'hier?-**(10)** Il faut que j'aille chez le pharmacien avant six heures.-**(11)** Je vais souvent chez elle.-**(12)** J'aime rester chez moi le dimanche.-**(13)** J'adore lire les journaux du dimanche au lit.-**(14)** La mère d'une amie de ma mère va me vendre sa voiture.-**(15)** Si j'avais beaucoup d'argent, j'achèterais un cheval de course.-**(16)** Elle passe la nuit chez son amie.-**(17)** Ferme la porte du garage!-**(18)** J'étais chez ma grand-mère quand il a téléphoné / appelé.-**(19)** J'ai trouvé cet article de journal dans le bureau de John.-**(20)** La mode de cette année ne me va pas du tout.

m) (1) J'étais très fatiguée hier après être rentrée du travail.-**(2)** Il était vraiment de bonne humeur après avoir reçu sa lettre.-**(3)** Je ne l'ai pas vue depuis au moins dix ans. Je regrette vraiment de l'avoir manquée.-**(4)** Brigitte a téléphoné ce matin pour nous remercier de l'avoir invitée.-**(5)** Je ne me souviens pas du tout de l'avoir rencontrée.-**(6)** Après avoir passé son baccalauréat, elle a l'intention de voyager à l'étranger pendant quelques mois. -**(7)** Après s'être cassé la jambe dans un accident de ski, elle a complètement arrêté de faire du sport.-**(8)** Après nous être consultés, nous avons pris la décision de ne pas donner suite à sa demande.-**(9)** Après lui avoir parlé pendant plus d'une heure, j'espère bien l'avoir convaincue de prendre des vacances.-**(10)** Ils se sont excusés de nous avoir dérangés et ils sont partis tout de suite après.

n) (1) I was very tired yesterday after getting home from work.-**(2)** He was in a really good mood after getting his/her letter.-**(3)** I haven't seen her for at least ten years. I'm really sorry to have missed her.-**(4)** Brigitte phoned this morning to thank us for inviting her. -**(5)** I don't remember at all meeting her.-**(6)** After taking her baccalauréat exam, she plans to travel abroad for a few months.-**(7)** After breaking her leg in a skiing accident, she has stopped doing sports altogether.-**(8)** After consulting each other, we have decided not to agree to his request.-**(9)** After talking to her for over an hour, I really hope that I have convinced her to take a vacation.-**(10)** They apologized for disturbing us, and they left a moment later.

Index to Exercises

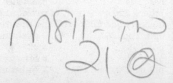